IMMUNITY
TO CHANGE

LEADERSHIP FOR THE COMMON GOOD

HARVARD BUSINESS PRESS

CENTER FOR PUBLIC LEADERSHIP
JOHN F. KENNEDY SCHOOL OF GOVERNMENT
HARVARD UNIVERSITY

The Leadership for the Common Good series represents a partnership
between Harvard Business Press and the
Center for Public Leadership at Harvard University's
John F. Kennedy School of Government. Books in the series aim
to provoke conversations about the role of leaders in business,
government, and society, to enrich leadership theory and
enhance leadership practice, and to set the agenda for
defining effective leadership in the future.

OTHER BOOKS IN THE SERIES

Changing Minds
by Howard Gardner

Predictable Surprises
by Max H. Bazerman and
Michael D. Watkins

Bad Leadership
by Barbara Kellerman

Many Unhappy Returns
by Charles O. Rossotti

Leading Through Conflict
by Mark Gerzon

Senior Leadership Teams
by Ruth Wageman,
Debra A. Nunes, James A. Burruss,
and J. Richard Hackman.

Five Minds for the Future
by Howard Gardner

The Leaders We Need
by Michael Maccoby

Through the Labyrinth
by Alice H. Eagly and
Linda L. Carli

*The Power of
Unreasonable People*
by John Elkington and
Pamela Hartigan

Followership
by Barbara Kellerman

IMMUNITY TO CHANGE

[HOW TO OVERCOME IT AND UNLOCK POTENTIAL
IN YOURSELF AND YOUR ORGANIZATION]

ROBERT KEGAN

LISA LASKOW LAHEY

HARVARD BUSINESS PRESS

Boston, Massachusetts

ISBN   978-1-4221-1736-1

Library-of-Congress cataloging information available.

The paper used in this publication meets the requirements of the American
National Standard for Permanence of Paper for Publications and Documents in
Libraries and Archives Z39.48-1992.

For Bernard and Saralee Kegan

For my guys, Bill, Zach, and Max Lahey

CONTENTS

PREFACE AND ACKNOWLEDGMENTS

This book has literally taken us our whole professional lives to write. Advance reviewers say you will find here an entirely novel but thoroughly "road-tested" approach to bringing about significant improvements in individuals and groups in the workplace.

Well, it's true that our road is well paved: The ideas and practices you will learn about here have been put to good use by a national railway in Europe, an international financial services company, one of America's most admired technology companies, the leadership of a statewide child welfare agency, superintendents and their principals in several U.S. school districts, senior partners in the world's leading international strategy consulting firm, and the fastest-growing labor union in America.

But it has also been a winding road, and to tell the truth, we didn't set out originally to work on the problem we are now getting credit for solving—how to close the gap between what people genuinely *intend* to do and what they are actually *able* to bring about. Twenty-five years ago we would have been of little use to these organizations. Though we knew then we were on a trail worth a lifetime of exploration, we had no idea or plan that it would bring us to leaders and their teams in public and private sectors in the United States, Europe, Asia, and Africa.

We began as academic psychologists researching the development of mindsets and mental complexity in adulthood. With one of us (Kegan) taking the lead in the development of a new theory, and the other (Lahey) taking the lead in developing the research method and assessment procedures to test and refine it, we proceeded, in the 1980s, to uncover something that has been fascinating us—and fellow researchers and practitioners all over the world—ever since.

We discovered the possibility of life after adolescence! Despite the popular—and, at that time, even scientific—belief that our minds, like our bodies, don't get any "taller" after adolescence, we found that some of our adult research subjects were able to evolve whole patterns of increasingly complex and agile ways of apprehending the world.

While few attained the most advanced growth patterns our investigations revealed, it was apparent through longitudinal research (carefully assessing and reassessing the same people over many years) that when people *did* evolve it was always in the same sequence. Each new mental plateau gradually overcame the systematic limitations of the prior one. Further research eventually demonstrated that each qualitative leap forward enhances not only people's ability to *see* (into themselves and their world) but to *act* more effectively as well. (You will learn more about these mental plateaus in the first chapter of this book.)

But we also saw that many people did not evolve a whole new mental system after adolescence, and if they moved at all it wasn't far. Since we have always been educators at heart (and have spent our university lives not in a school of management, but a school of education), we wanted to know whether one could do anything to support these shifts in the expansiveness and complexity of our mindsets. Were such advances just a matter of fate and random variation, completely out of our hands? Or could people actually be helped to grow? This took us further down our road, throughout the 1990s, and led us to a second discovery.

We had been studying the evolution of mental development from the outside, as it were, seeking to describe the structure of each way of meaning-making, why it created the reality it did, what changed in a structure when it evolved. But now, without our quite realizing it, we were finding our way into the inner dynamics, in particular a sort of "master motive" that keeps us on our current plateau. We uncovered a phenomenon we call "the immunity to change," a heretofore hidden dynamic that actively (and brilliantly) prevents us from changing because of its devotion to preserving our existing way of making meaning.

We first introduced readers to the concept of immunity to change in our 2001 book, *How the Way We Talk Can Change the Way We*

Work. There we presented a deceptively simple process—distilled and refined over many years—by which people can uncover the hidden motivations and beliefs that prevent them from making the very changes they know they should make and very much want to make (whether the goal is "being more courageous in my communications" or "losing weight").

The reception to that book has been enormously gratifying, as it has been to watch what happens when we personally guide people (now several thousand a year) through this process (as we will guide you, if you wish, in chapter 9). They repeatedly say things like, "I never saw that coming!" and "I got more out of that in three hours than three years in therapy!" But the truth is, what people are raving about is the power and clarity of a new *insight* they are having (and the speed with which they get to it). And we all know there is a big gulf between insight and the ability to act upon it.

We knew we had developed something powerful and practical, but we were still a long way from satisfying the reader's true goal (not just greater insight into *why* one person can't delegate or another can't deliver upward feedback, despite his firm resolve, but the ability to actually *do it*)—and a long way from satisfying our own (being able not just to see the internal mechanisms that perpetuate a current mindset, but also to help someone transcend its limitations).

Shortly after *How the Way We Talk* was published we went before a group of chief knowledge officers and human resource heads from *Fortune* 500 companies and large international NGOs. They belonged to a consortium that previewed promising new ideas and practices still in the development stage, and gave the "inventors" the frankest possible assessment of their value. We didn't talk to them about what we had found or invented; we simply asked them to try the process themselves for a few hours under our guidance.

When they were done they all said the same thing, but their reaction was best summed up by one CKO: "I've got good news and bad news. First, the good news: I've spent twenty years in the field of capability-building and performance improvement, and what you have just done with us is the single most powerful piece of learning technology I've ever seen. It's like you've conceived the jet engine in the era of the prop plane, and you've demonstrated here you can get the thing off the ground. Now the bad news: You haven't a clue what to do with the plane now that you've gotten it airborne—where to fly it or how to land it."

He was pretty much right. We have since learned from some readers of *How the Way We Talk* that, once given the boost to get airborne, they could fly their planes on their own to their desired destinations. But for most people greater insight, however exhilarating, is insufficient to bring about lasting change. We still had a big piece of work ahead of us, a third threshold that needed crossing, and this one took yet another seven or eight years—the time between the publication of our last book and this one.

One of the things we've had going for us in this last stretch has been our recognition that the goal of helping people to deliver on very specific improvements, changes that have proven resistant to thoughtful plans and heartfelt resolutions, is intimately related to the goal of helping people to develop a new meaning-making system that can transcend the limitations of their current one. Building on our colleague Ronald Heifetz's heuristic distinction between "technical" and "adaptive" challenges, we can say that some personal-change goals—especially those we know we must accomplish but still cannot—require that we ourselves "get bigger"; that is, we must *adapt* in order to accomplish them.

Thus we suspected that if we could build a successful "learning platform" that moved from *diagnosing* immunities to *overcoming* them, we might deliver on both goals at the same time. We knew our diagnostic process helped make the invisible visible, which our research showed to be the driver of increasing mental complexity (moving mental structures from "subject" to "object," from "master" to "tool"). The ability to enter and transform the mindset, we reasoned, should prove to be a crucial asset for meeting specific adaptive challenges. And conversely, the personal urgency to meet an adaptive challenge should make the challenge a kind of Trojan horse, a riveting object of attention that, once engaged, might break open and transform the whole (mental) field.

Immunity to Change presents the outcome of our pursuit of these hunches for the last several years. From our point of view, the best test of our learning platform asks more than, "Does it enable me to accomplish my specific improvement goal?" (e.g., "Did I become a more courageous communicator?" "Am I now a better delegator?"). Certainly it would be a valuable platform if the answer to this question, more often than not, were yes.

But we began with a bigger aspiration that prompts an additional question: "And does it also promote advances in mental complexity, the kind of change that will permit a whole *range* of new abilities, not just meeting the single initial improvement goal?" If the answer to this were yes, then the payoffs for investing in an *adaptive* approach to personal improvement would be many, many times the value of accomplishing a single goal.

It will be up to you, as you examine the cases and accounts in this book, to assess how strong our learning platform is. If you come to feel the answer to our second, tougher question is also yes, then a central message of this book—people *can* change—should take on a double meaning for you: yes, people—even adults—can make significant improvements in focused areas where they have many times before tried and failed; and yes, even "grown-ups" can continue to evolve more complex mental systems, analogous to the transformations from childhood to adolescence, enabling a more penetrating, more responsible, less egocentric grasp of reality.

If you have no familiarity with our earlier books, welcome! We have no expectation that you do, and they are not a prerequisite to getting the most out of this one. If you have ever tried—and failed—to make changes in your own life, or to help others make changes in theirs, read on: we wrote this book for you. Especially if you lead, manage, supervise, consult, counsel, train, coach, or teach—and *personal improvement* or *team performance* at work is one of your biggest concerns—this book is for you.

If you are familiar with our work, welcome back! Perhaps you read *How the Way We Talk Can Change the Way We Work* and wondered, "Now that you have uncovered the immunity to change and helped me see my problem, have you learned anything about how to help me *solve* this problem?" We wrote this book for you also.

If you have an interest in adult development, if you think about the possibility of significant forward leaps in psychological complexity after adolescence, if you have read Kegan's earlier books *The Evolving Self* or *In Over Our Heads,* and you wonder if we have learned anything new about how better to *support* these leaps, then you too are our target audience.

Finally, if you have known all along that our very practical work on immunities to change is founded on our theoretical and research work on the evolution of mindsets and meaning systems, and have been wondering when would we ever get around to explicitly bringing them together to shed new light on creating learning organizations or meeting adaptive challenges, then this book is for you, as well.

We had something else going for us during the years we worked on this book—the privilege of working for extended periods of time with courageous and generous leaders and their teams, in business, government, and education. These people were willing to try an entirely different way of working at improvement, individually and collectively—a way that was at times uncomfortable and scary. The organizations in which we sought to be of help were very different, but their leaders—whether CEOs, unit heads, or team leaders—all shared one thing in common long before they met us: A deep and abiding recognition that their people bring their humanity to work with them every single day; that the absolute division between the work realm and the personal realm is naive and unhelpful; and that twenty-first-century leaders must find a more effective way to engage the emotional lives of their organizations and their leadership teams.

We want to do more than express our appreciation to these people, many of whose stories you will hear in the pages ahead. We want to express our admiration, and to acknowledge that they became our thought partners as much as our clients, helping us to learn what we are trying to pass on in this book.

Another source of support to our learning in the years since we wrote *How the Way We Talk* has been our participation in the Change Leadership Group (CLG) at the Harvard Graduate School of Education. This group, founded initially through a grant from the Bill and Melinda Gates Foundation, was constituted to develop a more effective "change leader's curriculum" for education administrators seeking to bring about significant, systemwide reforms in America's public school districts.

Judging that many reform efforts foundered on an insufficiently powerful grasp of organizational dynamics or psychological dynamics or both, the Change Leadership Group deliberately drew together an interdisciplinary team and set to work in pilot districts to understand what leaders would need to sharpen both their external and internal lenses.

We obviously joined the team to lead the psychological side of the work, and you can see how the immunity-to-change concepts and practices have been integrated into a leadership curriculum in our collectively authored book, *Change Leadership: A Practical Guide to Improving Our Schools.*

But our experience working with our CLG colleagues and our district-leadership partners over several years has been an education for us, as well. Working at change for extended periods with an organization's leadership team and being forced to take an organizational view by colleagues whose thinking is shaped by that orientation, we have been led to a much more dialectical way of conceiving the relationship between the sociocentric and the psychocentric perspectives.

Where we formerly tended to view the organization, group, or social context in terms of the way it did or did not optimally support individual development ("How good a 'holding environment' is it? How can it be better?"), we are now inclined to ask as well, "How do these individual developments enhance the team's performance or help the organization to deliver on its goals?" (You will see the results of this new perspective early on in this book when we consider the use of the immunity-to-change practices in groups.)

We appreciate our consulting colleagues who collaborated with us on projects referenced here: Dr. Timothy Havens and Mark Sarkady joined us in our work with Peter Donovan and his executive staff. Dr. Robert Goodman was our partner in the work with the pharmaceutical team in chapter 7.

We are indebted to a host of wonderful friends and thought-partners who have contributed to this book in ways we trust they know: Karen Aka, Maria Arias, Elizabeth Armstrong, Michael Bader, Marwan Bizri, Connie Bowe, Sue D'Alessio, Herman De Bode, Peter Donovan, Conning Fannell, Pierre Gurdjian, Ron Halpern, Tim Havens, Ron Heifetz, Deborah Helsing, Annie Howell, Tsun-yan

Hsen, Jude Garnier, Robert Goodman, Barry Gruenberg, Jennifer Juhler, Michael Jung, Neil Janin, Art Kaneshiro, Jay Kaufman, Richard Lemons, Marty Linsky, Kati Livingston, Emily Souvaine Meehan, Beat Meyer, Frank Moretti, Patricia Murrell, Donald Novak, Micky Obermayer, Eric Rait, Wilhelm Rall, Barbara Rapaport, Mark Sarkady, Harry Spence, Mary Ellen Steele-Pierce, Willa Thomas, Tony Wagner, James Walsh, Laura Watkins, and Terri Weiland.

We want to thank our editors Jeff Kehoe, who began championing this book years before it was written, and Colleen Kaftan, who helped us reshape the forest and groom every tree. The book is far better because of you both.

Finally, in our prior book we thanked our immediate families, and they continue to be a life-sustaining source of stimulation, joy, and support. But before we invite you to read further, we want to say a word about our own parents. As it happens, both of us grew up in "business families." In twenty-some years of working together we have seldom paid much attention to this piece of shared history, but it is true. Both of our families owned small businesses, and all four of our parents were involved at one time or another in tending to them.

Now, although these parents certainly were and are proud of us, were they to be completely honest, they would also have to admit to some deep skepticism as to whether books and theories and "management science" really had anything of practical value to contribute to their work. (If your own work is more about running things than helping those who run them, we are guessing one or two of you share this skepticism.)

"I looked through a lot of that stuff," one of our parents once told us, "and it all reminded me of the story about the fisherman and the game warden. The game warden accepts an invitation to go fishing with a stranger who rows him out to the middle of the lake. As the game warden begins to fiddle with his fishing rod, he watches in horror as the stranger pulls out a stick of dynamite from his tackle box, lights it, and throws it into the lake. There's a big explosion and a huge geyser of water. Lots of fish—whole, intact fish—flop on shore, just waiting to be scooped up. The game warden can hardly contain himself. 'What in God's name are you *doing*?!' he says. 'I'm a

game warden, for goodness' sake! That's illegal! It's dangerous! It's . . .'
While the game warden is stammering away, the stranger reaches
back into his tackle box, pulls out another stick of dynamite, lights it,
and, this time, hands it to the game warden!

"'Just what in hell are you *think*ing?!' he says, holding the dynamite with its burning fuse as far from his face as possible. 'I can't
be*lieve* this! What am I supposed to *do* with this?!'

"The game warden keeps shouting and the fuse keeps burning.
Finally, the stranger looks at him and says, 'Listen, are you going to
just talk—or are you going to *fish*?!'"

According to that parent, all those books about management and
leadership "just talk," but the person running a business "fishes."
And *real* fishing, he seemed to be saying, doesn't exactly look like a
Norman Rockwell painting. "These books are like the game warden," his story seemed to say. "They have their rules and ideas about
the proper way that things should go. And they make a lot of good
sense, too, so long as you are in some neat and clean world that exists
in those books. But the real work of running a business isn't much
like the world of the books. The real world is very, very messy."

One of our favorite responses from the advance reviews of this
book was this one: "We are about as far as we could be here from the
clean room of the psychology experiment" (the place where our long,
winding road began). "These authors know about the real world of
work." We certainly had no conscious intention to be loyal to our
own enterprising parents' skepticism, but it seems that the work we
have ended up doing has brought us into the messiest and "real-est"
aspect of organizational life, the world of private meanings and inner
feelings as they play themselves out in the public arena of work.

We didn't intend to write a book our hard-working parents
would not dismiss—but it is interesting to us that that might be what
has happened. The cases and stories you will encounter in this book
are not about the Norman Rockwell version of work and leadership.
They are about the necessity of finding ways of surfacing the world
below the waterline—and hopefully with a much more effective technology than dynamite.

INTRODUCTION

N<small>O LEADER NEEDS CONVINCING</small> that improvement and change is at the top of the agenda. And no leader needs a book of sympathy for how hard it is to bring change about—whether in oneself or in others. We all know that change is hard, but we don't know enough about why it is so hard and what we can do about it. Most of the favorite explanations, while true in some cases, turn out to be weak answers to why the changes that are called for today are so difficult. Lack of urgency? Inadequate incentives? Uncertainty about what we really need to do differently? Are these really the primary barriers to change you see in yourself and in those who work and live around you?

Not long ago a medical study showed that if heart doctors tell their seriously at-risk heart patients they will literally *die* if they do not make changes to their personal lives—diet, exercise, smoking—still only one in seven is actually able to make the changes. One in seven! And we can safely assume that the other six *wanted* to live, see more sunsets, watch their grandchildren grow up. They didn't lack a sense of urgency. The incentives for change could not be greater. The doctors made sure they knew just want they needed to do. Still, they couldn't do it.

If people cannot make the changes they dearly want to when their very lives are on the line, then how can leaders at any level, in any kind of organization, expect to successfully support processes of change—even those they and their subordinates may passionately believe in—when the stakes and the payoff are not nearly as high?

Could it be any clearer that we need some new ways of understanding what prevents and enables our own change?

As with the heart patients, the change challenges today's leaders and their subordinates face are not, for the most part, a problem of will. The problem is the inability to close the gap between what we genuinely, even passionately, *want* and what we are actually *able* to do. Closing this gap is a central learning problem of the twenty-first century.

THREE PROBLEMS CREATE THE CONTEXT FOR THIS BOOK

This disjunction between our increased understanding of the need for change and our lack of understanding as to what prevents it is the first of three fertile problems that lay the foundation for this book. If you are like the leaders with whom we have been working over many years while developing these ideas and practices, you may be a little skeptical about how much anyone—yourself included—really can change. This brings us to a second fertile problem.

Every year, in response to increasing challenges and opportunities, organizations across all sectors collectively invest precious resources— billions of dollars and extraordinary amounts of time—trying to improve their people's capabilities. Anyone might be forgiven for imagining that the endless parade of professional development programs, personal-improvement plans, leadership trainings, performance reviews, and executive coaching reflects a deep-seated optimism among leaders about the prospects for personal change. Why else would they make such investments?

And yet, whenever we win the confidence and friendship of leaders, we are likely to hear—often over drinks or a good meal—"Let's face it. People don't really change much. I mean, at the end of the day Al is always going to be Al. By the time someone is thirty or thirty-five, he is who he is. I suppose you can hope for little adjustments around the margins, but really, I think the best you can do is leverage the hell out of the guy's strengths and hire around his weaknesses. Why wear yourself out and beat the poor guy up for changes he isn't going to make?"

Thus the interesting truth is that riding alongside the public optimism reflected in enormous organizational investments in people development is a deep-seated private pessimism about how much people really can change.

And we come by this pessimism honestly. On more than one occasion, in more than one country, working in more than one sector, we have heard essentially this same story:

> We take the year-end reviews very seriously around here. It's not like the Dilbert cartoons where people roll their eyes as they enter the room and wait for the psychobabble and pep talk to be over. People listen carefully to the feedback they get. A lot of company time and money goes into its gathering and debriefing; and a lot of heart and mind goes into attending to it on the receiving end. People sometimes cry in these meetings. They make the sincerest of pledges and the most careful of plans to change the things that need to be changed. Everyone leaves the room feeling like an intense and real conversation has occurred and the time was well spent. And then? A year later we are all back in the room looking at the feedback, and the picture really isn't that different. Something is wrong here.

It sure is, and that's why we wrote this book. We have a resounding answer to the debate about whether people and organizational culture really can change.

The changes you are going to read about here are not little adjustments around the margins. And their proof does not rest on the self-deception of self-evaluation. It comes from evaluations, often anonymous evaluations, by one's toughest critics—the people who live with you every day at work and at home. When clients, coworkers, or family members respond to our surveys by saying:

> "Whatever you're doing with Nicholas, can you do it with his partners, too?" (from a client)

"Our whole team senses an enormous shift in Martin; he has become a pleasure to work with; the team is much more productive. I would never have predicted this." (from a coworker)

"I've had the first real conversation with Mom I've had in years." (from a family member)

then we start to believe something of importance is really happening.

The evidence comes, too, in experiences like the recent one we had working with the leadership of a school district thousands of miles from our home. We have been working with them for a few years now, and since they are so far away we have been building up a local crew of change coaches to carry on the work. We had arranged for a promising new candidate to visit the offsite we were conducting. She was a highly experienced school professional, and we invited her to just sit in and observe, to get a feel for the kind of work these administrators were undertaking with us.

We were mostly absorbed in the work we were doing, but every time we looked at our visitor we couldn't help but notice what seemed to us a disturbed look on her face. About two hours into her visit, we saw her get up and, without warning, walk out of the room, with a slack-jawed expression of shock. She never returned. "Hmm, I guess that didn't go too well," one of us remembers thinking.

A few days later we checked in with one of our team members who had caught up with her. She had been shocked all right. "I've spent my whole life working with school leaders," she said. "I've never heard conversation of that sort. I've never heard people be as honest or as responsible. I've never heard people talking about things that are more likely to lead to real change." (Before you get too far into this book, you'll get a full picture of what this kind of conversation looks like.) She left because she had another appointment. She wanted to know how she could join the coaching team.

The materials in the pages ahead suggest a next generation of ideas and practices for leaders with an interest in the learning life of their organizations. It has been nearly twenty years since Peter Senge's

Fifth Discipline first inspired leaders to think about learning organizations, and more than twenty-five years since Donald Schön's *The Reflective Practitioner* rekindled the importance of attending, literally, to the mind at work. All over the world today, in every sector, leaders aspire to lead organizations that learn, and to be, themselves, personally reflective about what they do.

But we need to take individual and collective learning at work to the next level if we are to meet twenty-first-century change challenges. If we do not, we can learn and reflect as much as we want, but the changes we hope for, or that others need from us, will not happen because all the learning and reflecting will occur within our existing mindsets. This brings us to our third and last fertile problem.

Our MIT colleagues, Senge and Schön, inspired many leaders at the end of the last century to incorporate a responsibility for learning into their short list of leadership priorities. The theory base and set of practices associated with the concept of the learning organization is a rich and growing one. But it has always had a missing dimension that might be most noticeable to people like us who have spent our lives in the field of education: it lacks a sophisticated understanding of adult development.

When Senge and Schön wrote their books, the brain scientists were still insisting there were no qualitative changes in our mental equipment after adolescence. Meanwhile, like other "soft scientists," we were conducting our own research, which we came to feel suggested a quite different picture. Today the hard and soft scientists agree that the story of mental development does not need to end in adolescence. But we have yet to catch up to the implications of this dramatic revision of our possibilities.

This lack of an adult developmental dimension in organizational learning theory has never been more important than the present, as leaders increasingly ask people to do things they are not now able to do, were never prepared to do, and are not yet developmentally well matched to do. The field of "leadership development" has overattended to leadership and underattended to development. An endless stream of books tries to identify the most important elements of leadership and help leaders to acquire these abilities. Meanwhile, we ignore the most powerful source of ability: our capacity (and the capacity of the people who work for us) to overcome, at *any* age, the limitations and blind spots of current ways of making meaning.

Without a better understanding of human development—what it is, how it is enabled, how it is constrained—what passes for "leadership development" will more likely amount to "leadership learning" or "leadership training." The knowledge and skills gained will be like new files and programs brought to the existing operating system. They may have a certain value—new files and programs do give you greater range and versatility—but your ability to use them will still be limited by your current operating system. True development is about transforming the operating system itself, not just increasing your fund of knowledge or your behavioral repertoire.

If you are leading anything at any level, you are driving some kind of plan or agenda, *but some kind of plan or agenda is also driving you*. It is out of your awareness. You cannot yet take responsibility for it. And most of the time, that agenda will limit or even doom your ability to deliver extraordinary results. If you do not attend as much to "development" as to "leadership," then your leadership development will always be directed to the plan or agenda you have. It will not be about the plan or agenda that "has you," and therefore your capacity for change will inherently be limited.

The accounts and stories you will find here suggest a route to genuine development, to the qualitative expansions of mind that significantly increase human capability at work— not by rehiring but by renewing existing talent.

THE PLAN OF THIS BOOK

This book is divided into three parts. The first part provides a new way to understand change. The second shows you the value of our approach for individuals, work teams, and entire organizations. The third part invites you to try the approach for yourself.

Part 1 begins with a quick tutorial on what we have learned from thirty years of research on the development of mental complexity in adulthood and its meaning for work life. Chapter 1 provides the theoretical and empirical foundations for all the accounts and practices that follow. In chapter 2 we introduce our discovery of a previously hidden phenomenon that prevents us from making the very changes we passionately intend—the dynamic we call "the immunity to change." In chapter 3 you will learn from two leaders, one from business and one from government, how and why they brought this work into their organizations and the benefits they saw happening as a result.

In part 2 we provide extended accounts of the kinds of changes we have seen organizations and individuals make when they identify and work through their immunities to change. We choose people from a variety of sectors, working on the full range of improvement goals we typically encounter. In chapter 4 we explore what happens when groups assess their collective immunity to change; in chapters 5 and 6 we follow two individuals addressing their personal immunity to change; and in chapter 7 we show the most ambitious design— team members working to overcome their individual immunities in the context of an intact, ongoing work group seeking to improve its collective performance.

In part 3 we invite you into a direct experience of the phenomenon at the heart of this book, guiding you through your own individual and collective immunity-to-change journey. Chapter 8 identifies the ingredients needed to support this kind of change process. In chapters 9 and 10, we take you through a step-by-step process to diagnosis and then go to work on overcoming your individual immunity to change. Chapter 11 gives you the tools and process to help you bring the immunity work to your team or organization. In the conclusion we discuss the seven attributes of leaders who work successfully to make their settings a consistently fertile place for the growth of personal and collective capability.

We doubt you'd be reading this book unless some part of you; already knows how important it is for people to significantly enhance what they can do at work; hopes there is new reason to believe in this possibility; and wonders what you might do to help bring it about. We hope you find the book good company on all these fronts—a resource for your head, heart, gut, and hand—and that it helps you achieve the results you want.

PART ONE

UNCOVERING A HIDDEN DYNAMIC IN THE CHALLENGE OF CHANGE

$$\left[\ 1\ \right]$$

RECONCEIVING THE
CHALLENGE OF CHANGE

WHAT WILL DISTINGUISH your leadership from others' in the years ahead? As the subtitle of this book suggests, we believe it will be your ability to develop yourself, your people, and your teams. Throughout the world—and this is as true in the United States and Europe as it is in China and India—human capability will be the critical variable in the new century. But leaders who seek to win a war for talent by conceiving of capability as a fixed resource to be found "out there" put themselves and their organizations at a serious disadvantage.

In contrast, leaders who ask themselves, "What can I do to make my setting the most fertile ground in the world for the *growth* of talent?" put themselves in the best position to succeed. These leaders understand that for each of us to deliver on our biggest aspirations—to take advantage of new opportunities or meet new challenges—we must grow into our future possibilities. These leaders know what makes that more possible—and what prevents it.

The challenge to change and improve is often misunderstood as a need to better "deal with" or "cope with" the greater complexity of the world. Coping and dealing involve adding new skills or widening our repertoire of responses. We are the same person we were before we learned to cope; we have simply added some new resources. We have learned, but we have not necessarily *developed*. Coping and dealing are valuable skills, but they are actually insufficient for meeting today's change challenges.

In reality, the experience of complexity is not just a story about the world. It is also a story about people. It is a story about the fit between the demands of the world and the capacity of the person or the organization. When we experience the world as "too complex" we are not just experiencing the complexity of the world. We are experiencing a mismatch between the world's complexity *and our own at this moment*. There are only two logical ways to mend this mismatch— reduce the world's complexity or increase our own. The first isn't going to happen. The second has long seemed an impossibility in adulthood.

We (the authors of this book) have spent a generation now studying the growth of mental complexity in adulthood. We think what we have learned may help you to better understand yourself and those who work with you and for you. In gaining that awareness, you will begin to see a new frontier of human capabilities, the place where tomorrow's most successful leaders will focus their leadership attention.

AN UPDATED VIEW OF AGE
AND MENTAL COMPLEXITY

The ideas and practices you will find in this book begin by identifying a widespread misconception about the potential trajectory of mental development across the lifespan. When we began our work, the accepted picture of mental development was akin to the picture of physical development—your growth was thought fundamentally to end by your twenties. If, thirty years ago, you were to place "age" on one axis and "mental complexity" on another, and you asked the experts in the field to draw the graph as they understood it, they would have produced something similar to figure 1-1: an upward sloping line until the twenties and a flat line thereafter. And they would have drawn it with confidence.

When we began reporting the results of our research in the 1980s, suggesting that some (though not all) adults seemed to undergo

FIGURE 1-1

Age and mental complexity: The view thirty years ago

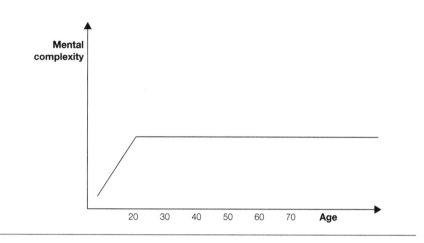

qualitative advances in their mental complexity akin to earlier, well-documented quantum leaps from early childhood to later childhood and from later childhood to adolescence, our brain-researcher colleagues sitting next to us on distinguished panels would smile with polite disdain.

"You might think you can infer this from your longitudinal interviews," they would say, "but hard science doesn't have to make inferences. We're looking at *the real thing*. The brain simply doesn't undergo any significant change in capacity after late adolescence. Sorry." Of course, these "hard scientists" would grant that older people are often wiser or more capable than younger people, but this they attributed to the benefits of experience, a consequence of learning how to get more out of the same mental equipment rather than any qualitative advances or upgrades to the equipment itself.

Thirty years later? Whoops! It turns out everybody was making inferences, even the brain scientists who thought they were looking at "the thing itself." The hard scientists have better instruments today, and the brain doesn't look to them the way it did thirty years ago. Today they talk about neural plasticity and the phenomenal capacities of the brain to keep adapting throughout life.

If we were to draw the graph showing age and mental complexity today? On the basis of thirty years of longitudinal research by our

FIGURE 1-2

Age and mental complexity: The revised view today

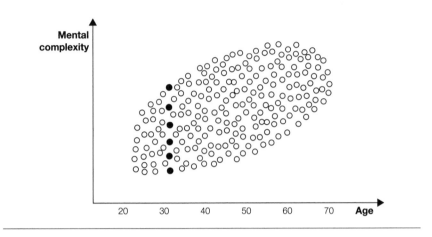

colleagues and us—as a result of thoroughly analyzing the transcripts of hundreds of people, interviewed and reinterviewed at several-year intervals—the graph would look like figure 1-2.

Two things are evident from this graph:

- With a large enough sample size you can detect a mildly upward-sloping curve. That is, looking at a population as a whole, mental complexity tends to increase with age, throughout adulthood, at least until old age; so the story of mental complexity is certainly *not* a story that ends in our twenties.

- There is considerable variation within any age. For example, six people in their thirties (the bolded dots) could all be at different places in their level of mental complexity, and some could be *more* complex than a person in her forties.

If we were to draw a quick picture of what we have learned about the individual trajectory of mental development in adulthood, it might look something like figure 1-3. This picture suggests several different elements:

- There are qualitatively different, discernibly distinct levels (the "plateaus"); that is, the demarcations between levels of

FIGURE 1-3

The trajectory of mental development in adulthood

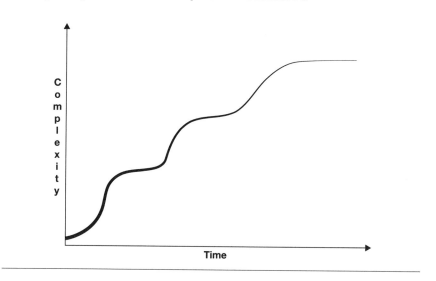

mental complexity are not arbitrary. Each level represents a quite different way of knowing the world.

- Development does not unfold continuously; there are periods of stability and periods of change. When a new plateau is reached we tend to stay on that level for a considerable period of time (although elaborations and extensions within each system can certainly occur).

- The intervals between transformations to new levels—"time on a plateau"—get longer and longer.

- The line gets thinner, representing fewer and fewer people at the higher plateaus.

But what do these different levels of mental complexity in adulthood actually look like? Can we say something about what a more complex level can see or do that a less complex level cannot? Indeed, we can now say a great deal about these levels. Mental complexity and its evolution is not about how smart you are in the ordinary sense of the word. It is not about how high your IQ is. It is not about developing more and more abstract, abstruse apprehensions of the world, as if "most complex" means finally being able to understand a physicist's blackboard filled with complex equations.

THREE PLATEAUS IN ADULT MENTAL COMPLEXITY

Later on in this book we will say more about these levels, but for now, let's begin with a quick overview of three qualitatively different plateaus in mental complexity we see among adults, as suggested in figures 1-4 and 1-5.

These three adult meaning systems—the socialized mind, self-authoring mind, and self-transforming mind—make sense of the world, and operate within it, in profoundly different ways. We can see how this shows up at work by focusing on any significant aspect of organizational life and seeing how the very same phenomenon—for example, information flow—is completely different through the lens of each perspective.

FIGURE 1-4

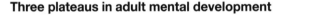

Three plateaus in adult mental development

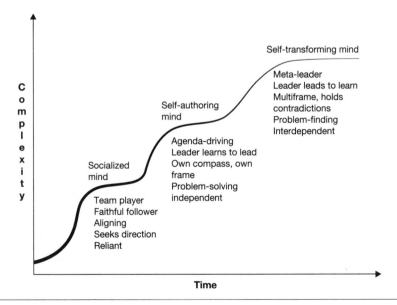

FIGURE 1-5

The three adult plateaus described

The socialized mind

• We are shaped by the definitions and expectations of our personal environment.

• Our self coheres by its alignment with, and loyalty to, that with which it identifies.

• This can express itself primarily in our relationships with people, with "schools of thought" (our ideas and beliefs) or both.

The self-authoring mind

• We are able to step back enough from the social environment to generate an internal "seat of judgment" or personal authority that evaluates and makes choices about external expectations.

• Our self coheres by its alignment with its own belief system/ideology/personal code; by its ability to self-direct, take stands, set limits, and create and regulate its boundaries on behalf of its own voice.

The self-transforming mind

• We can step back from and reflect on the limits of our own ideology or personal authority; see that any one system or self-organization is in some way partial or incomplete; be friendlier toward contradiction and opposites; seek to hold on to multiple systems rather than projecting all but one onto the other.

• Our self coheres through its ability not to confuse internal consistency with wholeness or completeness, and through its alignment with the dialectic rather than either pole.

The way information does or does not flow through an organization—what people "send," to whom they send it, how they receive or attend to what flows to them—is an obviously crucial feature of how any system works. Experts on organizational culture, organizational behavior, or organizational change often address this subject with a sophisticated sense of how systems impact individual behavior, but with an astonishingly naive sense of how powerful a factor is the level of mental complexity with which the individual views that organizational culture or change initiative.

Socialized Mind

Having a socialized mind dramatically influences both the sending and receiving aspects of information flow at work. If this is the level of mental complexity with which I view the world, then what I think to send will be strongly influenced by what I believe others want to hear. You may be familiar with the classic group-think studies, which show team members withholding crucial information from collective decision processes because (it is later learned in follow-up research) "although I knew the plan had almost no chance of succeeding, I saw that the leader wanted our support."

Some of these groupthink studies were originally done in Asian cultures where withholding team members talked about "saving face" of leaders and not subjecting them to shame, even at the price of setting the company on a losing path. The studies were often presented as if they were uncovering a particularly cultural phenomenon. Similarly, Stanley Milgram's famous obedience-to-authority research was originally undertaken to fathom the mentality of "the good German," and what about the German culture could enable otherwise decent, nonsadistic people to carry out orders to exterminate millions of Jews and Poles.[1] But Milgram, in practice runs of his data-gathering method, was surprised to find "good Germans" all over Main Street, U.S.A., and although we think of sensitivity to shame as a particular feature of Asian culture, the research of Irving Janis and Paul t'Hart has made clear that group-think is as robust a phenomenon in Texas and Toronto as it is in Tokyo and Taiwan.[2] It is a phenomenon that owes its origin not to culture, but to complexity of mind.

The socialized mind also strongly influences how information is *received* and *attended to*. When maintaining alignment with important others and valued "surrounds" is crucial to the coherence of one's very being, the socialized mind is highly sensitive to, and influenced by, what it picks up. And what it picks up often runs far beyond the explicit message. It may well include the results of highly invested attention to imagined subtexts that may have more impact on the receiver than the intended message. This is often astonishing and dismaying to leaders who cannot understand how subordinates could possibly have "made *that* sense out of *this*" communication, but because the receiver's signal-to-noise detector may be highly distorted, the actual information that comes through may have only a distant relationship to the sender's intention.

Self-Authoring Mind

Let's contrast all this with the self-authoring mind. If I view the world from this level of mental complexity, what I "send" is more likely to be a function of what I deem others need to hear to best further the agenda or mission of my design. Consciously or unconsciously, I have a direction, an agenda, a stance, a strategy, an analysis of what is needed, a prior context from which my communication arises. My direction or plan may be an excellent one, or it may be riddled with blind spots. I may be masterful or inept at recruiting others to invest themselves in this direction. These matters implicate other aspects of the self. But mental complexity strongly influences whether my information sending is oriented toward getting behind the wheel in order to drive (the self-authoring mind) or getting myself included in the car so I can be driven (the socialized mind).

We can see a similar mindset operating when "receiving" as well. The self-authoring mind creates a filter for what it will allow to come through. It places a priority on receiving the information it has sought. Next in importance is information whose relevance to my plan, stance, or frame is immediately clear. Information I haven't asked for, and which does not have obvious relevance to my own design for action, has a much tougher time making it through my filter.

It is easy to see how all of this could describe an admirable capacity for focus, for distinguishing the important from the urgent, for making best use of one's limited time by having a means to cut through the unending and ever-mounting claims on one's attention. This speaks to the way the self-authoring mind is an advance over the socialized mind. But this same description may also be a recipe for disaster if one's plan or stance is flawed in some way, if it leaves out some crucial element of the equation not appreciated by the filter, or if the world changes in such a way that a once-good frame becomes an antiquated one.

Self-Transforming Mind

In contrast, the self-transforming mind also has a filter, but is not fused with it. The self-transforming mind can stand back from its own filter and look *at* it, not just *through* it. And why would it do so? Because the self-transforming mind both values and *is wary about* any one stance, analysis, or agenda. It is mindful that, powerful though a given design might be, this design almost inevitably leaves something out. It is aware that it lives in time and that the world is in motion, and what might have made sense today may not make as much sense tomorrow.

Therefore, when communicating, people with self-transforming minds are not only advancing their agenda and design. They are also making space for the modification or expansion of their agenda or design. Like those with self-authoring minds, what they send may include inquiries and requests for information. But rather than inquiring only *within* the frame of their design (seeking information that will advance their agenda), they are also inquiring about the design itself. They are seeking information that may lead them or their team to enhance, refine, or alter the original design or make it more inclusive. Information sending is not just on behalf of driving; it is also to remake the map or reset the direction.

Similarly, the way the self-transforming mind receives information includes the advantages of the self-authoring mind's filter, but is not a prisoner of that filter. People at this level of mental complexity can still focus, select, and drive when they feel they have a good map. But they place a higher priority on information that may also alert them to the limits of their current design or frame. They value their filter and its ability to separate the wheat from the chaff, but they know it can also screen out "the golden chaff," the unasked-for, the anomaly, the apparently inconsequential that may be just what is needed to turn the design on its head and bring it to the next level of quality.

Those with self-transforming minds are more likely to have the chance even to consider such information, because people are more likely to send it to them. Why is this? Because those with self-transforming minds not only attend to information once it gets to their door; they also realize their behavior can have a big effect, *upstream,* on whether people decide to approach the door. Others are not left guessing whether to send potentially "off-mission" communication they judge to be important. They send it because people with self-transforming minds have found ways to let them know such information will be welcomed.

MENTAL COMPLEXITY AND PERFORMANCE

These descriptions, focusing on just a single important element of organizational life—information flow—should begin to make the different levels of mental complexity a little clearer. They also suggest a value proposition for mental complexity. Each successive level of mental complexity is formally higher than the preceding one because it can perform the mental functions of the prior level as well as additional functions. But the discussion of how information flow is conceived and handled also suggests that these formal mental properties translate into real actions with real consequences for organizational behavior and work competence. The implication is that a higher level of mental complexity outperforms a lower level.

Is this just a hypothesis, albeit with some plausible face validity, or has it actually been tested and systematically demonstrated? There are now a number of studies correlating measures of mental complexity with independent assessments of work competence or performance. We will consider these results in greater depth later in this book, but for now let's just take a peek at what these studies show.

Keith Eigel assessed the level of mental complexity of twenty-one CEOs of large, successful companies, each company an industry leader with average gross revenue of over $5 billion.[3] (He used a ninety-minute interview assessment measure that we and our colleagues developed. The Subject-Object Interview, described in "How Do We Assess Level of Mental Complexity?", has been used all over the world, across all sectors, over the last twenty years. It discriminates developmental movement between, and within, the levels of mental complexity with high degrees of interrater reliability.) Using separate performance assessments, Eigel also evaluated the CEOs' effectiveness in terms of the ability to:

- Challenge existing processes

- Inspire a shared vision

- Manage conflict

How Do We Assess Level of Mental Complexity?

OUR ASSESSMENT TOOL is a ninety-minute interview we call the Subject-Object Interview, so named because the complexity of a mindset is a function of the way it distinguishes the thoughts and feelings we have (i.e., can look at, can take *as object*) from the thoughts and feelings that "have us" (i.e., we are run by them, are *subject to* them). Each different level of mindset complexity differently draws the line between what is subject and what is object. Greater complexity means being able to *look at* more (take more *as object*). The blind spot (what is *subject*) becomes smaller and smaller. The assessment instrument has proven to be quite subtle: it can identify, with high degrees of interrater reliability, fully five different transitional places between any two mindsets.

The interview begins by handing the subject ten index cards, upon which are written the following cues:

- Angry
- Anxious, nervous
- Success
- Strong stand, conviction
- Sad
- Torn
- Moved, touched
- Lost something, farewells
- Change
- Important

In the first fifteen minutes, we ask the interviewee to make notes on each card in response to questions of the following form: "Think of some times, over the last few days or weeks, when you found yourself feeling really mad or angry about something [or nervous, scared, anxious, etc.], and jot down what comes to mind." The interview then proceeds as a systematic exploration: the interviewee tells us the *whats* (what made him feel angry, successful, etc.) and we probe to learn the *whys* (why would that make him feel angry or successful; just what is at stake?). We chose these prompts because earlier research showed them to be highly successful at eliciting the boundaries and contours of people's current way of constructing reality. A trained interviewer can probe such material to learn the underlying principle governing what the person can and cannot see (the blind spot).

The interviews are transcribed and analyzed according to a uniform process. Thousands of these interviews have now been conducted with people all over the world, with people of all ages and from all walks of life. Most people find the interview a highly engaging experience.

Source: L. Lahey, E. Souvaine, R. Kegan, et al., *A Guide to the Subject-Object Interview: Its Administration and Analysis* (Cambridge, MA: The Subject-Object Research Group, Harvard University Graduate School of Education, 1988).

- Solve problems

- Delegate

- Empower

- Build relationships

In addition, for comparison, Eigel did similar assessments in each of the same companies, interviewing promising middle managers nominated by their respective CEOs. Figure 1-6 summarizes his findings.

Several results stand out. The first obvious one is the clearly discernible upward slope, signifying that increased mental complexity and work competence, assessed on a number of dimensions, are correlated. So not only is it possible to reach higher planes of mental complexity, but such growth correlates with effectiveness, for both CEOs and middle managers. This finding has been replicated in a variety of fine-grained studies of small numbers of leaders, assessed on particular competencies.[4] Taken together, the cumulative data speaks anew to the problem of complexity: we begin to see how

FIGURE 1-6

Individual mental capacity and business effectiveness: Eigel's results

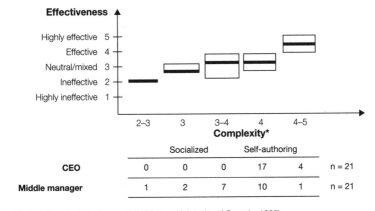

	Socialized			Self-authoring		
CEO	0	0	0	17	4	n = 21
Middle manager	1	2	7	10	1	n = 21

Source: K. Eigel, "Leader Effectiveness" (PhD diss., University of Georgia, 1998).
*3 = socialized mind; 4 = self-authoring mind; 5 = self-transforming mind

being at a given level of mental complexity can make a "complex world" more or less manageable.

SHIFTS IN THE DEMANDS ON FOLLOWERS AND LEADERS

We can also take a more sweeping view of the same issue by considering the new demands on leaders and their subordinates in the faster, flatter, more interconnected world in which we live. Take another look at figure 1-4, the chart of the various plateaus in adult mental complexity.

Now let's consider what was asked, and is now asked, of subordinates. In the world in which we *used to* live, it was enough in most cases if people were good team players, pulled their weight, were loyal to the company or organization where they worked, and could be counted on to follow conscientiously the directions and signals of their boss. In other words, the socialized mind would be perfectly adequate to handle the nature of yesterday's demands upon subordinates.

And today? Nathaniel Branden writes:

> In the past two or three decades, extraordinary developments
> have occurred in the American and global economies. The
> United States has shifted from a manufacturing society to an
> information society. We have witnessed the transition from
> physical labor to mind work as the dominant employee activity.
> We now live in a global economy characterized by rapid change,
> accelerating scientific and technological breakthroughs, and an
> unprecedented level of competitiveness. These developments
> create demand for higher levels of education and training than
> were required of previous generations. Everyone acquainted
> with business culture knows this. What is not understood is
> that these developments also create new demands on our
> psychological resources. Specifically, these developments ask
> for a greater capacity for innovation, self-management,
> personal responsibility, and self-direction. This is not just
> asked at the top, it is asked at every level of a business enter-
> prise, from senior management to first-line supervisors and
> even to entry-level personnel . . . Today, organizations need not
> only an unprecedentedly higher level of knowledge and skill
> among all those who participate but also a higher level of
> independence, self-reliance, self-trust, and the capacity to
> exercise initiative.[5]

What is Branden—and many others who write about what we
are now looking for from our workforce—really saying, as it relates
to level of mental complexity? He is saying, without realizing it, that
it used to be sufficient for workers to be at the level of the socialized
mind, but today we need workers who are at the level of the self-
authoring mind. In effect, *we are calling upon workers to understand
themselves and their world at a qualitatively higher level of mental
complexity.*

And what is the picture if we look not at subordinates but at
bosses and leaders? Organizational theorist Chris Argyris raises similar issues about the ever-growing insufficiency of traditional concep-
tions of managerial and leadership effectiveness that still dominate

our thinking today. There may have been a day when it was enough for leaders to develop worthy goals and sensible norms, cultivate alignments around them, and work "to keep organizational performance within the range specified"—all the while exercising the strength of character to advocate for one's position and hold one's ground in the face of opposition.[6] Skillful as such managers may be, their abilities will no longer suffice in a world that calls for leaders who can not only run but reconstitute their organizations—its norms, missions, and culture—in an increasingly fast-changing environment. For example, a company that chooses to transform itself from a low-cost standardized-products organization to a mass customizer or a provider of organization-wide solutions will need to develop a whole new set of individual and team capabilities.

Argyris and Schön described the challenges of a similar organizational transition thirty years ago:

> This, in turn, requires that members of the corporation adopt new approaches to marketing, managing, and advertising; that they become accustomed to a much shorter product life cycle and to a more rapid cycle of changes in their pattern of activities; that they, in fact, change the very image of the business they are in. And these requirements for change come into conflict with another sort of corporate norm, one that requires predictability in the management of corporate affairs . . . A process of change initiated with an eye to effectiveness under existing norms turns out to yield a conflict in the norms themselves.[7]

For more than a generation, Argyris (and those who have been influenced by him) has unwittingly been calling for a new capacity of mind. This new mind would have the ability not just to *author* a view of how the organization should run and have the courage to hold steadfastly to that view. It would also be able to step outside of *its own* ideology or framework, observe the framework's limitations or defects, and *re-author* a more comprehensive view—which it will hold with sufficient tentativeness that its limitations can be discovered as well. In other words, the kind of learner Argyris rightly looks for in the leader of today may need to be a person who is making meaning with a *self-transforming* mind.

Thus, we are asking more and more workers who could once perform their work successfully with socialized minds—good soldiers—to shift to self-authoring minds. And we are asking more and more leaders who could once lead successfully with self-authoring minds—sure and certain captains—to develop self-transforming minds. In short, we are asking for a quantum shift in individual mental complexity across the board.

So how big *is* the gap between what we now expect of people's minds and what their minds are actually like? Are we expecting something that is so big a reach? After all, if the world has gotten more complex over the last half century, then perhaps the world has become a better incubator of mental complexity as well, and the supply of mental complexity has risen with the demand.

We now have two sophisticated, reliable, and widely used measures for assessing mental complexity along the lines we are talking about here. (This is something quite different, obviously, from IQ testing, which has only the most modest correlation with mental complexity; you can have an above average IQ, say 125, and be at any of the three plateaus.) These are the Washington University Sentence Completion Test (SCT) and the Subject-Object Interview (SOI) we introduced earlier.[8] Two large meta-analyses of studies using one or the other of these measures have now been performed, with several hundred participants in each study. Figure 1-7 presents a quick summary of results.

Two observations stand out from the data in figure 1-7:

- Both studies, each done with completely different samples, arrive at the same finding—that in a majority of respondents, mental complexity is not as far along as the self-authoring mind (in fact, in each study exactly 58 percent are not at this level)—and since both studies are skewed toward middle-class, college-educated professionals, the actual percentage in the general population is likely even higher.

FIGURE 1-7

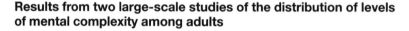

Results from two large-scale studies of the distribution of levels of mental complexity among adults

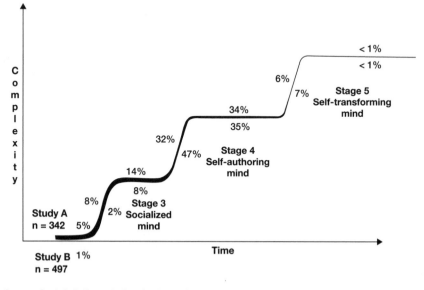

Sources: Study A: R. Kegan, *In Over Our Heads* (Cambridge, MA: Harvard University Press, 1994). Study B: W. Torbert, *Managing the Corporate Dream* (Homewood, IL: Dow-Jones, 1987).

- The percentages of people *beyond* the plateau of the self-authoring mind are quite small.

These data suggests that the gap between what we now expect of people's minds (including our own minds) and what our minds are actually like is quite large. We expect most workers to be self-authoring, but most are not. We expect most leaders to be more complex than self-authoring, and very few are.

We can see these same macro trends confirmed at the micro level if we return for a moment to the Eigel study (have another look at figure 1-6). Note here that only about half of the "promising middle managers" are self-authoring (and those who are do better than those who are not), and only four of the twenty-one CEOs from industry-leading companies are beyond self-authoring (and those who are do better than those who are not).

MENTAL COMPLEXITY AND "TECHNICAL" VERSUS "ADAPTIVE" CHALLENGES

Our colleague and friend Ronald Heifetz makes an important distinction that helps us summarize the central points we have made so far. Heifetz distinguishes between two kinds of change challenges, those he calls "technical" and others he calls "adaptive."[9] Technical changes are not necessarily easy, nor are their results necessarily unimportant or insignificant. Learning how to remove an inflamed appendix or how to land an airplane with a stuck nose wheel are examples of largely technical challenges, and their accomplishment is certainly important to the patient on the surgeon's table or the nervous passengers contemplating a crash landing.

They are nonetheless "technical" from Heifetz's point of view because the skill set necessary to perform these complicated behaviors is well known. The routines and processes by which we might help an intern or novice pilot become an accomplished practitioner are well practiced and proven. While it is entirely possible that an intern or a pilot in training will become qualitatively more complex over years of training, such mental growth is beyond the scope of their technical training. Novice surgeons, for example, become sufficiently skilled surgeons without anyone worrying about their adult development or mental growth.

However, many, if not most, of the change challenges you face today and will face tomorrow require something more than incorporating new technical skills into your current mindset. These are the "adaptive challenges," and they can only be met by transforming your mindset, by advancing to a more sophisticated stage of mental development.

Heifetz says the biggest error leaders make is when they apply technical means to solve adaptive challenges. In other words, we may be unable to bring about the changes we want because we are misdiagnosing our aspiration as technical, when in reality it is an adaptive challenge. The implication is that we must find *adaptive* (nontechnical) means of supporting ourselves and others to meet adaptive challenges.

Distinguishing adaptive challenges from technical ones again brings our attention back from the "problem" to the "person having the problem." We've said that "complexity" is really a story about the relationship between the complex demands and arrangements of the world and our own complexity of mind. When we look at this relationship we discover a gap: our own mental complexity lags behind the complexity of the world's demands. We are in over our heads.

This naturally brings us to a next question: can we actually do something to incubate mental complexity, and to accelerate it? We have spent more than twenty years actively exploring this question in a "laboratory" that has taken us all over the world. In the next chapter we bring you into this laboratory to show you what we have found.

[2]

UNCOVERING THE
IMMUNITY TO CHANGE

So WHAT WOULD IT MEAN to meet an adaptive change adaptively, rather than technically? In other words, what would it mean to intentionally support the development of complexity of mind? In many respects the rest of this book is an answer to that question.

We have learned that meeting adaptive challenges requires, first, an adaptive *formulation* of the problem (i.e., we need to see exactly how the challenge comes up against the current limits of our own mental complexity), and, second, an adaptive *solution* (i.e., we ourselves need to adapt in some way).

This chapter is devoted to the first task, creating an adaptive formulation of an adaptive challenge. Seeing how a challenge brings us to the current limits of our own mental growth is obviously not a cognitive matter alone. Instead, it will connect head and heart, thinking and feeling. An adaptive formulation requires some new means of perceiving that at once gives us a sharper analytic reading than we have had before and reveals the "emotional ecology" underlying the challenge.

This chapter introduces an explicit method for acquiring this new means of perceiving. (In chapter 9 you'll have an opportunity to develop an adaptive formulation of one of your own challenges.)

Once we've discussed how to develop an adaptive formulation, we will turn to adaptive solutions: we will show you how to make changes—in yourself and your organization—enabled by developing greater mental complexity.

To teach you our method, we first want to bring you into our "laboratory" to show you what we have discovered—a phenomenon we call the immunity to change. Our lab does not exist in a single space in a university, and we don't wear white coats as we do our work. Our lab is out in the world, in real work settings in business, government, and education, in the United States and abroad, where, in every case, courageous leaders—CEOs, senior managers, commissioners, superintendents—have invited us to collaborate with them and their senior teams over many months on a novel learning journey.

We are going to hold this phenomenon in front of you and turn it around in our hands, so that you can see it from several angles. If our demonstration succeeds, you will see a previously hidden dynamic in the problem of change. Each person's particular version of this dynamic is made visible through drafting a mental map that functions something like an X-ray, a picture of the invisible made visible. The X-ray or immunity map helps us all to see not just how things are at the moment, but why they are this way, and what will actually need to change in order to bring about any significant new results. The best way for us to help you see the phenomenon is to show you a few of these immunity maps.

PETER'S IMMUNITY MAP

Meet Peter Donovan, a CEO colleague of ours. Peter is a cofounding CEO of a multibillion-dollar financial services company based in New England. By the time we met him, in his fifties, he had grown the company from a minor player in a suite of holdings into one of the undeniable jewels in the corporate crown. He's a contagiously stimulating, energetic, and funny guy whose curious mind, interest in people, and love of the work all contributed mightily to his company's success. As the company's first leader, he inevitably gave it the imprint of his personality.

Though gifted in many ways, Peter, like all of us, had his limitations. These were becoming more noticeable, he'd be the first to say, because he had decided, not long before we started working with him, to dramatically increase the size of his company, acquiring two competitors in different parts of the country. Of course, this also meant acquiring the organizational challenges of melding different corporate cultures, taking on new senior players who themselves needed to assume different roles, and redefining, to some extent, his own way of operating. Foremost among Peter's personal challenges in these new circumstances was the need for him to evolve a more distributed leadership model, to be less hands-on everywhere, to be a better delegator, to let more thinking—other than his own—into the executive region of the company brain.

Drawing on his self-awareness, but also taking seriously the feedback he had received from those around him, Peter identified a set of personal change goals he felt a strong commitment to fulfill. He said it was imperative, not just desirable, for him to make these changes if he was going to successfully lead the company into its next stage of being. In his own words, he wanted to:

- Be more receptive to new ideas.

- Be more flexible in his responses, especially regarding new definitions of roles and responsibilities.

- Be more open to delegating and supporting new lines of authority.

Developing an X-ray around these aspirations required Peter next to create a candid and honest list of the things he did (and failed to do) that ran *contrary* to these goals. His initial list looked like this:

- I often give curt responses to new ideas, taking on a "closing off," "cutting off," or overruling tone.

- I don't ask open-ended questions or genuinely seek out others' opinions often enough.

- I too frequently communicate to others the message that they need to touch back to me.

- I am too quick to give my own opinions when that may not be what people are asking for.

Figure 2-1 displays the first two features of Peter's X-ray.

Trying to solve our problems by fixing the behaviors of the second column is a perfectly understandable and commonplace response. It is also a perfect example of trying to solve a problem by technical means. If Peter's column 1 goals represent for him an adaptive, rather than a technical, challenge, then trying to solve his problem by fixing the column 2 behaviors is also a perfect example of trying to solve an adaptive challenge via technical means.

In developing our X-ray further, we take a counterintuitively respectful stance toward the obstructive behaviors of the second column. Instead of regarding them as things that just need to go away, we look at the behaviors as a precious resource, valuable information that can be mined to develop a more satisfying picture of what may

FIGURE 2-1

Peter's Emerging X-ray: Columns 1 and 2

1 Commitments (improvement goals)	2 Doing/not doing instead (behaviors that work against the goals)
Be more receptive to new ideas Be more flexible in my responses, especially regarding new definitions of roles and responsibilities Be more open to delegating and supporting new lines of authority	Giving curt responses to new ideas; "closing off," "cutting off," or overruling tone Not asking open-ended questions or seeking opinions of others often enough Communicating to others too much/ too frequently that they need to touch back to me Being too quick to give opinion when that may not be what people are asking for

really be happening. Another way of putting this is to say that we regard the entries in the second column more as symptoms of something else, rather than "the thing itself." Thus, for the moment, we are less interested in making these behaviors go away, and more interested in how they can lead us to a picture of the real challenge.

Here we are reminded of what the psychologist William Perry once said are the two most important things to know about people you are trying to help change: "What do they really want [column 1], and what will they do to keep from getting it?" [column 2]. The advantage of our X-ray technology is that it also provides a window into a third element: *why* do they persist with the column 2 behaviors that keep them from getting what they want? For the answer, we must look to the competing commitments of column 3.

Using our X-ray technology, we are able to make visible those "hidden" commitments that "have Peter"—commitments that hold him captive, in their thrall (even if Peter is partially or completely unaware of them), and compete with Peter's stated goals in column 1.

What commitments "have Peter"? He listed the following:

- To have things done *my* way!

- To experience myself as having a direct impact.

- To feel the pride of ownership (of how we do things); that is, to see my stamp on things).

- To preserve my sense of myself as the super problem solver, the one who knows best, the one who is in control—yesterday, today, and tomorrow.

This last commitment came to feel most influential.

If we enter this component into the X-ray, as shown in figure 2-2, we see not just a collection of separate entries but a single system at work.

The arrows in figure 2-2 suggest that what we are looking at now is not simply a set of entries in three separate columns. We are looking at an expression of a single, dynamic system; a system in equilibrium; a system of countervailing forces that preserves and sustains

FIGURE 2-2

Peter's X-ray: The hidden dynamic in columns 1 through 3

1 (Behavior goals) Visible commitments	2 Doing/not doing instead (Behaviors that work against the goals)	3 Hidden competing commitments
Be more receptive to new ideas Be more flexible in my responses, especially regarding new definitions of roles and responsibilities Be more open to delegating and supporting new lines of authority	Giving curt responses to new ideas; "closing off," "cutting off," or overruling tone Not asking open-ended questions or seeking opinions of others enough Communicating to others too much/too frequently that they need to touch back to me Being too quick to give opinion when that may not be what people are asking for	To have things done my way! To experience myself as having a direct impact To feel the pride of "ownership" (of how we do things); that is, "see my stamp" To preserve my sense of myself as the super problem solver, the one who knows best, the one who is in control

itself for a very good reason. We call it an *immune* system, because it gives us a glimpse into what we call the immunity to change. This phenomenon, which the X-ray makes visible, begins to reveal a crucial missing piece in the puzzle of why change is so difficult.

We use the medical metaphor of immunity quite mindfully to signal that, first of all, this phenomenon is not in itself a bad thing. On the contrary, an immune system is, most of the time, a beautiful thing, an extraordinarily intelligent force that elegantly acts to protect us, to save our lives. Every immunity to change can be seen as an asset and a source of strength for that person. As a member of Peter's senior staff said approvingly when he first looked at Peter's X-ray, "The stubbornness and relentlessness displayed in your picture has had a lot to do with the success of this company and the size of my house!"

WHEN AN IMMUNE SYSTEM BECOMES PART OF THE PROBLEM

However, in some instances an immune system can threaten our continued good health. When it rejects new material, internal or external to the body, that the body needs to heal itself or to thrive, the immune system can put us in danger. In these instances the immune system is no less focused on protecting us. It is just making a mistake. It does not understand that it must alter its code. It does not understand that, ironically, in working to protect us, it is actually putting us at serious risk.

Peter's immunity to change helps us to see why a technical solution will not, in his case, suffice. A technical approach to his current limitations would involve plans or strategies for eliminating his obstructive column 2 behaviors. He doesn't ask enough open-ended questions? He gives people the feeling they need to check back with him on everything? Surely we can figure out some effective solution to this. After all, Peter is a strong-willed guy, with lots of self-discipline. When we first started working with him, Peter decided that he needed to lose ten pounds. He cut down on second helpings and desserts, and in two months he lost ten pounds. We just had lunch with him, some four years later, and he has kept the weight off.

So why shouldn't he be able to handle this challenge in the same way? Suppose he vows to monitor the way he asks questions, and keeps track of how often he reframes a question to be more inviting of an undetermined response. Suppose he never ends a meeting with his direct reports before inquiring about their action plans, and then sees whether the number of times they feel they need to get his sign-off (when they don't need it) goes down. If a guy can lose weight without having to discover any fancy new phenomenon, couldn't the same approach work here as well?

We have always told our clients that if they can make the changes they need to by recipe, by willpower, by creating some plan to extinguish certain behaviors and amplify others—like submitting to a diet—then by all means that is exactly what they should do. Nothing we have to offer is as quick and easy as a straightforward technical solution—*if it works.*

But in reality nearly all the people we have ever had the privilege to serve have already tried simply changing their column 2 behaviors, as any intelligent person would, and they have discovered *it doesn't work*. They tried a technical means to solve their problem or meet their challenge, as well they should. It is a good way to discover whether the problem or challenge *is* a technical one. You can't always tell just by looking at it. For Peter, losing ten pounds apparently was *not* an adaptive challenge. A diet, a technical means, solved what for him was a technical problem. But in this respect Peter is something of a rarity. For most of us—since research shows that the average dieter regains 107 percent of the weight he or she takes off—losing weight is *not* a technical challenge; it is an adaptive one. Solving it with a technical means—dieting—will not work.

Peter had already tried to alter his tone of voice and do a better job releasing his direct reports. He may even have had some temporary success. But before long the old behaviors were back—plus 7 percent, by Peter's own admission. This is a clear signal that for him these challenges are adaptive ones, and the X-ray shows us exactly why: the behaviors of his second column are not some weak failings arising from some insufficiently developed moral muscle. *They are brilliant, highly effective behaviors serving exactly the purpose another part of him intends!* He makes everybody check back because he is in the thrall of a hidden commitment to feeling like the indispensable guy who knows best (perhaps even more so at this time, with so many new players on the scene, some of whom have "known best" themselves).

But make no mistake: Peter is *also* sincerely and deeply committed to being a better delegator. The X-ray does not peel back some insincere commitment to reveal the real one. The phenomenon we have spent the last twenty years exploring would be far less interesting and important if we were simply identifying the gap between what people say and what they mean. Change does not fail to occur because of insincerity. The heart patient is not insincere about his wish to keep living, even as he reaches for another cigarette. Change fails to occur because we mean *both* things. It fails to occur because we are a living contradiction. "My immunity map," Peter said, "is a picture of me with one foot on the gas and one foot on the brake!" He wants to make a change, but he also wants to "save his life," and underneath his commitment to being the guy who knows best is a deep-running assumption that his "life" would be at risk were he not to remain in complete control.

Organizations all over the world, as we said, are spending billions of dollars and committing enormous amounts of time to evaluation processes in order to grow greater capabilities in their personnel. People bravely listen to feedback about what they need to change. They often commit, with the utmost sincerity, to make the changes. They may even start out putting a lot of emotional energy into that commitment. But a year later, they are back looking at a picture of very little change.

Too often, these sincere avowals to change become the work equivalent of New Year's resolutions. Most New Year's resolutions *are* sincere. That is precisely what makes their dismal record of accomplishment so perplexing. But Peter's X-ray shows us why New Year's resolutions so seldom yield lasting results. When we make a New Year's resolution, we look at the behaviors we seek to extinguish as bad; we look at the behaviors we want to amplify as good. But until we understand the commitments that make the obstructive behaviors at the same time brilliantly *effective,* we haven't correctly formulated the problem. Einstein said the formulation of the problem is as important as the solution. Creating an X-ray can help Peter uncover and address his problem as an immunity to change, a way that he protects himself from accomplishing his goal in order to "save his life."

RON'S IMMUNITY MAP

Let's take a look at another immunity X-ray. Ron Halpern is Peter's president and COO, and he has been with him almost since the day Peter started the company. A bright, warm, and gentle guy, Ron has over thirty years' experience in financial services and was trained originally as a lawyer. He and Peter are more than good colleagues; they are good friends.

As the person in charge of day-to-day operations, Ron regularly has to make decisions, often without consultation, often risking the unhappy reactions of others. He does this without serious difficulty, except in one very significant situation—making decisions within the executive staff. He was therefore not surprised by what he heard after consulting those around him for frank feedback as to the single most important kind of improvement he could make. He identified his first-column commitments like this:

- Be a more forceful and direct communicator.

- Be a more effective decision maker within the executive staff, especially when it may involve unpopular decisions.

- Stop being overly conciliatory.

- Get better at pushing back with the CEO, less oriented to his approval and support.

Like Peter, he was frank and candid when he filled in his second column:

- Not being direct

- Checking in too often, overconsulting, overinsuring no negative reactions

- Trying to please everyone, especially CEO

- Overly tuned in to CEO's point of view

When Ron completed the third column, his immunity X-ray looked like figure 2-3.

Ron's adaptive challenge certainly has a whole different ring to it than Peter's. Yet like Peter's, his immunity X-ray reveals a powerful equilibrium, an immune system balancing the countervailing forces of contradictory commitments. There is always "a foot on the brake and a foot on the gas."

Some people refer to our X-rays as pictures of a particular person's internal status quo. We don't use this term, because it tends to connote stillness, stasis, a lack of energy. Actually, when there is a foot on the gas and a foot on the brake there is an *enormous* amount of energy

FIGURE 2-3

Ron's initial immunity X-ray

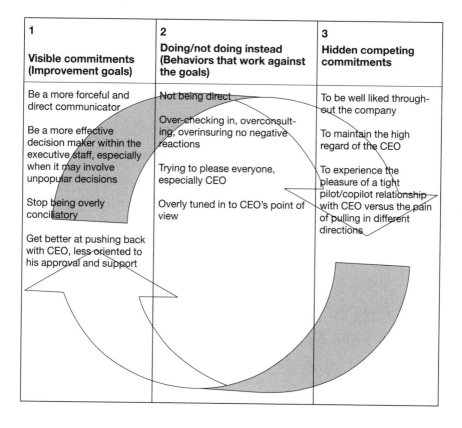

1 Visible commitments (Improvement goals)	2 Doing/not doing instead (Behaviors that work against the goals)	3 Hidden competing commitments
Be a more forceful and direct communicator Be a more effective decision maker within the executive staff, especially when it may involve unpopular decisions Stop being overly conciliatory Get better at pushing back with CEO, less oriented to his approval and support	Not being direct Over-checking in, overconsulting, overinsuring no negative reactions Trying to please everyone, especially CEO Overly tuned in to CEO's point of view	To be well liked throughout the company To maintain the high regard of the CEO To experience the pleasure of a tight pilot/copilot relationship with CEO versus the pain of pulling in different directions

cycling through that system. But because the energies are cycling in opposing directions, the car is not moving. Imagine if Peter or Ron were able to release some of the energy trapped inside his immune system. Imagine if *you* (or your colleagues) were able to release the energy that is trapped in yours (or theirs). What might Peter and Ron—what might we as individuals within our organizations—be able to do with this energy that they and we cannot do today? (This is the subject of part 2 of this book.)

Ron's obstructive behavior (column 2) cannot be eliminated by a New Year's resolution any more than Peter's can, because the X-ray shows us that Ron's lack of directness, overconsulting, and constant effort to please are brilliant and effective behaviors on behalf of his own third-column commitments. Notice that those third-column commitments are not necessarily predictable from looking at the second-column behaviors alone. They never are. In Ron's case, he discovered (through means we will later explain) that he had a commitment to being well liked and well regarded, and to preserving, at all costs, his close relationship with Peter.

But these aren't the only third-column commitments that could generate such behaviors. Another person with similar first-column goals and second-column obstructions might discover his third-column commitment is to avoid being held responsible for bad decisions and company failures (so he essentially works to have others, rather than himself, make key decisions). Still another person with similar first and second columns might discover that the commitment that "has her" is a commitment to not be envied or resented, to not stick out too far above the rest, or to not be seen as having "gone over to the other side" and become more of a "boss" and a "suit" than "one of the gang." (These happen not to be Ron's third-column commitments, but they could be.)

SAME ISSUE, DIFFERENT MAPS FOR DIFFERENT INDIVIDUALS

As we will see, the third-column commitments are the most powerful entry points to adaptive change, so it is important to recognize that while many people can share the same obstructive behavior, the real motivation for that behavior (the thing that makes it brilliant) might be quite different.

We can see this more clearly by returning to the subject of weight loss. (We know we left you hanging on this one, right? You were hoping for a little help with your own waistline battles.) We said that for Peter, this apparently was not an adaptive challenge, but for most of us it is. Americans collectively lose millions of pounds of body weight every year in diets—and then regain even more. Why might this be, by the light of these ideas?

The entries for the first and second columns in figure 2-4 are ones that many, many of us could identify with. Column 1: we would sincerely like to lose weight—for health reasons, for vanity, so our

FIGURE 2-4

A multiperson X-ray of the challenge of weight loss

1 **Visible commitment**	2 **Doing/not doing instead**	3 **Hidden competing commitments**
I am committed to losing weight.	I eat too much. I eat when I'm not even hungry. I eat food with too much fat. I eat food with too much carbohydrate.	Person A: I am committed to not being bored, to feeling stimulated and energized. I am committed to not feeling empty. Person B: I am committed to feeling well connected to my people, to receiving love when it is offered to me. Person C: I am committed to not being seen, and related to, as a sexual object. I am committed to not feeling overwhelmed and enraged.

clothes don't feel so tight, for whatever reason. Column 2: asked to identify our behaviors that work against this goal, most of us get around to seeing that—wait for this—the problem has something to do with the way we are eating! We eat more than we should, when we are not even hungry; we eat food that is too fatty or too carb-rich, and so on.

We try to solve this problem by going directly at the second-column behaviors. A diet is a good example of this. The reason a diet will not work for most of us is that we need a better (nontechnical) formulation of our problem. We need to see that we are in the grip of an adaptive challenge. We need to see how our second-column behaviors are also brilliant and effective (not just obstructive).

But as widely shared as the first two columns might be, the actual immune systems of several dieters—uncovered by accurate entries in their third columns—might all be quite different.

We have worked with a number of people whose first-column goal concerned weight loss. (There is a project underway in Copenhagen assessing the efficacy of our approach on the treatment of obesity.) One person discovered that his overeating was not a solution to hunger, but to the unwelcome feelings of emptiness and boredom that frequently arose, and for which food had become the treatment of choice.

Another person described himself as "a member of a loving tribe of people that engages in weekly, multicourse, multigenerational eating extravaganzas—in other words, I'm an Italian-American!" He was referring to the Sunday meal, and he proceeded to explain, "You won't really be able to understand this if you're not Italian, but whenever I would diet, and refuse my loving aunts' tenderly offered extra helpings of manicotti or whatever, they would have the most hurt expressions on their faces, and they would say things that just cut right through me, like, 'What? So you are too good for us now? You're not one of us anymore?' I love my aunts, and what they are offering me isn't just an extra portion. They are offering me love. Turning this down becomes too painful. I guess you could say I have a third-column commitment to feeling well-connected with my people."

A third person regularly wanted to lose twenty pounds. She would bravely take up a diet, lose twenty pounds, and before long, regain it. She discovered she had a third-column commitment to "keeping my relationships desexualized." As soon as she lost weight, she found herself being approached by men she felt were no longer relating to her as a person but as a sex object. Given her personal history, she had good reason to find this kind of experience deeply disturbing.

However similar the improvement goals and obstructive behaviors of these three people may be, the specific (adaptive) formulations of their weight-loss issues are quite different (see figure 2-4). For each of them, losing weight will be an adaptive challenge, but for each a *different* adaptive challenge. None of them is likely to succeed by dieting. The route to success for each will be different because each person's immune system is unique.

We have just begun to acquaint you with the process by which we uncover the immunity to change. But before we examine this phenomenon further, we imagine a reaction you might be having right now. It is possible, as you look at these first pictures from our lab, especially the third columns of maps like Peter's and Ron's, that you're thinking something like this:

"Where are they finding these people who are so willing to open their kimonos? I don't know whether to admire these people's honesty, candor, and lack of defensiveness, or to be appalled at their willingness to bare themselves, warts and all. It doesn't really matter. The point is I can't see the people I work with— hell, I can't even see *me*—revealing all this stuff! It's interesting, and it does give you a deep look inside. I can even begin to think about what might be in the third columns of some of the people around me, but practically speaking, I don't see where we can go with this, because I just don't think there are very many people who are going to willingly reveal themselves at this depth. I think Kegan and Lahey must be working with a very idiosyncratic sample of people who go in for this kind of thing."

We think we might feel the same way if we were just looking at these X-rays without understanding how they get developed. We will show you how that happens in a later chapter, but for now we should say quite confidently that the people who produced these X-rays, and others like them, are not idiosyncratic at all. They are men and women like you. They work in the same sector that you do. They are the same age and level of seniority as you are right now. And, if asked, they would tell you they are no more inclined to share such personal information than you are.

We can say this because the full sample of people with whom we developed these X-rays now includes thousands of people, every kind of person you can imagine, across all professional and leadership levels. They are engineers and educators, CEOs and the CIA, surgeons, sitting judges, physicians, and university provosts; they are assistant commissioners of child welfare, assistant high school principals, and corporate vice presidents; they are bankers, legislators, drug company executives, attorneys, international business consultants, and librarians; they are managers, senior managers, line managers, account managers; they are graduate students in business, education, government, and medicine; they are professors and retired persons, army colonels, labor union leaders, and software developers; they are executives from *Fortune* 500 companies and small businesses; they live in the United States, Western Europe, Eastern Europe, South America, India, Japan, the Mideast, Singapore, Shanghai, and South Africa. While they are skewed to the college-educated, middle-class ranks, they are certainly not idiosyncratic in relation to issues of self-disclosure, self-awareness, or emotional expressiveness. They are no more or less likely than you to have spent time in psychotherapy or other self-reflective activities. (They may be no more interested in introspection than the fellow in the following cartoon; see figure 2-5.)

Almost none of them had any clue when they began the process of developing their X-rays that they were going to create a picture that would be so revealing—or intriguing—to them. If we had told

FIGURE 2-5

"Look, call it denial if you like, but I think what goes on in my personal life is none of my own damn business."

them beforehand what they were going to produce, some might have declined to participate, and most might have been skeptical. So do not assume there is anything unusual about the people who produced the pictures you have seen so far.

THE EMOTIONAL ECOLOGY
OF AN IMMUNE SYSTEM

At the simplest level, any particular expression of the immunity to change provides us a picture of how we are systematically working against the very goal we genuinely want to achieve. But this dynamic equilibrium is preventing much more than progress on a single goal. It is maintaining a given place on the continuum of mental complexity. The immunity to change provides both an "outside" and "inside" perspective on what it means to say that the adult mind is a still-developing organism.

We can avail ourselves further of these outside and inside perspectives by looking more deeply at something we said earlier, that every immune system is an intelligent force that seeks to protect you, even to save your life. Considering more fully these ideas of self-protection and intelligence gives us a deeper understanding of what the immunity to change really is. Moreover, doing so brings to life the idea that development simultaneously implicates the workings of the head and the heart. We said that an adaptive formulation will grab us at the limits of our mindsets, and that our mindsets always say something about the worlds of our feeling and our thinking. How exactly does the phenomenon of the immunity to change deliver on this dual demand? What does it tell us that we may not have known before about our hearts and our heads?

Let's begin with our hearts. It is not possible to spend twenty years constantly exposing ourselves to the phenomenon we have uncovered without developing a whole new appreciation of human courage.

Courage involves the ability to take action and carry on even when we are afraid. No matter how big or consequential a given step may be, that step cannot be said to involve courage if we are not somehow afraid to take it. It may show how smart we are, how energetic, how focused; but not how brave. It is action in the face of fear that demonstrates courage. We have come to this new appreciation for human courage because we have learned something that may be very hard for successful, capable people to believe: more than we understand, most people deal constantly with fear.

"I'm not afraid," we know you are saying to yourself right now. "I feel fine." And you are right. You do not feel your fear. The reason you do not is because you are dealing with it. Though you are not aware of it, you have created a very effective anxiety-management system, and that system is what we call the immunity to change.

Anxiety, we have gradually come to appreciate, is the most important—and least understood—private emotion in public life. When you look at an immunity X-ray such as Peter's or Ron's, you are seeing a dimension of a person's mindset that is usually invisible. This hidden dimension resides at the level of feelings rather than cognitive thought. It is not itself anxious but is devoted to managing anxiety. The immunity X-ray offers a schematic representation of the way a person is handling not an acute or episodic anxiety, but a constant, if unrecognized, anxiety running continuously through his or her life.

Peter's immune system may manage a constant anxiety about his possible dispensability and his fear of losing control. Ron's may manage a constant anxiety about putting important relationships at risk. But neither of them experiences this anxiety consciously or constantly because the immune system is working beautifully to manage it automatically. Successful people—like Peter and Ron, like us, like you—develop anxiety-management systems that are very robust and self-sustaining, and they permit us to function in a wide variety of situations.

But we run these systems—even highly successful anxiety-management systems—at a cost. Inevitably, they create blind spots, prevent new learning, and constantly constrain action in some aspects of our living. These costs show up when we are unable to deliver on some genuinely desired change, the realization of which would bring us to a new, higher level of functioning in ways we truly want to attain.

Most self-improvement efforts take place in too constricted a psychological space, blind to these bigger dynamics at play. Without benefit of the X-ray, a conscientious Peter or Ron will go to work trying to alter his column 2 behaviors. The person who wants to lose weight will go on a diet. However hard they work, however sincerely they seek to extinguish their obstructive behaviors, everything will go on *within* the existing mindset. No new learning can occur. It is simply not possible for Peter or Ron, or any of us, to retain our current immune systems and still accomplish our first-column commitments. So how can we get beyond this quandary?

OVERCOMING IMMUNITY: THREE PREMISES

We can summarize much of what we've learned about overcoming the immunity to change in a series of premises:

- Overcoming immunity does *not* require the elimination of all anxiety-management systems. We will always need some kind of anxiety-management system. When a physical immune system gets us in trouble by rejecting something the body needs, we don't think the answer lies in wiping out the whole immune system. The solution for Peter or Ron, or anyone, lies in transforming this immune system, in building a bigger and more complicated immune system, one that can permit the accomplishment of the column 1 commitment. Of course, transforming an immune system is a difficult thing, because . . .

- It is not change that causes anxiety; it is the feeling that we are without defenses in the presence of what we see as danger that causes anxiety. That "change makes us uncomfortable" is now one of the most widely promoted, widely accepted, and underconsidered half-truths around. If we told you that tomorrow you would win the lottery, find the love of your life, or finally be promoted to partner, we think you'd agree any of these would entail big changes for you. But you'd probably also agree that anxiety is unlikely to be most people's first emotion in response! So it is not change by itself that makes us uncomfortable; it is not even change that involves taking on something very difficult. Rather, it is change that leaves us feeling defenseless before the dangers we "know" to be present that causes us anxiety. Overturning an immunity to change always raises the specter of leaving us exposed to such dangers. We build an immune system to save our lives. We are not easily going to surrender such a critical protection.

However, as you will see in the pages ahead,

- Our immune systems *can* be overcome. Too constricting an anxiety-management system can be replaced with a more expansive one (the limits of which may eventually be discovered, and the prospect of overcoming may arise again).

When we overcome an immunity to change, we stop making what we have come to see is actually a bad bargain: our immune system has been giving us relief from anxiety while creating a false belief that many things are impossible for us to do—*things that in fact are completely possible for us to do!* In testing his own false beliefs, Peter began to yield to others in ways he learned facilitated the integration of the new, more complicated company he was creating. Ron began delivering much more effective feedback within the executive staff and discovered he did not, for the most part, jeopardize his relationships, but in many instances actually strengthened them.

Thus, the immunity we have uncovered is not just an explanation of why people have so much difficulty bringing about a change they dearly want to make. It also shows us a whole *system* at work. The immune system is a way of managing an extraordinarily powerful feature of emotional life—the deep sense, often well founded, that life is dangerous, and that any sensible person must attend to the human version of national security. An X-ray of one's immunity to change is like a page from the top-secret playbook of a personal national defense system. The implication is that we cannot succeed with adaptive challenges without recognizing that we are putting at risk what has been a very well functioning way of taking care of ourselves.

So exploring the phenomenon of the immunity to change brings us more deeply into the world of our feelings, as we said any adaptive formulation of the problem must do. An immunity to change, as the name implies, is a system of self-protection.

TOWARD A MORE EXPANSIVE WAY
OF KNOWING

But an immunity to change is also more than a system for self-protection. We conclude this chapter by giving you a glimpse of something we think is very exciting. If we are successful, over these next few pages you will see how the phenomenon that animates the rest of this book—the immunity to change—brings together all the elements we have been discussing in these first two chapters—reconceiving the challenge to change, the prospect of increasingly sophisticated levels of mental complexity, and the continuous need to manage anxiety.

The root of any way of knowing (what philosophers call an *epistemology*) is an abstract-sounding thing called the "subject-object relationship." Any way of knowing can be described with respect to that which it can *look at* (object) and that which it *looks through* (the "filter" or "lens" to which it is subject). Young children, for example, are still *subject to* their perceptions, so when something *looks* small to them (like cars and people viewed from the top of a tall building), they think it actually *is* small. Three-, four-, and five-year-olds will look down and say, "Look at the tiny people!" Children of eight, nine, and ten can *look at* their perceptions. They will say, "Look how tiny the people *look*!"

A way of knowing becomes more complex when it is able to *look at* what before it could only *look through*. In other words, our way of knowing becomes more complex when we create a bigger system that incorporates and expands on our previous system. This means that if we want to increase mental complexity, we need to move aspects of our meaning-making from subject to object, to alter our mindset so that a way of knowing or making meaning becomes a kind of "tool" that *we have* (and can control or use) rather than something that *has us* (and therefore controls and uses us).

Each of the levels of mental complexity we first began to explore in chapter 1 incorporates a distinctly different subject-object relationship, a successively more complex way of knowing that is able to *look at* what the prior way of knowing could only *look through*. Figure 2-6 summarizes the subject-object relationship at each level of adult development.

FIGURE 2-6

The subject-object relationship becomes increasingly expansive at successive levels of mental capacity

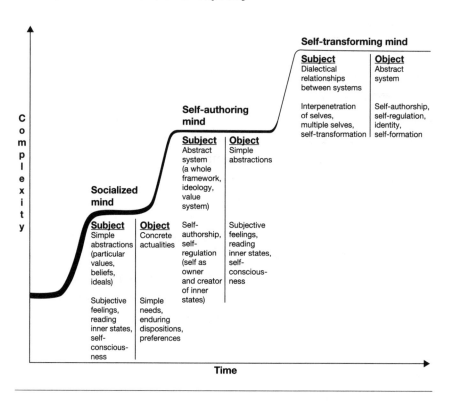

For example, a person who perceives the world through a socialized mind is subject to the values and expectations of his "surround" (be it his family of origin, his religious or political reference group, or the leaders of his work setting, who set terms on his professional and financial reality). The perceived risks and dangers that arise for such a person have to do with being unaligned, or out of faith, with that mediating surround; being excluded from it and thereby cut off from its protections; or being evaluated poorly by those whose regard directly translates into his regard for himself.

At the next level of mental complexity, the self-authoring mind, a person is able to distinguish the opinion of others (even important others) from her self-opinion. She might certainly take other views into account, but she can *choose* how much, and in what way, to let them influence her. People who advance to this more complex mental capacity can take the whole meaning-making category of others' opinions as a kind of tool, or something they have, rather than something that has them. In other words, this more complex way of knowing allows us to take others' opinions as object rather than subject.

The ability to subordinate or relegate opinions, values, beliefs, ideas (our own or others') to a more complex system—to prioritize them, combine them, create new values or beliefs we didn't even know we had—enables us to be the author of our own reality, and to look to ourselves as a source of internal *author*ity—hence the "self-authoring" mind.

Notice that this new way of knowing does not remove the specter of risk and danger from psychological life; rather, it changes the basis or context from which such a sense of alarm arises. Ultimate anxiety is no longer a function of being excluded from or disdained by one's tribe but instead may be about the threat of falling short of our own standards, of being unable to realize our agenda, of losing control, or of having the pen with which we are writing the script of our life run dry.

And if one is not to be forever captive of one's own theory, system, script, framework, or ideology, one needs to develop an even more complex way of knowing that permits one to *look at*, rather than choicelessly *through*, one's own framework. In such a case, that framework becomes more preliminary than ultimate, more in-process than magnum opus. This breaks through to a bigger emotional and mental space that can seek out the framework's current limitations rather than merely defend the current draft as a finished product and regard all suggestions to the contrary as a blow to the self.

These three qualitatively different levels of complexity—the socialized mind, the self-authoring mind, and the self-transforming mind—thus represent three distinct epistemologies. Each way of knowing maintains an equilibrium between what is subject and what is object. Growth in our way of knowing—adapting—involves disturbing this balance, and learning to *look at* what before we were *looking through*.

Well and good, you might say, but the question still remains, "*How* are we assisted or enabled to make that move from subject to object? What prompts the development of mental complexity? Can we use such an understanding to intentionally incubate or accelerate its development?"

THE IMPORTANCE OF OPTIMAL CONFLICT

It should be clear by now that the work of increasing mental complexity is not a cognitive matter alone. The language—"increasing mental complexity"—does conjure up some picture of exclusive attention to *thinking,* or perhaps submitting ourselves to some didactic discipline, where if we study hard, and *concentrate,* we will somehow grow our mental complexity. However, we have been saying from the beginning that this is messy work, that it draws on head and heart, on thinking *and* feeling. So what produces greater mental complexity?

If we were to summarize the answer that arises from seventy-five years of research on the question—begun long before our time in the laboratories of developmental psychologists like Jean Piaget and Barbel Inhelder in Switzerland or James Mark Baldwin, Heinz Werner, and Lawrence Kohlberg in the United States—it would be *optimal conflict*:

- The *persistent* experience of some frustration, dilemma, life puzzle, quandary, or personal problem that is . . .

- Perfectly designed to cause us to *feel the limits* of our current way of knowing . . .

- In some sphere of our living that we *care about,* with . . .

- *Sufficient supports* so that we are neither overwhelmed by the conflict nor able to escape or diffuse it.

Our goal in this chapter has been to show you what it means to formulate an adaptive challenge *adaptively* (so we do not mistakenly address it *technically*). If we've succeeded, you might only now be in a position to see why developing an X-ray, putting it in front of a person, and providing the support to do the work the X-ray calls for turns out be a powerful means of supporting the development of mental complexity, enabling people to meet adaptive challenges. Creating a picture of our immunity to change surfaces an *optimal conflict.*

Take another look at Peter's immunity X-ray in figure 2-2. The process of building this picture around a change Peter very much wants to make but is unable to achieve helps him see a conflict perfectly designed to highlight the limits of his current way of knowing. It takes the contradiction he is subject to (the contradiction between his first and third columns) and gives it to him as an object of his attention. It takes the contradiction he *is* (which is why he systematically cannot achieve what he has set out to do) and converts it into a contradiction he *has,* which he can now go to work on. Only by seeing the systematic *im*possibility of achieving his first-column goal can Peter put himself—for the first time—in a position to realize that goal.

When people first see their X-rays developing before their eyes, they often have a mix of emotions: "revealing," "uncomfortable," "intriguing," and "scary" are common responses. This might be what it feels like to glimpse the world through a wider aperture.

Can we say *which* level of complexity Peter's map is beginning to reveal for him? A single X-ray, and a first draft at that, does not always make a person's position on the continuum of mental complexity (the slopes and plateaus) absolutely clear. (Do not be surprised if your first picture, which you'll develop in chapter 9, is ambiguous in this respect. How much you care to know where you are on this continuum will vary, depending on whether your interest is limited to progress on the column 1 goal or includes a bigger personal growth project.)

But Peter's third column hints at the issues he was subject to, and now can face. Do they suggest a particular epistemology to you? In comparison, have another look at Ron's X-ray in figure 2-3. Do you notice any contrast between the two? Peter's immunity to change seems highly related to his need to maintain control of the definitions and workings of a company he himself has authored. You could substitute the word *self* for the word *company* in the prior sentence and it would effectively describe the workings of the self-authoring mind. It may only be by expanding this epistemology in some way—a scary activity inevitably threatening to the economies of the heart and the head—that Peter will be able to meet his adaptive challenge.

Ron, in contrast, seems to be systematically preventing his own desired change because it would threaten a self that derives its deepest satisfactions from alignment, the watchword of the socialized mind. Peter and Ron are both gifted leaders in many ways. They have each made distinct contributions to the success of their company, and their differing talents complement each other. They worked hand-in-hand on the acquisitions that tripled the size of the company. If you spent a day with either one of them you would also conclude that both are smart guys. If these tentative hunches about their levels of mental complexity are right (and they may not be), we are saying that Peter is, in a very particular way, more "complex" than Ron, but this doesn't mean he necessarily has a higher IQ or that it is going to be any easier or harder for one or the other to meet his adaptive challenge. Each will have to put at risk a way of knowing the world that also serves as a way of managing a persistent, fundamental anxiety. But note that the *kind* of persistent anxiety each is managing is *distinctly different*. Each epistemology has its own world of dread.

THREE DIMENSIONS OF IMMUNITY

You may now gradually come to see the immunity to change as a multidimensional phenomenon, as illustrated in figure 2-7. First, at the most practical level, an immunity map gives us a picture of how we are actively preventing the very change we wish to make. But it also shows us how a given place in the continuum of mental development is at once a way of knowing the world and of managing a fundamental anxiety. Thus it reveals a second dimension in the way persistent anxiety is managed, and a third, the epistemological

FIGURE 2-7

The three dimensions of the immunity to change

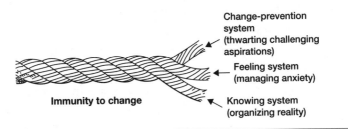

Change-prevention system (thwarting challenging aspirations)

Feeling system (managing anxiety)

Immunity to change

Knowing system (organizing reality)

FIGURE 2-8

A junior partner's immunity X-ray

1 Visible commitment	2 Doing/not doing instead	3 Hidden competing commitments	4 Big assumptions
To be more excited and inspired in my work by connecting more with my own passions, and trusting more my own distinctiveness	I work at things I am not that interested in (because I feel I must). I work in ways that are more routine, more established (because I feel that is what is expected).	To being well regarded by those who evaluate me To not running any reputational, social, economic risks To not looking unsuccessful To not pushing an unknown/unproven trail	I assume my safest route to success is to perform exceptionally well in ways that are expected and well established. I assume that if I am not highly regarded I will be a failure.

balance that must be preserved if we are to maintain our way of knowing the world and ourselves.

You can test your own grasp of all three dimensions by considering two more X-rays. These two maps, like those of Peter and Ron, are not fabricated. They come from the work of real clients we have been privileged to serve. If certain things start to jump out at you when you look at these fresh specimens, it is not because we engineered them to show all three dimensions at once. It is because you are beginning to see these dimensions yourself!

The maps in figures 2-8 and 2-9 come from two partners in an international strategy consulting firm. The first one, figure 2-8, comes from a junior partner. You may look at this map and think, "Ironically, this fellow's strategy of playing it safe may actually be much more dangerous personally than if he were to run whatever he thinks of as a risk, since playing it safe will almost certainly lead ultimately to failure within the firm." But if you are saying this to yourself, you are looking at it from *outside* the socialized mind. While it may not be possible for him to realize his first-column commitment without

FIGURE 2-9

A senior partner's immunity X-ray

| 1

Visible commitment | 2

Doing/not doing instead | 3

Hidden competing commitments | 4

Big assumptions |
|---|---|---|---|
| To better develop the "being" side (vs. the "doing") specifically, to develop a stance oriented just to deep understanding (without instrumentality or ulterior purpose) | Tendency to drive toward solution, jump in with "the answer," save the day

Look for (maybe even set up) situations where I am needed to make the difference

Don't listen well once I've made up my mind | To be the hero

To feel indispensable | I assume I will not feel deeply satisfied unless I am being the hero.

I assume the metric I currently use for "satisfaction" is the only one that will work for me. |

developing beyond the socialized mind, the map actually suggests some valuable ways to support exactly that move.

To plant seeds for that exploration, we direct your attention to a part of this map you have not yet seen in prior pictures. The full development of all our immunity maps includes this fourth column: what are the "big assumptions" (tenets in our mental models) that sustain the whole immune system? We call them "big assumptions" because they are not currently viewed as "assumptions" at all. Rather, they are uncritically taken as true. They *may* be true, and they may not be, but as long as we simply assume they are true, we are blind even to the question itself.

If this fellow could experiment with behaviors that put his big assumptions to the test, there is a good chance that he will modify these assumptions. That modification may not only begin to release him from the grip of his current immune system; it may actually start to build the more complex mental structures that make up the self-authoring mind.

In the junior partner's map of his immunity to change we can see:

- The systematic way in which he is preventing the very progress he hopes for (connecting more with his passions; trusting more his own distinctness)

- The way this "change-prevention system" is being employed to protect him from his brand of terror (e.g., being regarded poorly by important others)

- The way his map (and his anxiety protection) reflects a broader personal epistemology or knowing system, which in his case makes the self cohere through its alignment with externally provided values and expectations

The map in figure 2-9 comes from a senior partner in the same firm. You can see all three elements at work in this map as well, despite the fact that the *way* these elements express themselves is so different. This person also has an adaptive formulation in front of him. He wants very much to be able to take up a different kind of stance in relation to those he might seek to serve or join, what we might call a more *accompanying* (vs. analytic and problem-solving) stance. He wants to be able to join others with less of an "agenda," or with a quite different agenda from the one he has mastered.

His map shows him why a technical fix (taking a course to learn some counseling skills, for example) will not by itself enable him to make much progress on his goal. The behaviors in the second column cannot simply be altered because they are serving an important purpose. He can see better how he is systematically poised to produce exactly the results that prevent the change he desires, and he can see why. His change-prevention system does a good job protecting him from a different family of anxieties than those of his junior colleague; namely, the fear of no longer knowing oneself as the hero who comes to the rescue, a way of seeing himself that has apparently become quite precious to him.

In addition, his map could be a foundation for a bigger project than accomplishing his first-column goals. It could support development *beyond* the self-authoring mind in general. Were he able to alter, even somewhat, the big assumptions of column 4, he might begin to include both the "doing self" *and* the "being self" into his active identity. With this more complex system (the self-transforming mind) he would not only be less captive of the doing self; he would also be less inclined, in general, to identify himself so onesidedly with just one pole in any of life's great dialectics (e.g., being independent vs. relying on others; being an elder vs. being the child).

———————

Now that we've introduced you to this multidimensional phenomenon—the immunity to change—let's hear from leaders themselves how and why they chose to engage it in their own leadership teams.

$$\left[\ 3\ \right]$$

"WE NEVER HAD A
LANGUAGE FOR IT"

Engaging the Emotional Life of the Organization

OUR CLIENTS ARE OUR TEACHERS. We want you to hear from some of them—so you can learn what we did—before we go any further in this journey. Remember Peter Donovan, the CEO of the expanding financial services company we introduced in chapter 2? Let's join him at a critical moment in an immunity-to-change offsite with his senior executive colleagues.

"I hear what you're saying, but that's really not the way I want to do it," Peter said on that occasion, in a tone just adamant enough to create an awkward, eyes-down silence among the half-dozen people sitting in a circle in a corner of a large living room at the conference retreat center.

He was speaking to Bill, one of his three executive vice presidents. Bill was trying to get Peter to change his mind as to how we should end the offsite the following morning with the company's executive committee (EC), a now eighteen-person group who had gathered in New England from as near as Boston and as far as the West Coast. Five years earlier the company and its EC were considerably smaller, but as the company's cofounder, Peter had decided his business needed to grow, and grow rapidly.

"We needed to get much, much bigger," he said later, recounting the story of how he eventually came to bring the immunity-to-change work into the top team in his company. "And I couldn't do it organically. I needed to buy. Fortunately I had two competitors who became available. The first one, in Washington, D.C., doubled the size of our business, and, a few years later, another one in California increased our business again by 50 percent. So we had gone, in the course of three and a half years, from a company of about a hundred people, doing about a billion dollars' worth of commercial mortgages, to a three-hundred-person company doing about three and a half billion dollars' worth of commercial lending all throughout the country.

"This rapid growth through acquisitions posed a real challenge for us, as you can imagine, in terms of integrating the senior management team to make sure we were all on the same page. We needed a common language and a common definition of leadership within our organization, given that we had a relatively new senior management team—both because of the acquisitions as well as promoting some people as we grew as a company, and because we were three separate platforms, geographically distant and dispersed. And finally, our leadership development work had stagnated. We had taken on a leadership development initiative about three years earlier, and I realized we really weren't where we needed to be in order to help the company grow.

"Initially, I focused on our middle management and their development, and then I realized—after I debated for an hour the definition of leadership with one of my senior managers!—that we had a lot of work to do at the top. To paraphrase Pogo, "We looked in the mirror and the enemy was us." We were the ones who really needed to develop first before we could develop the next level of management, and I felt we just weren't making the kind of progress we needed, and I was scratching my head as to why that was."

The impasse at the offsite arose after an unusually intense day. The living room was otherwise empty as the rest of the EC members were off unwinding before dinner while we, the planning group, had been reviewing the day, and were now turning to a design for closing well tomorrow. We soon discovered that Peter and his EVPs were certainly not, at this moment, on the same page.

We had already spent several weeks working with the team to prepare the workshop. Peter and his most senior lieutenants had come to us after reading about our immunity-to-change work in the *Harvard Business Review*.[1] Peter recalled:

> I was on a flight going out to California, and the article immediately hit a nerve for me. And I handed it to my COO, whom I was traveling with, and said, "You've got to read this. We need to apply it," and we instantly started going through a mental checklist of key people in our company, and thinking, "Yeah, this applies to this person." We put it down for a while, came back to Boston, picked it up about six months later, read it again, were as excited the second time as we were the first. We passed the article around to our senior management, sat down with Bob and Lisa, and started to map out a plan as to how we were going to bring this into our organization.

Peter quickly intuited something about our approach that was not sufficiently clear to us at the start, and has only proven truer as our work has progressed: it is of the utmost importance to get the *right* improvement goal in the first column. "It doesn't matter how great your learning technology is," Peter said. "To figure out your immunity to change around some improvement goal that isn't the most important thing for you to change is a waste of everybody's time and money."

IDENTIFYING EACH PERSON'S ONE-BIG-THING

Peter and his cabinet wanted all the members of the executive committee to create their own immunity maps, but not to be the *sole* deciders of what would go in their first columns. "None of us should just decide for ourselves," he insisted. "We should all get inputs from the people around us." For weeks before the offsite, each member of the EC had conversations—with the person to whom they reported, with peers, with someone who reported to them. The topic of the conversation, in all cases, was the same: "What's the *single thing* you think is most important for me to get better at?"

The narrow focus was an unprecedented approach to leadership development in the company. People were used to getting wide-ranging feedback, to identifying a full profile detailing many strengths and areas for improvement. Here they were doing something quite different. A shorthand phrase developed naturally that eventually became a part of senior management lingo—"one big thing," as in: "What is the one-big-thing I should work on?" "What is Harold's one-big-thing?"

To learn what their boss thinks is the one thing that will make the biggest difference with regard to receiving a top bonus, or being promoted, or, in some cases, to being *retained,* certainly captured the interest of the EC members. In different ways, so did learning what their own direct reports and their peers would say. As you can imagine, all this external input led to prospective entries for first-column improvement goals in which people were considerably invested.

But Peter had a second insight. He was not satisfied that he or his colleagues should consult only the people around them at work:

> As people would dig around and start coming up with a possible one-big-thing, I started to realize this cannot be just about work. I'd say, "You've got to give it the spousal test." They'd say, "Well, what's that?" I went to my wife. I said, "Dear, I'm focusing on one-big-thing, and you might be surprised to know I've got a little bit of a problem with control." We're in bed and she looks at me and she starts to laugh. She says, "You've got to be kidding me!" I said, "No, really." She says, "I've been married to you for twenty-three years. You're *just* figuring this out? 'A *little* problem with control,' you say? You are a control *freak*!" All right, so we are getting somewhere, right? I think I'm on the right path. This is what I call passing the "spousal test."

We don't know how much Peter understood it at the time, but his insistence that people conduct not just 360-degree feedback, but what we might call 720-degree feedback—including key people in your private life as well as your public life—dramatically increased people's attachment to improving on their first-column goals. They knew the payoffs could be big at work and at home, if only they really could find a way to make dramatic strides on their one-big-thing. He upped the ante for choosing what went in the first column, but he also greatly upped the size of the pot to be won.

So when the EC showed up at the offsite, each member had a first-column improvement goal that really mattered to him or her. The day had been spent developing powerful maps of their immune systems. They each saw how their own immunity was doing a brilliant job protecting them from some dread threat and, in return, was extracting its familiar charge for all its good work—namely, zero real progress on their now urgently desired improvement goal. As usual, the experience was quite illuminating, but the day's intensity was compounded by the fact that the EC members were sharing their maps with their entire subgroup rather than with a single partner, as is our usual practice.

They had been divided into subgroups intended to maximize safety and comfort. Although they were one executive committee, leading one now national company, they were still a somewhat balkanized collection on a trust map. EVP Bill, for example, only a few years before had been the beloved and trusted CEO of one of the companies Peter had acquired. He was close to retirement, and not uncomfortable being Peter's lieutenant for a few years, helping blend his own senior team into the enlarged EC. He had just skillfully and sensitively guided his own longtime colleagues through a process in which they not only came to powerful personal realizations concerning their own improvement goals but also shared these discoveries with each other.

He had found the day very valuable and exciting, but he also wanted to take good care of his people, whom he sensed were feeling quite vulnerable from the depth and openness of the immunity work. "We'd known each other for years," Bill later said. "But we were coming to know each other in a whole new way." It was Bill's concern for his own people that led to the impasse with Peter. And it was Peter's *third insight* that provoked the impasse in the first place.

"Here's my sense of how we should end tomorrow," Peter said, with characteristic enthusiasm. "It's the best way I can think of to take this work out of here, and carry it forward so it eventually makes a difference in who we are as an executive committee. What we have done so far today is a big step, but we have only shared with the members of the EC with whom we are already the most comfortable and familiar. Tomorrow morning, I think we should go around—and probably we should be the ones to start—I think we should each go around and let each other in on what we have each learned about our immune systems."

It wasn't Bill's style to get directly in anyone's face, let alone Peter's, but everyone could read loud and clear that his cautionary response was deep-felt. Bill countered, "Hmm, well, I'm not too sure about that. Ah, I don't know how it went in the other groups, but I've got a crew of people who took some very deep dives today. I'm proud of every one of them, but this is very new ground for them. We've got some folks who have quite a lot to think about right now. My sense is that they are feeling pretty vulnerable. I just can't see them going around tomorrow and telling everyone what's in their four columns."

Peter was clearly disconcerted when he saw the others giving nonverbal assents to Bill's words. "So, what are you proposing exactly?" he asked.

"I think the day might come when we *could* all share these things," Bill said, quickly sensing Peter's disappointment. "And I feel this has been a very important, very good day. I just don't think we're ready quite yet for the step you're proposing. I think the next place for each person to take what they've learned is to their coach, and that it's very good we have made these one-on-one coaching relationships available."

This is when Peter said, "I hear what you're saying, but that's really not the way I want to do it." When the eyes went down in the awkwardness of the impasse, Peter went on: "Look, what we are trying to do here is bring this whole executive committee to a new level. I've made very clear that we are raising the bar for what it means to be on the top team."

Silence.

"I'm just not interested in launching eighteen separate leadership development projects! That's not going to get it done. I'm trying to do something here with *the whole team*!"

"I don't think you realize, Peter," another of his colleagues said, "that not everyone is as comfortable jumping into this kind of thing as you are."

"You don't get great by staying comfortable. People need to step up!"

More silence.

The hapless consultants (that would be us) were reluctantly coming to the conclusion that we needed to step in and say something, if only we knew what that was. Our obvious hope, that our clients could work this out for themselves, was fading fast.

And then something happened that didn't just break the evening's impasse. It probably created the turning point of the entire project.

"Ah, excuse me, Peter," said Bill, finally breaking the silence. "And I mean no disrespect here, but, um, I wonder if what's happening right now isn't maybe an example of *your own* big thing?"

FROM INSIGHT TO IMPACT: MAKING REAL CHANGE HAPPEN

"What happened in that meeting," another member of the senior management team later told us, "was that we actually started using this stuff! Suddenly it wasn't about an offsite exercise anymore. It had crept into the way we worked together. And we were starting right at the top!

"I give Bill and Peter, both, all the credit in the world. There was Peter wanting people to step up, and Bill stepped up all right! And Peter, to his everlasting credit, backed off. I think we might have lost the whole project right there, had he stuck to his guns and jammed this thing down people's throats . . . because Peter can be a force of nature when he gets going on something. He can be very hard to stop."

As Peter later said, "I was insisting we do this, and I was not willing to compromise, not willing to pull back. And quite frankly, had we not laid the groundwork we did, I don't honestly know that I would've pulled back. I may have done what I usually do, which is just to sort of put my head down and keep on blasting forward. I swallowed hard. I took a deep breath. It was a real-life case of trying to absorb and to exhibit the same kind of behavior I was hoping I would see out of our senior management team."

Pogo's maxim had likely never felt so *personally* true—"We have met the enemy and he is us!" But when Peter talks about what really helped him to stop, to listen, and, ultimately, to make a different decision despite his passionate convictions to the contrary, it is interesting that his experience of Bill's words seems completely devoid of feeling accused of something, or caught in the act, or on the short end of a game of "Gotcha!"

"He was very direct," Peter said, "but he wasn't personalizing it at all. He was just referring me to my one-big-thing."

This may sound like a strange statement. After all, what Bill was referring to—Peter's intense need for control—was extremely personal. Yet when Peter looks back from the vantage point of a few years and sums up the effect of the work on his senior management team, this same theme—of finding a way to appropriately and effectively engage the personal and the private in the public life of work—is exactly what stands out.

He begins by talking about his relationship with his COO, Ron, whom you also met in chapter 2.

> My one-big-thing is control, okay? The one-big-thing for the COO was to please. He is the nicest man in the world, bar none. My wife tells me that all the time. She says, "Why can't you be like him? He's the nicest man!" And he is. I love him, okay. I love him. But there's an interesting dynamic that goes on. I need to control. He needs to please. So, what's that really mean? I make the decisions and he lets me make the decisions. But sometimes, when he didn't agree, he wouldn't confront me, but he wouldn't follow through either. He would end up being a buffer or a cushion between me and whoever

else might have been involved in the decision. Sometimes he would actually do the opposite of what I asked him to do in the thought he was pleasing me by not saying no, and serving the company by doing what he thought was really the right thing to do.

And so you've got this dynamic going on where we weren't always in sync. And so we're sitting in a conference room, looking at our immunity maps together, and all this sort of comes out. I turned to him and said, "Let me see if I've got this straight. I'm an abuser and you like it!" He started chuckling, kind of laughed. I laughed too, but then I said, "This is very, very counterproductive. We really do need to change this behavior."

Now understand: we've been working together for fifteen years. Fifteen years! It wasn't like he just joined six months ago. And I think we knew, deep down inside, that this kind of dance was going on, but we never had a language for it. We never had permission. We probably never had the courage to really sit down and face it directly, and the "one-big-thing" approach, as we called it, really gave us the structure and the language, the ability to address this in a way that was seen as positive and not simply a personal attack.

Then Peter turned to other changes in people's relationships with him as CEO. "You know the term 'the canary in the mine'?" Peter asked, referring to the miners' warning device to detect a dangerous lack of oxygen in the mines. He said he had come to see the work we were doing as creating another kind of warning system, what he called "the canary in the *mind*." "By that I mean you have given permission to others on your senior management team to talk about these things, to talk about the behavior that they see exhibited, whether it's by me or by others, because we've laid the groundwork for that. And I thought that that was very, very powerful. We need to just nip this in the bud the first time I do something dysfunctional. The first time that I do something negative. Not let it build up. It can be a real problem as the CEO to get any kind of feedback, particularly negative feedback, from your senior management team."

Next he addressed changes in relationships among the team as a whole:

People need to give each other permission to have that conversation, and so often that's not the case, and certainly in business and in senior management. You know, "We can't talk about that." "We can't go there." "We don't know how to go there." "We don't know how it's going to be received." All that, quite frankly, gets removed when you create this kind of a framework.

The work that we did really provided a common language for us all to be able to talk about the challenges of personal development. And that was so important for us, to be able to talk about the issues in a way that we'd all agreed on, as to how they'd be addressed and to talk about how we'd try to change behavior individually and collectively, and why. And I found so many times before we really struggled with, "What's the language that we're supposed to use?" "How are we supposed to address an issue?" "Do I have permission to address the issue?" As the CEO, do I have permission to address the issue in a way that I think is going to be constructive and not be received as a personal attack? That's a very tricky line to walk, and I found the language of the one-big-thing, the immunity-to-change matrix, if you will, really provided the stability to do that. It's a very personal thing in terms of leadership development and yet I found it was actually able to depersonalize, in some ways, some of the things we were talking about, and very, very effectively.

I think it made us a much more cohesive management team, much better at communication. We were able to get to the heart of issues right away because a language and construct had been created. We didn't have to dance around the issue. "How am I going to approach so-and-so about this?" No. It's the one-big-thing. We know it's the one-big-thing. He knows it's his one-big-thing. You can just go and talk to him about it in those terms, in a very supportive, sort of matter-of-fact way. He'll accept it in the same way and we move on. So, at times, as I say, it became really a very effective way to help address personal and collective development.

Peter cautioned that it takes time and patience.

Not everyone gets it. Not everyone gets it in the same way, or at the same time. And so, as with any development effort, you have to expect that you're going to have people in very different places through this whole process, emotionally and intellectually, and certainly in terms of commitment, as a result. I had one guy say to me, "Will this be used against me? I'm exposing my weakness." So you had to be careful that it wasn't seen as sort of the end-all, be-all.

Over time people became more accepting, better understanding of what we were trying to do, energized, emboldened, engaged, at times courageous. And we saw some real courage. We saw tears in meetings, men and women. We saw people take bold steps. We saw people trust us in terms of what our motivations were and where we're going with this. In the end many of them—not all of them—became enthusiastic advocates. This brought senior management closer together. I don't think there's any question about that.

Finally, Peter talked about the effect the work had on those beyond the senior team.

I think, in turn, our senior management gained greater credibility within the organization because there was this openness about their own challenges in terms of behavior that others in the organization saw and applauded and tried to emulate over time. We created a corporate buzz. People started to come to me. "I want to know what my 'one-big-thing' is." People who were not involved with senior management. People sometimes who were not involved in management at all, because they could hear the excitement of what was going on. Everybody wanted to discover and work on their one-big-thing. And, you know, obviously that's a very, very positive thing for the growth cycle.

And what about that offsite? How did it end? The next morning Peter and Bill told the group about their whole conversation, about the decision they ultimately came to, not to push anyone before he or she was ready. And they talked about exactly how they arrived at this decision, about the way bringing up the one-big-thing—even the CEO's—can alter familiar patterns of behavior—even the CEO's—that sometimes need altering.

Thirty days after the offsite, every member of the executive committee voluntarily shared their immunities with each other. We were there when it happened, and we remember Peter's words at the end: "I don't think I've ever been prouder of the people in this group."

"IF YOU CAN'T GET THAT STUFF OUT FROM UNDER THE TABLE, IT'S GOING TO BLOCK YOU ALL THE WAY": WHAT WE LEARNED FROM HARRY SPENCE

Serving at the pleasure of the governor of the Commonwealth of Massachusetts, Harry Spence was, when we first met him, the commissioner of the Department of Social Services, the state's child welfare organization. Harry says he took the job thinking his task was "to make the Massachusetts child welfare system as good as any other state in the country."

But after about eighteen months into his job, he changed his goal. He says, "I realized that the field of child welfare nationally was so grossly underdeveloped that anyone with a leadership opportunity had a huge responsibility to bring the field itself to a better position. This is a system that lives in constant terror of the high-profile case. It is therefore an organization in an endless defensive crouch, which is, of course, the worst possible posture from which to learn."

We'll let Harry continue the story in his own words, as Peter did for his company: "So we had been trying to figure out how one can actually turn a child welfare organization into a learning organization. How can you take an organization in constant fear and help it be deeply committed to learning? Because this is what it will take to further develop an enterprise that is so underdeveloped nationally."

We got the chance to work with Harry for reasons that sound a lot like Peter's, as different as their two organizations may be. Harry, too, felt his senior team was stuck in some way. After months of leading the agency, his experience with his senior staff mirrored what he had been hearing indirectly since he arrived: the senior staff as a group was just not effective at all. He describes what he means by this:

> We struggled over what to put on the agenda. We tended to discuss administrative and political topics only. And one of the fundamental rules I have is that most organizations like this spend about 80 percent of their time on politics and administration and about 20 percent of their time on practice. And a kind of core rule I have is you've got to flip that. You've got to make it 80 percent of the time on practice and 20 percent of the time on politics and administration. And we couldn't get it to happen.
>
> We just somehow couldn't get the senior staff off of issues of politics and administration, and even then, warily. And what was clear was the "warily" piece, how deeply wary we all were of each other on the senior staff.
>
> Why? Some of this I inherited. There were very divisive internal dynamics going on within the central office and there were lots of places where competition had been set up among central office staff. And then this is work in which everyone operates under this constant anxiety that if someone makes a mistake, not only do they carry the blood of a child on their hands, but they will be publicly crucified. And so there's endless anxiety about that issue. And, of course, that drives tragically bad child welfare practice, not good practice. It actually drives the bad practice. So people are already in a very anxious state, and they are competing with each other. There were specific clear axial lines along which there were fights going on, some of which I'd inherited, and they just continued as I came in and I tried to settle them. But there was just this enormous sense of "we can't," "we're fearful."
>
> And then there was a lot of the stuff that goes on generally in senior staffs in lots of organizations. After the senior staff

meetings—little clusters and cliques who would discuss together the infuriating things, a stupid thing that somebody else did and so on, lots of the back-channel stuff that goes on.

This challenge created the context for us to begin working with Harry. Like Peter, Harry contacted us because the immunity-to-change approach resonated with him:

I deeply believe that organizations are incredibly impeded by the covert dynamics that are never acknowledged around the emotional life of the organization. It was a premise I came to this work with, that in order to really alter the dynamics of organizations, if you can't get that stuff out from under the table, it's going to block you all the way.

You know, you'd think in a clinical organization, in a child welfare organization—all these folks are trained psychiatric social workers or various kinds of social workers, and have master's degrees and two years of training in clinical theory, and use it easily in some ways—and yet, that premise is a hard premise for any organization, I think, to absorb.

So I was fascinated with the question of how in this organization, which so clearly had so much dysfunction throughout the organization—because it's trauma work really, because the emotional content of the work is so intense and our social workers and staff are constantly engaging trauma day in and day out. It's not unlike doing EMT work except it's psychological EMT work. They're walking into households that are horrific. They're encountering children in circumstances that are horrifying, all of this stuff. And it's driving a lot of emotional stuff in the organization. How do we get beyond that?

And I kept thinking to myself, you know, I can't send every one of them to California for a yearlong program to develop their personal leadership skills. I can't send them out endlessly on training programs. I just don't know how to do this.

And when I came across the book what was wondrous about it was that it held the core complexity of all the training I had done in this incredibly small and highly accessible compass.[2]

I said to people, "You know, if I had four hours in which to take all of my personal development work and all of my training in California and all of that, and I had four hours to get someone to 'get it'—there's this astonishing distillation in the four-column exercise. And it's so brilliantly accessible. There's no one who *can't* get it. We're not talking about high-flown clinical terms. We don't need to spend days building a shared conceptual frame. It's really incredibly simple. And it feels like it could be very powerful." So I talked to Bob and Lisa and proposed to the senior staff that we try it.

And there were some mixed feelings, some uncertainty, and everybody read the book, and it upped the anxiety of the event occurring. And then we started the work. Early in the work, the second meeting or so, we did the four-column exercise. We actually spread it out over two sessions because there were too many people in the room to do it all at one time. They jumped into it in many ways, a number of them, at least—and it was immensely powerful.

Two three-hour meetings where there were tears, where people moved to places that I think startled them, in a setting where they had not trusted to even talk about a matter of minor disagreement for fear of the conflict that would ensue or the ridicule that might follow or whatever. And yet here they were, sitting around a table, and, in a few cases, really going deep, back into their childhood experiences about where this came from and the like.

And what was powerful is, not only is this occurring, but it's occurring in a setting in which each of the people in the room is sharing it. And so a bond was very quickly built among the group around the vulnerability they had shared together.

And secondly, there was a sudden easing of compassion for each other around the things that drove each other crazy. We have a litigator in the senior staff, for example, a terrific person, but she would just go into sort of litigation hyperdrive periodically and the person who was the object of it would feel assaulted. We came to understand what that dynamic was. Once you understood where that dynamic came from, people could stop saying, "Oh, my God. Did you see what she did again?" and say instead, "Oh." And then be able to say to her, "Whoops. Are we back in that? Wait a minute. Red flag. Isn't this what we've seen?" And for her to be able to say, "Oh, my God. Yeah."

And so for each of us to be able to do that, to both support each other because of the commitments around a set of changes we needed to make, and the shared vulnerability of having shared some deep feelings in the course of that time, built the beginnings, the foundation, for what then became really almost two years' worth of work of building our capacity as a senior staff to hold increasingly conflictual, intense, challenging, difficult conversations.

I think the core focus was for the senior staff to build itself as a container for really powerful conversations that included lots of risk taking, deep disagreement and the like. And so for the last six months or so, we explicitly focused on hot topics. "Let's keep building our capacity." "Let's list the hot topics that we can't discuss in the group." "Let's take them up, one by one, and start building our capacity to do that." And over the course of really two years, I think, the group has moved to the point now where our senior staff meetings are just overrunning with incredibly powerful discussions that we don't have time for. I mean, we're literally trying to keep the agenda. How do we keep the agenda manageable, because the group now can do such a powerful job of taking up any number of tasks within the organization and has become a central forum for thinking about practice?

LINKING PERSONAL AND ORGANIZATIONAL DEVELOPMENT

As Harry reflects on the work we did together, and his increasing clarity as to what it actually means to lift the field of child welfare to a more developed place, he considers the relationship between the two.

The work of child welfare is, far and away, the most complex public work that I've ever encountered in my life. It is fundamentally therapeutic work trying to be done by a public bureaucracy. And so what we're trying to do, really, is we're trying to create a professional services organization, a *public professional services organization,* and those don't exist. And one that is as complex as the complexities of the families that we're encountering, because when we make the task simplistic and then encounter complex circumstances, we do huge damage. If you oversimplify in the face of complexity, you do enormous damage. You bring a sledgehammer to bear in circumstances where what's needed is a scalpel or whatever. So we're trying to make this a far more complex professional services firm.

Bringing about this kind of development, Harry realizes, requires instilling an organization-wide habit of self-reflection. Key to this, he says, is recognizing certain parallel processes between the very personal nature of the work the organization does with its clients and the very personal nature of the work that professionals—from the commissioner on down—need to do with *themselves* in order to increase the chances they are part of the solution rather than the problem. What do these parallel processes look like? Here's what Harry had to say.

One of the famous sayings in child welfare is, "You can't do this work unless you believe that families can change." This is kind of a given. But if I am a child welfare worker, often I can be saying I absolutely believe this, but at the same time I will tell you about Joe, "that SOB in the office next to me, who's been yelling on the phone every time he talks for the last five years. I can't get him to quiet down. That SOB will *never* change!" Families can change, but my coworker cannot. Now one of those two statements is false. So, central to the work is an understanding that if you want to understand the dynamics of change in families, the best place to start is with Joe. You've got a constant laboratory in your relationships with each other around the issue of change. How might we as a public organization train people, support people, to develop their capacities to work with others to change? Well, they could start with their fellow employees.

So the work we did together as a senior staff is about change. And one of the learnings from that is how difficult change is and how much support is needed for change. After all, we weren't families involved in the child welfare system for neglect or abuse. We were just working together and even then we had a terrible time. It was incredibly hard to change. So, we developed respect for the difficulty of the task and an appreciation of what it is that best supports us in change. All that work together can easily be taken to the work with families. So we began to see there's a wonderful parallel process.

And there's a second parallel process, what's known in the world of clinical work, of course, as transference and countertransference. The whole set of issues around if I'm trying to assist someone to change, what am I bringing to that interaction, to that engagement that's getting in the way? What aspects of this relationship in which I'm trying to assist and support someone to change, where am I getting in my own way and in our way in this process?

But the language of transference and countertransference is, you know, this big, heavy, weighty language that's filled with Freudian baggage. The wonderful thing about the four-column exercise is that the language of the "one-big-thing" allows you to get at something very similar. Actually, maybe even precisely the same. It's the question of what is my core dynamic that is likely getting in my way here?

And so we have the same set of issues in which I am considering, "How am I getting in the way of my commitment to making the senior staff work as a really powerful and effective and functional group?" I could say to a social worker, the same question arises: "How am I getting in the way of my efforts to support this family to strengthen and improve?"

Self-reflection is a central aspect of any organizational work. Self-reflection is particularly critical in the kinds of relationships that arise between family and social worker in child welfare. We needed, we knew, a framework for self-reflection. And we've come to realize that the four-column work provides what we have come to call a kind of "scaffolding." We can't regulate this business but we can scaffold this business. I can't give you rules about how you interact with a family in order to produce change. I can't write it up as a set of bureaucratic rules, hand it to you, and say, "Comply." It won't work. The complexity of human misery, among other things, is so great. There is no simple set of rules. This is immensely discretionary work. It's a professional services firm, not an industrial model.

We're trying to build a set of values, a set of principles, around how you do the work, some core conceptual frames for the work you do, and values to support them. So we're now very excited at the notion that we can take the four-column exercise and use it both as a managerial practice with management teams in our twenty-nine area offices, where they both develop the language of the four-column exercise, have a conceptual frame for their self-reflection in their team-building work with their colleagues, but it's the same language that the social workers in their office will be trained in and thinking about in their relationship with the families. That's spectacular!

When he stands back from all the work we have done together, Harry returns us to the very place we began in chapter 2—the hidden role of emotion in meeting the challenge of change, the need for us to find a way to bring what we have tended to think of as private experience into the public realm of work:

What I've come to understand more and more deeply, actually, is the function of emotion in this work. What's striking about child welfare is that people go off to social work school, right? They learn a whole bunch of things, the core of which is the idea of "the return of the repressed," right? The idea that emotion that isn't dealt with comes back in a dysfunctional form in some way, will show up in dysfunctional form. A central principle of all clinical work. And then you go into the organization and the organization ruthlessly suppresses all emotion. It's a social work organization that seems to act in absolute defiance of the core principles of social work!

More than anything, in work like this—but I suspect to differing degrees in all organizational work—we need to find ways to reverse this dynamic of suppressing emotion. At the end of the day, this is what the four-column work helps us to do.

TACKLING TWO BIG PROBLEMS AT ONCE: WHAT PETER AND HARRY UNDERSTOOD BETTER THAN WE DID

Peter Donovan and Harry Spence lead organizations that could not seem more different. One is a private business connected to a market economy; the other is a public government agency charged with providing social services. Peter's company is not without social value: focusing almost exclusively on multiunit home lending (and sound lending practices, in contrast to the circumstances that led to our recent mortgage crisis), it has, in its own way, contributed to the reality that today, for the first time, a majority of Americans now enjoy this aspect of our national dream. But at the end of the day, he would be the first to say he is running a bottom-line-oriented business, beholden to a private ownership group; and Harry is running a public human-service business, beholden to the citizenry and its elected representative, the governor of the state.

Different as their situations may be, there are also some striking similarities—in their challenges, in their leadership, and in their outcomes. They both have a hunger to significantly improve the performance of their organizations, and—strong personalities though each may be—they both clearly recognize that no one heroic actor can by himself bring about the development they seek. They know they need partners. Each of them looks to his senior team as the critical unit for bringing about change, and each feels frustrated with the current state of that team.

But even more important, neither of them leaves himself out of the equation in his assessment of his team. In both cases, their willingness to "go first," to be as visible about their own immunity to change as they were asking their team members to be, made a crucial difference.

We have felt privileged to work with leaders as courageous as Peter and Harry, and we have certainly learned, from our collaboration with them and others, that the person at the top needs to be a champion of this kind of work. The leader must be more than a mere supporter of an approach like this one; he or she needs to be an active advocate. We cannot succeed if the leader is only authorizing our participation, if he or she is merely a sponsor of work being led by outsiders. We rely on the leaders we work with to be genuine partners in our approach, and when the resistance mounts, as it nearly always does, it is the leader, not the outside consultant, who must help the group to renew its commitment to the journey of personal learning for public results.

Peter did this on more than one occasion, and he made clear the source of his conviction:

> Basically, I said to people, "Look, if this really is your 'one-big-thing,' if you've really dug deep enough, if you've really gotten personal, everybody already knows. I know. Others know. So, there's this sort of illusion out there that you are sharing something so private, that nobody knows. Trust me, they know! They know and they talk about it. Now, where do they talk about it? Behind closed doors, at lunch, after work, but they talk about it."
>
> So, I had to do a little bit of a reality check. The reality is, they already know, it's the elephant in the room. And when you have eighteen or twenty senior managers, it's a herd of elephants and it's getting in the way. Right? It's getting in the way. So I had to convince them that it was better to create a language and a forum to talk about it positively than to have people taking about it behind their backs, and I think, over time, that resonated with people.

Similarly, at a critical point in our work with the Department of Social Services, Harry needed to find words to explain to his colleagues just why he felt this kind of work—as hard, as risky, and as time-consuming as it was—was really necessary for them to engage:

> I found myself saying, "Haven't we all had the experience of working for someone whose ego structure just means we have to spend huge amounts of time working around it?" We've all had that experience, the amount of energy we have to expend "managing up" to the personal predilections and character and style of one or another particular boss. I've yet to run into someone who has not had some version of this experience.
>
> And then I say, "Well, here comes the hard part: the shocking thing is that there are other people who experience *us* exactly the same way! The hard part to accept is—that person we experienced who just drives us crazy? Well, *we* are that person for someone else!" And if we can, kind of, get this, we can begin to do the work.

Harry's words have had an impact on people in a variety of other settings in which we have worked. But we can imagine that when he was saying these things to *his own senior team*—to some people for whom "the boss who drives you crazy" might well have been Harry himself, and when he was publicly committing himself to work on his own personal-learning agenda, including the very things that could well have made *them* crazy—his words had an especially powerful impact.

So there are real similarities in the challenges each leader faced, in the reasons they thought to work with us, in their willingness and ability to be effective champions of the work, and in their own courage to make themselves a vulnerable part of a shared learning journey. But the most striking similarity has to do with something we feel Harry and Peter understood better than we did: the purpose of our work, however we went about it, was to grow the organization's ability to better deliver on its aspirations.

The fact that the work in both settings got its start, and was continuously renewed, in the social context of a real work team (not private coaching relationships or a class brought together for the temporary purpose of imparting learning one hopes will later be transferred to the real work setting) promised to set up a number of novel and valuable conditions for staying with the hard work of personal learning, despite the fact that ongoing reflection and personal experimentation seem to run against the grain of most work settings, in both corporate and social sectors. Letting people in on your improvement goal (your column 1 commitment) immediately puts you "on record" as working at something that your colleagues can:

- Confirm will be valuable for you to work on

- Want you to succeed at, for the good of the group

- Witness whether you did or did not progress

- Be in a position to acknowledge your changes (providing powerful motivation when and if you make them)

- Feel spurred on to stay with their own improvement projects, inspired (or usefully "pressured") by your progress

Indeed, all this has proved to be true, and we are very encouraged about the power of the work team approach as a way to keep people involved in their own learning. We think it is a significant step toward solving a vexing practice problem, and, as we will discuss later in this book, it begins to yield a more complicated picture for best practices in organizational learning in the new century.

We know our CEO collaborators give us a lot of credit for bringing them a powerful, accessible, and professionally appropriate way of putting adult developmental issues on the table at work. But whether they know it or not, they also contributed something crucial to what we did together. After all, we originally came to this work from the perspective of psychologists supporting individual adult development. As organizational leaders, they were far more talented than we at thinking organizationally and systemically.

As Peter once said, in thinking about the need to transcend an individualistic orientation to leadership development, "If you've got a better phone, and somebody else has a better phone, but you're not connected, it still doesn't do you any good. You just sit there talking to yourself. I used to do that a lot as the CEO anyway. I didn't want to do that anymore." Our CEO partners intrinsically thought about building a new kind of network.

If you see through only one eye, you can still make out a lot of what is in front of you, but the key impairment is a lack of depth perception. Binocular vision allows you to look with depth. The complementarity of our two approaches—each of us taking as figure what the other took as ground—gave the work its distinctive depth. As developmentalists, we were most interested in the problem of sustaining people's involvement in processes that would lead to advances in their individual psychological complexity so that they could be more successful. As leaders of organizations, our CEO partners were most interested in the problem of how to effectively and appropriately engage the emotional life of the organization so that *it* could more successfully deliver on its purposes. Yet it was only by each of us also taking up the other's unsolved problem that we were ultimately able to deliver on both.

We hope Peter and Harry have piqued your curiosity, and that you'd like to have a look for yourself at what this is all about. What actually happens when individuals and teams take on this work? And what difference does it make? The people and organizations you will meet in part 2 provide a variety of opportunities for you to answer those questions.

PART TWO

OVERCOMING THE IMMUNITY TO CHANGE IN ORGANIZATIONS, INDIVIDUALS, AND TEAMS

$$\left[\; 4 \;\right]$$

OVERCOMING THE GROUPWIDE IMMUNITY TO CHANGE

A Collective Approach

As you consider this phenomenon we call the immunity to change, it will no doubt occur to you that it is not just individuals who are in the grip of competing commitments and constraining big assumptions. Collectivities—work teams, leadership groups, departmental units, whole organizations—also unknowingly protect themselves from making the very changes they most desire.

This chapter brings you into a number of teams and work groups that have explored immunities they may *collectively* enact in order to save themselves from unspoken dangers revealed in their *collective* third-column commitments and big assumptions. Often taking up this work after first identifying their individual immunities, the members of these groups saw value in also unearthing the core contradiction and constraining mindset that lived, not only within given members of their group, but within their group *as a whole*.

To give you a flavor for these kinds of explorations, we begin with three brief scenarios from widely varying organizations. You'll be meeting the senior faculty of a major research university's humanities department, a branch of the U.S. National Forest Service responsible for very dangerous work, and a troubled school district in Southern California.

THE HUMANITIES DEPARTMENT: "WE HAVEN'T PROMOTED A PERSON FROM OUR JUNIOR RANKS IN ELEVEN YEARS!"

The senior faculty of a large department in the humanities wondered if we might be able to help them with a problem they said they were getting nowhere solving on their own. "We haven't tenured a person out of our junior ranks in eleven years! I'm serious!" the chairman said. "We are one of America's most highly regarded research universities, but junior candidates are getting wary about accepting our job offers. It is true that when our junior faculty *do* leave us, they go on to great jobs elsewhere, but still, if you are a promising young person, you will understandably think twice about starting out here if you feel there is zero chance of tenure."

We initially wondered if this concern extended much beyond that of a conscientious chairman. But when we talked with other tenured members of the department it was clear this was something that had really grabbed the attention of the group. Unlike state universities, in which there is typically stronger departmental allegiance, it is not uncommon in private, high-profile research universities for individual senior faculty members to be primarily (if not exclusively) concerned about the progress of their own research and writing rather than the welfare of their department. But this issue seemed to have become alarming enough to be an exception.

"We've been 'round and 'round on this for years now," one of them said. "And it is frustrating not to be getting anywhere. I don't like feeling we are running a toxic place for the younger faculty. I'm a researcher, yes, but I'm a teacher, too, and I get satisfaction out of advancing the careers of the next generation. We do that for our doctoral students and we should be doing that for our younger faculty colleagues as well. *Everyone* is not going to be promoted, all right? I mean, that is an understood fact of life in a Research 1 university, and it should not be otherwise. But, my goodness, *someone* should be promoted!"

"We don't promote them," another one said, "because, despite our high hopes when we hired them, when it comes time to review them for promotion their research is too thin or not judged to be of the highest quality. So, over the years, we say we have to do a better job recruiting young faculty who *are* going to be more likely to produce. And, over the years, we do a better job of that. But then they get here and they don't! We can't have such terrible judgment! There must be something that goes on here after they come. We must have something to do with it."

"Well," still another said, "we mentor them; we tell them how important it is for them to publish; we give them semester leaves so they can write. I mean, what more are we supposed to do?"

This idea that "we might have something to do with it" is probably a prerequisite for a group to get anywhere in a shared consideration of its *collective* immunity to change. We asked the group to agree on how they wanted to frame their improvement goal, and together we entered this commitment in the first column of their collective map: "We want to do a better job by our junior faculty. We want them to experience the place as a support to their career development, and, in particular, we want to increase significantly the number of people we are able to tenure from our junior ranks."

We then asked them to collectively create a "fearless organizational inventory" of obstructive behaviors: "What are the things you *collectively* do (not just a few of you) or fail to do that work *against* your improvement goal?" They eventually had quite a lot to say on this front (see column 2 in figure 4-1):

- We load them up with too many advisees and committee assignments, and then they don't have the necessary time to do their research and publish.

- We give them too big a teaching load.

FIGURE 4-1

The collective immunity to change in a humanities department: Why junior faculty so rarely get promoted

1 Collective commitment goal	2 Collective inventory of doing/not doing	3 Collective hidden competing commitments
We want to do a better job by our junior faculty. We want them to experience the place as a support to their career development, and, in particular, we want to increase significantly the number of people we are able to tenure from our junior ranks.	We load them up with too many advisees and committee assignments, and then they don't have the necessary time to do their research and publish. We give them too big a teaching load. We tell them publishing is important, but we also tell them or show them that everything else is important, too—their teaching, their advising, their being on a governance committee. We don't give the right message about priorities.	We are committed to not increasing our workload on advising, teaching, and committee fronts. We are committed to preserving the privileges of seniority.

- We tell them publishing is important, but we also tell them or show them that everything else is important, too—their teaching, their advising, their being on a governance committee. We don't give the right message about priorities.

As you saw in chapter 2, the big "aha" of mapping one's individual immunity to change comes with the third column—the commitments that "have us" (as opposed to the first-column commitments "we have"). Think of Peter identifying his commitment to being in control or to Ron insuring he continues to be liked. In a similar way, when a group succeeds in creating a powerful collective map, it is the third column that produces an unaccustomed bigger space for a group to reflect on itself. Without warning, the group will find itself lifted to a new level of understanding. Seeing the whole forest—an inevitably tangled forest—rather than being immersed in the trees almost always provides something novel to think and talk about. If nothing else, the familiar "round and round" has been interrupted and something new emerges for group consideration.

How do we help people (whether individuals or groups) to make their third column commitments visible? We begin by surfacing the biggest fears that arise in considering doing the *opposite* of any or all of the second-column behaviors. In this case, the question for the senior faculty is, "What would we *collectively* be most concerned or worried about if we were to try to do the opposite?" You can probably guess the form these replies took, sometimes with laughter by the speaker or the listeners, or both:

"If they didn't take on all those advisees, then *we'd* have to!"

"If they taught less, we'd have to teach more!"

"If they didn't do the heavy lifting on the governance committees, then we'd have to!"

The worries people produce bring us to the doorway of their hidden commitments. They can then enter this unexplored room by considering that they may not only have worries; they may also be in the grip of unrecognized "commitments" to *prevent* the things they worry about from occurring. For the senior faculty members this led to third-column entries that brought a single, equilibrated system into view—their collective immune system, in all its glory. (See figure 4-1.)

As soon as this collective immune system came into focus it seemed to create a rush of reactions that had not been heard before. The same people who, an hour earlier, were sincerely and passionately sharing their consternation over the plight of destined-to-fail junior faculty were now bemused to hear themselves saying—with equal sincerity and passion—things like, "No one looked out for *us* when we were junior faculty—and *we* got tenured! Why can't *they*?!"

Then one of the members, laughing a little and shaking his head at this picture of the group with one foot on the gas and the other on the brake, told this story:

I want to tell you what this makes me think about. You know how one of our New Year's resolutions concerning this problem was that we would all be much more proactive in our mentoring? So this fall I decided to be a good citizen and take this agreement seriously, and I reached out to Laura. I consider her, and I still do, a very promising young scholar, and I really think that if she can get going in her research she has the chance, in a few years, to be tenured.

So I had a meeting with her and talked with her about the difficulties she faces in getting on with her work, and she tells me—no surprise!—that one of the biggest problems is when she is invited by one of us to join a time-intensive committee. "You're the same people who will be evaluating me for promotion," she says. "How am I supposed to say no to that?" So I tell her, "Completely understandable. I wonder what you'd think of this idea: from now on, when a senior faculty member invites you onto one of the time-consuming committees, you listen carefully, thank the person for thinking of you, and then you say, 'I think I'd really like twenty-four hours to sleep on this. Is it okay if I get back to you tomorrow?' No one will refuse such a reasonable request on your part," I tell her.

"And then what I want you to do," I say, "is give me a call. We will look this over together, see if there is any way we think it would be good for you personally to do this, and when we decide, most likely, there is not, then we'll figure out a way to get you out of it. How would that be?" Her eyes light up. "Oh," she says, "that would be just great!"

You probably know where this story is going, right? Two weeks later, I am on the phone with her, wearing my admissions chairman hat, and saying, "Laura, is there *any* way you could *possibly* find time to be on this committee? You would be just *so* good for this job!"

The picture of the group's core contradiction—its immunity to change—enabled the group to laugh at itself, one of its members to tell a refreshingly honest story about himself, and everyone else to see that their self-defeating routines were not some kind of damning evidence that they didn't really care enough about the junior faculty (their sneaking, unspoken, shameful suspicion). They saw instead that their genuine concern for the junior faculty lived along side an equally powerful and underacknowledged concern for preserving a work life they *assumed* could not be favorably altered by rethinking the allocation of faculty duties.

THE NATIONAL FOREST SERVICE: "OUR PEOPLE ARE DYING AND WE CAN'T DO A THING ABOUT IT!"

We worked for several years with a branch of the U.S. National Forest Service whose responsibilities included intentionally setting huge fires and burning thousands of acres every year. If that sounds like a strange kind of employment then perhaps you, too, grew up in the era of Smokey the Bear ("Only *you* can prevent forest fires!"), and believed that all forest fire was a bad thing. In fact, as we learned, many of our ecologies are "fire deprived," and it is occasionally necessary to get fire into them to promote their healthy regeneration.

It is, however, very dangerous work. Try as the fire starters might to contain the fires, they occasionally burn out of control, and when that happens they can cause millions of dollars of property damage, and even the loss of life. The people who die when the fires escape are most likely to be our clients, the people who set them. We attended their annual meetings, where a time is regularly set aside to remember the dead, and in the hallways during breaks, we heard the gallows humor: "I wonder who won't be here next year—and not because they have something better to do."

If ever a first-column commitment were starker we haven't seen it: "We are committed to reducing our own fatalities." However, we were warned by some who knew these folks that the chance of their even engaging in the diagnostic exercise was slim. (We have heard this warning, by the way, about many of the supposedly formidable, buttoned-up groups we have been privileged to work with over the years—sitting judges, CEOs, the CIA, surgeons, school superintendents, Israeli leaders. We have *never* had a group that was ultimately unwilling to take a deep dive into the work.)

Why was this group supposed to contain such unlikely candidates for collective introspection? "You've got to understand," we were told, "these are not social workers, and they don't spend much time thinking about their feelings. These are, for the most part, *men*—and I'm talking big, strong, scratch-where-it-itches, physically oriented, outdoorsy men!" We were told to think of a group of retired linebackers and were wished all sorts of semisincere good luck.

Again, we didn't turn to the idea of a collective immunity map until each of the participants had gone through his own personal version. These maps tended to have the familiar first-column goals you might find in any profession—aspirations to improve aspects of one's leadership or management. By the time we turned to their collective work, the subgroup that had chosen to work on the "reducing fatalities" goal had no trouble whatever producing a map (figure 4-2) that put tears in their eyes and a lump in their throats.

As you can imagine, these were wholly novel thoughts and feelings for the fire starters to be sharing with each other. They were moved and we were moved to listen to them. Today this branch of

FIGURE 4-2

**The collective immunity to change in the fire-starter service:
Why it's so hard to talk about reducing fatalities**

1 Collective commitment	2 Doing/not doing instead	3 Collective hidden competing commitment	4 Collective big assumption
We are committed to reducing our fatalities.	We are not completing rigorous after-action debriefs in most important cases. We are not publicizing our errors—to the public or internally. We are not looking hard at our mistakes.	We are also committed to not having to face the possibility that our people may die, and we may not be able to do anything about it!	We assume that if we do face the possibility of our helplessness we may become overwhelmed, and may not recover.

the Forest Service has an active, thriving Lessons Learned operation, and the number of fatalities has gone down. We have no idea if we had anything to do with that result, but we like to think we may have played a small part.

THE SCHOOL DISTRICT LEADERSHIP: "WE DON'T HOLD HIGH ENOUGH EXPECTATIONS OF OUR KIDS"

We worked with the leadership team of a hard-working school district in Southern California—the superintendent, assistant superintendents, and several school principals.[1] The student body was over 80 percent Latino; the professional staff was over 80 percent white. The majority of students came from families needing financial assistance. After all of the leaders had worked through their personal immunities to change, we invited them to diagnose a collective one.

As shown in figure 4-3, the group had no trouble identifying a shared first-column commitment that felt important to all of them: "Accelerating the rate of academic achievement of our English Language Learners (ELLs)." Although filling out the second column—identifying behaviors that work against that goal—was a less comfortable experience, they arrived fairly quickly at their answer,

FIGURE 4-3

The collective immunity to change in a school district: First draft

1 Collective commitment	2 Doing/not doing instead	3 Collective hidden competing commitment	4 Collective big assumption
We are committed to accelerating the rate of academic achievement of our English Language Learners (ELLs).	We do not hold high expectations for English Language Learners.	We may also be committed to not having to take on the additional work of revising what we teach and how we teach our ELL students.	

indicating, "We do not hold high expectations for our English Language Learners."

As is usually the case, they found the third column (the collective hidden competing commitments) to be the most difficult to complete, and ultimately their biggest learning opportunity. On their first try, they identified concerns about the new kinds of work they would have to take on if they were really to hold higher expectations of the ELL students—the need to create new kinds of curricula and new ways of teaching, lots of additional hard work for a group already feeling stretched to the limit.

Although the third-column commitment they settled on technically did create a picture of an immunity to change (see figure 4-3), the exercise—unlike what happened with the senior faculty of the university—did not seem to produce much energy for the group or usher in a productive new vantage point. It was late in the day, and we decided to adjourn until the following morning.

The next morning, an agitated assistant superintendent came to find us at breakfast. "I've been thinking about that exercise since we ended yesterday. I thought about it last night, and I dreamt about it. We are not telling each other the truth about what really should be in that third column!" We asked him what he thought was going on.

"The hardest thing for us to really talk about, in this mostly Anglo group," said the assistant superintendent, who was himself Latino, "is race. We all get along, and we are all people of good will, and we are all committed to helping these kids—but that may be exactly why we can't say what really belongs in that third column."

We asked him what he thought should go in the third column.

"If we were honest, it should say something like, 'We are also deeply committed to preserving a *povrecito* culture around here.' But I'm not sure I can say that to this group." He explained that a "povrecito culture" (*povrecitos,* or "poor little ones," is a term of endearment) was full of protective concern and sympathy. "It's a stance that says, 'These kids are already facing so many obstacles, bearing so many burdens, how can we possibly increase their suffering by holding them to rigorous academic expectations?'"

We kept talking, and eventually he concluded that he owed it to the group to suggest a revision of their third column. "If I can't raise this, who can?" He decided that, however difficult it would be for him, "it would be impossible for one of the white administrators to raise it. They would fear they'd end up looking racist, or offending us, or damaging the spirit of goodwill on our team."

When he brought this to his team that morning, "it was like putting a match to dry tinder," he said. It was as controversial as he'd expected it might be, and although not every member of the group was immediately willing to sign on to the new picture, they all agreed they had taken an important next step in their joint leadership. As one of them said, "The idea that low expectations could come, not only from a place of discrimination or disregard, *but from love and concern*—that was a big eye-opener!"

A previously unilluminated side of the group's operations was now in plain view. They could see more deeply and accurately how they worked against their genuine commitment to English Language Learners. The group was now in a position for the first time to address the crucial question of whether pushing these students *will* always lead to failure and suffering, as they had unknowingly assumed. And, finally, their revised map (figure 4-4) created the possibility of revising this assumption and overturning a protracted immunity to change.

These three scenarios illustrate how the immunity-to-change practices can begin to build upon, and go beyond, the focus on

FIGURE 4-4

A better draft: Why we don't hold high expectations for our English Language Learners

1 Collective commitment	2 Doing/not doing instead	3 Collective hidden competing commitment	4 Collective big assumption
We are committed to accelerating the rate of academic achievement of our English Language Learners (ELLs).	We do not hold high expectations for English Language Learners.	We are committed to preserving a *povrecito* culture—to protecting our students by not being too demanding.	We assume if we really did push our students they would not succeed; they would be crushed; we would feel terrible for them and personally defeated.

individual improvement. As you can see, at the very least, they can create new spaces for group reflection and interaction that have the potential to "unstick" the familiar behavioral and conversational routines that leave groups feeling "we aren't getting anywhere on this" or "we are going in circles." In such situations—and who among us does not have myriad first-person experiences of exactly this phenomenon?—we often also feel, "We probably are not talking about the real thing." But it is often hard to know what the real thing *is,* or how to raise it without creating debilitating defensiveness or intragroup conflict.

In chapter 11, we will discuss the practicalities of how to help a group or subgroup create a collective X-ray. But before you consider trying something like this yourself, you might be thinking, "Yes, deeper, more open conversation is all well and good, but how about taking it further to bring about an actual desired *collective result?* Does the senior faculty actually change its ways to create a more tenurable junior group? Does the school district raise its expectations and do the kids rise to the new challenge? Even the fire starters—is there a way to do this group-oriented work so you are not just left *hoping* you have made a difference?"

Indeed there is. To give you a picture of the way groups have engaged their collective immunities to bring about new results, we invite you to consider three fuller accounts. This time you'll meet a partnership group of a professional services firm, the medical staff of an outpatient clinic, and the faculty of a U.S. medical school.

THE PROFESSIONAL SERVICES FIRM: "WE ARE NOT A COHESIVE LEADERSHIP GROUP!"

The leadership team of a professional services firm wanted to take their group to the next level. Their self-assessment matched the feedback from their younger associates: they had many strengths; the firm was currently doing quite well under their leadership; but their lack of genuine cohesion, mutual trust, and internal support was costly for every level of the organization. Younger associates often felt caught in the middle and were uncertain whether joining their ranks was a happy prospect. The leaders themselves felt personally productive, even creative, but they were also worn out by the factional, competitive, and openly critical quality of their interaction. The managing director felt torn, on the one hand, by a desire to deliver on the group's wish for a less hierarchic, more shared form of team leadership, and on the other by the obvious inability of the group to be sufficiently collaborative to make such a governance structure work.

First the twenty partners had the opportunity to diagnose their individual immunities to change (more about working at this level in the next chapters). They chose personal improvement goals related to their team challenge of becoming a more cohesive leadership group (e.g., "to be less critical," "to be more open-minded," "to be more trusting," "more personal," "more empathic"). Then we invited them into an analysis of their *collective* immunity. They decided to frame the collective improvement goal as "creating a culture of mutual trust and unwavering support" within the partnership group.

We divided them into four subgroups for increased participation and interaction, and asked each group to map the collective immune system that was impeding their progress on this goal. When they reconvened as a full group, they combined the smaller groups' maps to create a very rich single picture (see figure 4-5) that captured everyone's attention.

What were they doing that ran counter to the goal (column 2)?

- We don't listen very well to each other; we'd rather tell each other.

- We talk behind each other's backs.

- We feel that if we haven't been personally consulted it wasn't a decision.

- We let our individual agendas trump the collective agenda.

- We don't assume the best intent in ambiguous situations; on the contrary, we often tend to assume bad intent.

- We avoid difficult conversations with each other.

FIGURE 4-5

Collective core contradictions in a professional services firm

1 Collective commitment	2 Doing/not doing instead	3 Collective hidden competing commitment
Create a culture of mutual trust and unwavering support	We don't listen very well to each other; we'd rather tell each other. We talk behind each other's backs. We feel that if we haven't been personally consulted, it wasn't a decision. We let our individual agenda trump the collective agenda. We don't assume the best intent in ambiguous situations; on the contrary, we often tend to assume bad intent. We avoid difficult conversations with each other. We don't extend ourselves to really understanding each other's agendas. We don't share information. We create and perpetuate an incentive structure that rewards individual over collective achievements. We are very judgmental and critical of each other. We form cliques and continue to collaborate within our small circles. We are all out there scurrying for clients, staying busy, hedging against downturns and lean times. We compete for junior associates to join our particular projects.	We are each committed to not having to follow anyone else's directions; to being "free"; to preserving our entrepreneurial passions; to our own selfish independence. We are committed to winning, even if it means others in the group will lose. We are committed to not having to rely on others, to never having to depend on others. We are committed to overbooking ourselves now so that we will never be back in lean times (storing up during the seven fat years). We are committed to having the people resources we need when we want them. We are committed to not working through conflicts directly, to not wearing ourselves out. We are committed to preserving the pleasure of harshly criticizing and judging each other.

- We don't extend ourselves to really understanding each other's agendas.

- We don't share information.

- We create and perpetuate an incentive structure that rewards individual over collective achievements.

- We are very judgmental and critical of each other.

- We form cliques and continue to collaborate within our small circles.

- We are all out there scurrying for clients, staying busy, hedging against downturns and lean times.

- We compete for junior associates to join our particular projects.

And what collective competing commitments (column 3) make all these behaviors perfectly sensible, even brilliant?

- To not having to follow anyone else's directions; to being "free"; to preserving our entrepreneurial passions; to our own selfish independence

- To winning, even if it means others in the group will lose

- To not having to rely on others, to never having to depend on others

- To overbooking ourselves now so that we will never be back in lean times (storing up during the seven fat years)

- To having the people resources we need when we want them

- To not working through conflicts directly, to not wearing ourselves out

- To preserving the pleasure of harshly criticizing and judging each other

The group members took a good hard look at their core contradictions and began to formulate the various possible big assumptions that sustained them. They listed these in the spirit of, "If we keep holding these views we will *never* become the higher-performing group we want to be!" "We seem to assume," they said

- That there is an inherent conflict between entrepreneurship and collective collaboration; this is an either-or.

- That we are essentially living in an "every man for himself" world; if things go badly for any one of us, the firm won't be there to back us up; if we reach out for help, we will not get it; if we do not look out for ourselves no one else will.

- That in the presence of limited data, our individual judgments are superior to any collective judgment.

- That taking our team to the next level is a *choice*; that we actually have an option; that we do not *have to* take this next step.

- That our present prosperity will not last; that the lean times will come again, and when they do there will be massive casualties.

- That there is ultimately more safety in breadth of work (hedging, overbooking) than depth (concentrating on the big client).

- That "entrepreneurialism" is only a matter of landing the new work (hunting) rather than going deeper with established clients (farming).

- That if we are not personally involved in a decision it can't be a very good one.

- That good people, strong people, don't need support.

As the group carried on this discussion the whole apparatus of the four-column exercise wonderfully disappeared, the way a catalyst disappears from the precipitate in a chemical reaction. The partners were no longer merely participating in an exercise. They had broken through to big glimpses of a collective mindset they could see was holding them back. Nearly every assumption was put forward and/or received in the spirit of strong doubt that the assumption was valid, but with an acknowledgment that the group was operating as if were true: "We are talking as if we can really afford to rest on our laurels, and that just staying as we are is one reasonable alternative, when actually I think we know that we have no choice in this matter, that we have to take the next step or eventually decline and fail."

When a partner would get too drawn into contesting a given assumption ("But look, folks, it's just not true that we don't help each other out . . . "), he would be met by another partner (not by the facilitators), who would remind him of what they were doing. ("But wait, Ben; we aren't problem solving right now. We aren't trying to argue ourselves out of these beliefs. We are trying to figure out what the beliefs really are. We can go to work on them later.") They saw they were getting a handle on *why* their change-prevention system was so robust.

They next identified the four most critical of these assumptions (knowing they could return to the others on another occasion). They broke into small groups again, and this time their job was to invent ways they could systematically explore—and possibly win some distance from—each of these big assumptions. This was a first step toward turning them into just what they were, *assumptions,* no more and no less, rather than uncritically accepted truths.

For example, the group that took up the first big assumption, about the incompatibility of the entrepreneurial and collaborative aspirations, devised a number of interesting experiments to test that assumption. For starters, as a thought experiment, they planned to unpack the whole category of entrepreneurialism, recognizing it had multiple meanings for different individuals within the firm. They set out to examine and assess whether each different component of entrepreneurialism would really be hampered by the constraints of collaboration, and in what fashion. Could a collaborative ethic actually *support* any aspects of entrepreneurialism?

As an action test, they decided to identify ten entrepreneurial projects (new clients they wanted to serve, or new projects they wanted to pursue with existing clients), which they would "hunt in packs" to test whether they could form new coalitions and succeed at generating new business while breaking down familiar cliques and looking out for the individual agendas of each member.

When the offsite ended, the closing comments sounded like this:

"I can't tell you how glad I am that we did not end in the usual fashion of standing and making pledges, as if with hand to heart, about how we each promised to be better boys and girls! We all know that such declarations can be pretty inspirational at the time; and we all know how discouraging it is that very little comes from them."

"We tell our own clients all the time that they should not rush too quickly to the solution, but need to spend some time really understanding what is going on. You folks made us take our own medicine."

"It's true nothing as yet has actually been solved, but I feel much more optimistic than when we started. It's not just how we have been talking with each other, but the way that a disarmingly simple process has helped us to get our arms around something that had felt like trying to punch your way out of a big paper bag. I see a way forward, and now that we have identified the kinds of thinking that get us in trouble, we have to keep paying attention to this and exploring it."

THE OUTPATIENT CLINIC: "WE ARE A SOFT TOUCH FOR DRUG-SEEKING PATIENTS!"

Peter Ham and his colleagues work in an outpatient clinic in an academic medical center.[2] Doctors and nurses there agreed to meet out of their joint dissatisfaction with inconsistencies throughout the department in how they were handling narcotic pain medications.

There had been a lot of discussion and concern about this issue for a long time prior to the meeting. Various stakeholders had complained for several months; the following descriptions are typical of their concerns:

- Some family physicians within the clinic believed their clinic was getting a reputation as an easy place to obtain narcotic pain medications.

- Some physicians objected to covering the clinic in-boxes for other physicians because of the high volume of requests they received for refills of narcotics.

- Nurses complained that the doctors were a "soft touch" and patients were manipulating the clinic. They complained that the doctors often undermined their hard line on narcotics refills by writing the prescriptions anyway. (A recent example occurred when nurses told patients they needed to wait for refills until the date specified on a chronic pain "contract," but doctors refilled the prescription early when the patient was able to get through to them.)

- Postgraduate physicians in training complained about the amount of "drug seeking" they saw during their clinical sessions.

The clinic had clear policies and procedures for how to handle requests for narcotics, but, as you can surmise, there was no consistency in enacting them. Several prior attempts to clean up how they dispensed narcotics had failed, and there was only increased frustration among many providers and staff over this issue. The department chair was particularly concerned and open to a new method to address the problem and improve the clinical practice. A new faculty member, recently exposed to the immunity-to-change model, volunteered to facilitate the meeting.

In the room were both physicians and nurses. They briefly discussed the narcotic problem as a group and then split up to work in pairs. The facilitator explained the four-column model, including the risk taking it involved for a few participants, and reassured the group that they were being invited to try the approach to see whether they found it useful.[3]

Each pair worked through an individually based four-column map. The only initial ground rules were that all information shared within the pairs would be confidential, and that the initial commitment (column 1) had to relate to the narcotic problem. In this way, individuals were invited to look at their personal contribution to what was a collective problem. Two doctors and one nurse volunteered to share their entries with the group.

FIGURE 4-6

Prescribing narcotics: The doctors' immunity map

1 Commitment	2 Doing/not doing instead	3 Hidden compet-ing commitments	4 Big assumptions
Prescribe narcotics appropriately Treat pain appropriately	Not taking the time to establish narcotic contracts Writing the narcotic prescription without taking a full history (e.g., when approached by a patient in the waiting room, in a hallway, by phone, or by e-mail) Not taking time to take a better pain history when the request for medica-tion comes at the end of a visit Not "firing" patients from the practice who are rude to nurses or staff around the narcotics issue Not discharging patients who violate narcotics contracts	Need to stay on time Need to believe patients Need to be liked by patients Need to avoid stress of confronting patients	If I'm late, I am an inefficient physician. If I don't believe patients, I can't be an ally in helping them. If I respond thor-oughly to every request, I will fail at my other important work. If I'm not liked by patients, my reputation will suffer. If I don't ensure that any possible pain is treated, I may fail to reduce suffering. If I feel stress, I will be unprofessional.

Let's first see what the doctors said; take a look at figure 4-6. Asked about the relationship between their column 1 commitments and the clinic's policy for prescribing narcotics, both doctors said that they were one and the same. In other words, these doctors were committed to adhering to the clinic's policy. But as you can well see, they acted inconsistently with this commitment. (Of course, they did often adhere to policy, but they were honest in acknowledging that many times they did not.) As you can also see from their map, those behaviors were serving other important purposes for them, including

FIGURE 4-7

Prescribing narcotics: A nurse's individual immunity map

1 Commitment	2 Doing/not doing instead	3 Hidden compet-ing commitment	4 Big assumptions
Consistently enforce clinic rules on narcotic prescribing	Not telling physi-cians about feeling undermined	Need to avoid discomfort of criticizing doctors	If I criticize the doctors they will get angry, avoid me, criticize me in return. If I feel discomfort, I will not enjoy my job.

a need to avoid the negative outcomes (at least the perceived outcomes) of following the clinic's policy. There you have an immune system: one foot on the gas, the other on the brake.

Now let's turn to the nurse's personal immunity around this same issue. Take a minute to read the map in figure 4-7.

What is most striking to us is how similar the nurse's immune system is to the doctors': all engage in behaviors counter to their commitment to fully exercise the clinic's policy so that they can avoid the discomfort of facing other people's reactions. Of course, what differs is the people they worry about getting a reaction from: for the doctors, it is the patients, and for the nurse, it is the doctors. (And, as is the nature of a system at play, the nurses—assuming this one nurse is speaking for more than just herself—don't reveal that they're upset about being undermined by the doctors, thus enabling the doctors to not worry about the nurses' reaction.)

At the close of the meeting, the facilitators asked everyone *not* to try to change the behaviors they listed in column 2, but to contemplate their big assumptions (column 4) over several months. They asked the partners to be available to each other to check in on progress with their consideration of their assumptions and column 3 commitments.

But of course the intent of the meeting was not simply to air the doctors' and nurses' contributions to the current problem. The facilitators hoped that eventually they would change their behaviors and attitudes. Thus they also made plans for assessing whether any changes occurred. For the month prior to the meeting, when a patient called in for a narcotic prescription, the nurses added the patient to a database and determined whether the patient had a valid narcotic contract or not. These patients' charts were then reviewed five months later to determine whether patients without narcotic contracts were put on contracts, given narcotics without a contract or outside the bounds of a contract, or refused prescriptions.

Also, during the next five months, the clinic monitored the number of patients discharged from the practice for narcotics issues such as forging prescriptions, rude or threatening behavior related to a narcotic request, or violation of a narcotic contract.

This rigorous assessment in follow-through was itself impressive, but the results were even more so:

- By the end of five months, fourteen patients were discharged from the practice for violating narcotics contracts, compared to *no discharges* in the prior two years.

- Rates of narcotic contracts increased from 30 percent during the first month to 65 percent during the last month for any patient requiring a narcotic refill.

- One hundred percent of nurses working the phone prescription line reported feeling supported in enforcement of narcotic rules (when previously very few did).

We think these are remarkable results. So did the facilitator and his colleagues, who concluded that a relatively small investment in meeting time produced substantial measurable outcomes. While other interventions within the clinic may also have contributed to the reported changes, the participants considered the meeting in which people mapped their barriers and assumptions around pain management to be the turning point. Following that meeting, they said, they could chart an evolution from complaining privately, to making public commitments to change, to examining underlying assumptions that tended to prevent their changes, to actually changing their behavior.

THE MEDICAL SCHOOL: "WE AGREE WHAT AND HOW IT WOULD BE BEST TO TEACH FUTURE DOCTORS—BUT WE AREN'T DOING EITHER!"

Constance Bowe and her colleagues used the immunity-to-change approach in an organizational transformation context—an ambitious curricular reform effort at an American medical school.[4] The memories of most higher education institutions are littered with failed efforts and broken dreams on the schoolwide reform front, as one idealistic aspiration after another runs into the reality that it is far easier for small factions to impede a process of change than for a larger, like-minded group to bring it about.

The steady, step-by-step process Bowe reports seems to have led to a very different result, because the reformers' adaptation of the immunity-to-change approach held the group, at each step, in an inclusive exploration of its *shared* contradictions, preventing the "us versus them" splintering that often derails and undermines well-intentioned organizational change efforts.

Ron Heifetz once wrote that Martin Luther King Jr.'s leadership brilliance was his ability to reconstruct the civil rights movement from a struggle between white people and black people (which divided the nation) to a struggle between America's national ideals as represented in the Constitution and her then-current realization of those ideals—a struggle in which, at least potentially, all could join together.[5] Such a shift doesn't immediately reduce conflict but transforms its nature by aligning attention to *a gap*, the closing of which is everyone's responsibility, rather than aligning people with one side or the other. Since there will never be enough charismatic leadership geniuses to support every worthy change challenge, it would be useful if mere mortals, working more conscientiously than charismatically, could learn to bring about such a shift in collective attitudes. Bowe and her colleagues demonstrate that the immunity-to-change process might deliver on this more workmanlike goal.

The group began by engaging the entire faculty in a consideration of the core capabilities they wanted to instill in an ideal graduate that would enable that person to succeed in research or practice in the world of twenty-first-century medicine. When they next considered the greatest gaps between these aspirations and their graduating students' actual capabilities, they were able to identify their collective first-column improvement goals (the short form of each goal that appears in figure 4-8 is given in brackets):

- We are committed to promoting the development of comprehensive professional competencies, attitudes, and skills in our graduates. [Professional competencies]

- We are committed to encouraging self-directed, active learning in our students as preparation for becoming lifelong learners. [Active learning]

- We are committed to enhancing the integration of basic and clinical science concepts essential for the practice of medicine. [Integration]

- We are committed to expanding our students' familiarity with the identified underserved topics. [Underserved topics]

Having found a way to help the faculty collectively name their first-column commitments (rather than having some top-down force impose goals on them), the reformers then turned to the even more difficult task of having the group collectively own the "fearless inventory" of their obstructions to these goals (the second column).

Once again, the reformers went about this task by helping the whole group to experience another gap. This time it was not the gap between where they wanted their students to be and where they actually were, but the gap between the way they as a faculty tended to teach and the way they knew they *should* teach. How did they do this?

The reformers surveyed all faculty who directed required courses and clerkships, soliciting their views on optimal instructional and assessment designs for various learning objectives. (Tables 4-1 and 4-2 describe the results in detail.)

TABLE 4-1

Survey of faculty views on optimal instruction methods for various learning objectives (n = 44, 98% return)

Learning objectives	Lectures	Large-group discussion (with preparation)	Small-group discussion (no preparation)	Small-group discussion (with preparation)	Independent projects (with oversight)	Experiential learning	Tutoring
Identify critical information and concepts	4.2*	3.3	3.0	4.1	3.4	3.5	3.9
Efficient presentation of information	4.6	3.2	2.4	3.4	3.1	2.7	3.3
Encourage self-directed learning	1.6	2.4	2.4	4.3	4.6	4.1	3.4
Problem-solving skills	1.4	2.3	2.8	4.2	4.0	3.6	3.4
Critical thinking skills	1.7	2.7	3.0	4.2	4.2	3.7	3.7
Communication skills	1.4	2.5	3.2	4.5	3.2	3.3	3.3
Information integration	2.6	3.3	3.0	4.4	3.8	3.8	3.4
Information management	2.6	2.8	2.7	3.9	4.0	3.4	3.5
Familiarity with reliable information resources	2.7	2.7	2.3	3.8	4.6	3.1	3.1
Ability to work in teams	1.1	2.3	3.0	4.3	2.5	3.6	2.0
Application of concepts	2.3	2.9	3.0	4.3	4.1	4.0	3.5

TEACHING METHODS

TABLE 4-1 (CONTINUED)

Survey of faculty views on optimal instruction methods for various learning objectives (*n* = 44, 98% return)

TEACHING METHODS

Learning objectives	Lectures	Large-group discussion (with preparation)	Small-group discussion (no preparation)	Small-group discussion (with preparation)	Independent projects (with oversight)	Experiential learning	Tutoring
Integration of learning	2.4	3.0	3.0	3.9	4.2	3.7	3.8
Retention of information	2.6	2.8	3.0	4.2	4.3	4.1	4.0
Overall rankings	2.4	2.8	2.8	4.1	3.8	3.6	3.4

Source: C. M. Bowe, L. Lahey, R. Kegan, and E. Armstrong, "Questioning the 'Big Assumptions': Recognizing Organizational Contradictions that Impede Institutional Change," *Medical Education* 37 (2003).

*Excerpt from Course/Clerkship Director Survey. *Instruction read: "Different teaching methods have distinctive advantages for specific educational objectives. From your perspective and experience, rank each of the teaching methods (columns) in terms of its efficacy (5 = optimal; 1 = minimal) in promoting each of the learning objectives (rows)."

TABLE 4-2

Faculty views on optimal assessment designs for various learning objectives (*n* = 44, 98% return)

Learning objectives	EVALUATION METHODS					
	Multiple-choice exam	Essay	Oral	Open-book or take-home exam	Performance	Interval comprehensive
Factual knowledge	4.3*	4.0	3.8	2.7	3.4	4.0
Conceptual knowledge	2.8	4.3	4.2	3.3	3.3	3.0
Self-directed learning	2.4	3.5	3.6	3.5	3.3	2.9
Problem-solving abilities	2.7	4.1	4.1	3.7	3.6	2.8
Critical thinking	2.4	4.0	4.1	3.4	3.2	2.8
Communication skills: written, oral, and listening	1.4	3.8	4.3	2.6	3.2	2.1
Integration of information	2.5	4.0	4.0	3.2	3.5	2.8
Information management	2.2	3.3	3.4	3.4	3.3	2.8
Knowledge of information resources	2.7	2.9	3.2	3.1	2.3	2.6
Working in groups	1.3	1.3	2.1	2.8	2.3	1.6
Knowledge retention and accessibility	3.3	3.4	3.8	2.6	2.7	3.4
Organizational skills	2.0	4.0	4.0	3.2	3.2	2.0

TABLE 4-2 (CONTINUED)

Faculty views on optimal assessment designs for various learning objectives (*n* = 44, 98% return)

EVALUATION METHODS

Learning objectives	Multiple-choice exam	Essay	Oral	Open-book or take-home exam	Performance	Interval comprehensive
Basic clinical exam skills	2.0	2.4	3.1	2.1	3.8	2.1
Self-assessment abilities	2.2	2.7	2.8	2.3	3.2	2.5
Technical skills	1.7	2.1	2.2	1.7	3.9	1.9
Overall rankings	2.4	3.3	3.5	2.9	3.2	2.6

Source: C. M. Bowe, L. Lahey, R. Kegan, and E. Armstrong, "Questioning the 'Big Assumptions': Recognizing Organizational Contradictions that Impede Institutional Change," *Medical Education* 37 (2003).

*Instruction lead: Different evaluation methods have distinct advantages for specific learning objectives. From your perspective and experience, rank each of the evaluation methods (columns) in terms of its efficiency (5 = optimal, 1 = minimal) in promoting each of the learning objectives (rows).

Survey responses showed that most faculty considered teaching methods other than formal lectures (group discussions, individual projects, experiential learning, and tutorials) to be more appropriate for meeting all their learning objectives (of which there were thirteen) other than "identifying critical information and concepts" and "efficiently presenting information." For example, they ranked "small-group discussions with student preparation" as a much more valuable method than lectures for every other learning objective. Yet small-group discussions composed only 12 percent and 11 percent of the preclinical and clinical programs, respectively, while formal lectures constituted 65 percent of the preclinical and 20 percent of the clinical programs.

Similarly, faculty members recognized the limitations of multiple-choice examinations compared to essay, oral, and performance assessments for all objectives except factual recall, but objective tests remained the mainstay of evaluation in most courses and many clerkships.[6]

The survey also enabled the reformers to identify a number of other contradictions in faculty behavior relative to the four primary improvement goals, which led to a rich rendering of column 2 that came, not from the reformers, but from the faculty representatives themselves—a genuine "telling on ourselves," exactly the kind of fearless collective inventory we seek.

The reformers then helped the collective to identify the hidden competing commitments (column 3) and big assumptions (column 4) that account for these obstructive behaviors. Working in separate task forces around each of the four improvement goals (and including students in each group, since they had less at stake and could honestly raise possible sources of self-protection), the faculty were able to come to a much more powerful picture of *why* they had so far been unable to make much progress on goals like those in their first column. (See the full immunity X-ray in figure 4-8.)

As Bowe and her colleagues explain, "Some of the competing commitments were laudable in their own right. Who could take issue with insisting on adequate preparation of students for licensure examinations, protecting faculty time and academic advancement, and acknowledging the limitations of the institution's resources for

FIGURE 4-8

The medical school faculty's collective immune system: Why we're not consistently using the best methods to achieve important learning objectives for students

1 Collective commitments	2 Doing/not doing instead	3 Collective hidden competing commitments	4 Big assumptions
	What is the curriculum currently not doing (or doing) that prevents this commitment from being fully realized?	*(What is the fear if we do other than this?, and thus ...)* "We are also committed to..."	*"We assume that"*
Professional competencies	Overemphasizing factual information at the expense of other aspects of professional development	**Not having our students be unprepared** (Reduced attention to factual information will result in ill-prepared students)	Students learn essential factual information only when it is formally taught in the current time allotments.
	Not effectively monitoring student's professional attitudes, behaviors, and competencies; providing constructive feedback; and consciously role modeling desired behaviors throughout all four years of training	**Not threatening residents and students** (Factually, residents and students will be threatened by monitoring and evaluating professional competences)	Assessment of professional competencies, especially attitudes, is unreliable and too subjective to be applied as a criterion for advancement.
	Not integrating clinical contextual issues into clinical problem-solving discussions	**Maintaining departmental control of curriculum** (Integration of professional competencies into a department-based curriculum will distract from discipline-specific content)	The individual departments' learning objectives need to take precedence over the school's overall training goals.
Active learning	Setting arbitrary limits on learning; using overly detailed syllabi; primarily focusing on assessment of factual learning Not coordinating teaching/assessment	**Getting good teaching evaluations** (Students become frustrated if learning expectations are not clearly delineated; confusion will result in poor	Students require a highly structured teaching setting in which to learn. Student evaluations of teaching are based on the

	formats with learning objectives	teaching evaluations)	amount of information that is taught rather than on what is learned.
	Not providing sufficient opportunities to monitor how well students can apply acquired concepts to clinical cases	**Maintaining school's reputation and accreditation** (Learning of factual material needed to pass licensure exams would suffer; school accreditation could be jeopardized)	Licensure exams stress retention of factual information rather than concepts.
	Limiting opportunities for faculty development in new teaching and assessment methodologies	**Limiting/protecting faculty teaching effort; avoiding faculty rebellion** (Faculty will rebel if expected to broaden their teaching and their teaching and assessment styles)	Teaching excellence is not a high priority among faculty; their research and clinical responsibilities take precedence over their role as teacher.
Integration	Allowing poor faculty communication and collaboration around educational planning	**Limiting institutional demands on faculty teaching effort** (Recognizing and integrating multiple disciplines will unduly increase unsupported faculty workload)	Faculty teaching responsibility does not extend beyond presentation of discipline-specific material.
	Permitting a compartmentalized presentation of learning content in which individual disciplines vie for control of teaching their own concepts, often beyond a level appropriate for students		Students learn best when topics are presented separately as department-based disciplines; they are incapable of coping with simultaneous from information disparate disciplines.
	Not providing more interdisciplinary teaching and evaluating students on their abilities to recognize and apply generalizable biomedical concepts	**Avoiding student confusion** (The disorganization inherent in an integrated teaching approach will confuse students and compromise learning)	
		Insuring the accuracy of what is taught; preserving "the experts'" turf (Misinformation and misunderstanding will	Faculty members cannot teach outside their expertise at a level appropriate for medical students; they have neither

FIGURE 4-8 (CONTINUED)

		arise if "nonexperts" are allowed to teach material from other disciplines)	the time nor interest to update their understanding in other fields.
Underserved topics	Not developing a stage-appropriate curriculum for each of these times	**Protecting curricular turf for "core" material** (Expanding the coverage of the underserved topics would result in radical cutbacks in time allotted to core material currently presented)	The current core curriculum cannot be reduced to accommodate new disciplines and themes.
	Not integrating material from these topics into existing courses where relevant		General faculty competencies in the underserved topics cannot be augmented sufficiently to address curriculum needs at the medical student level.
	Not creating additional venues for expanding these themes as needed	**Retaining discipline-specific teaching by experts** (Teaching and evaluation in these areas would greatly exceed available faculty expertise)	

education? Such concerns were responsible and logical. Other competing commitments were more self-serving: insuring good teaching evaluations, maintaining departmental control of educational resources and curriculum objectives and excluding additions to the curriculum to protect current time allocations. Many of the task force members were reluctant to personally espouse these more negative and reactionary mindsets. Instead, they dutifully voiced them on behalf of their constituencies."[7]

As always, whether in an individual or collective immunity map, the emergence of the third column simultaneously provides a *cognitive* awareness of a change-prevention system at work, and the *emotionally* unsettling insight that the true barriers to change come from within the system. Describing the third-column worries and the competing commitments they motivate, Bowe and her colleagues write: "These heartfelt concerns, if left unaddressed, would certainly compromise any reform proposals or, more likely, perpetuate the status quo. The group had based its primary commitments on educational goals and curriculum data. It now examined the sources and rationales supporting the institution's equally powerful collective competing commitments."[8]

It was similarly useful for the group to identify possible big assumptions that preserve this immunity to change. As always, once these beliefs are shifted from "the truth" to "only possibly true," a way forward to overturn the immunity to change appears.

> Many of the initial big assumptions underpinning the competing commitments proved to be truisms commonly operative at many medical schools. The advancement of medical training during the last century, as well as the stability and well-being of medical schools in general, was attributed to the adherence to some of these maxims. It is not surprising that curriculum proposals seeming to fly in the face of these axioms prompted deep rooted concern and resistance among some faculty. Participants could not remember a time when these organizational mindsets were not generally accepted but admitted that their validity had not been recently questioned. Holding curriculum development hostage to truisms from the past seemed indefensible.[9]

To their credit, the reformers were not content to stop here. Though they had helped the group to an uncommonly powerful diagnostic, they did not trust that this would by itself lead to a successful "treatment." They grouped the big assumptions into four broad areas, seeing how their collective immunity was protecting the institution from a raft of presumed inadequacies:

- Assumed limitations of our students

- Assumed limitations of the faculty

- Assumed limitations of the departments

- Assumed limitations of our institution

They then set about to design and run a series of tests in each of these categories, keeping in mind that the purpose of the test was not primarily to "get better" but to "get information," especially information about the validity of their assumptions (see figure 4-9).

As figure 4-9 indicates, these tests constituted a set of pilot projects, which the reformers acknowledge could seem to some a plodding pace toward change. Their cautious approach, they say, "contrasts sharply with more dramatic transformations attempted in other schools' reforms." They believed it would, however, "permit the collection of data to support or debunk the legitimacy of the big assumptions and allow for adjustments along the way in the institution's educational and administrative infrastructure in order to sustain the reforms as they expanded into the curriculum."[10]

So what were the results of this way of going slow to eventually go fast—and last?

- Much to the naysayers' surprise, more than eighty interdisciplinary faculty from seventeen departments (including six department chairs and four deans) volunteered to participate and be trained in discussion teaching and performance assessment in the first year. The involved faculty's effort and newly acquired teaching skills were peer evaluated and documented in letters to their department chairs to insure adequate recognition in the promotion process. The student reception of the reform projects was enthusiastic and encouraging.

- The positive experience from the supported pilot projects seriously challenged the validity of several institutional assumptions. Both faculty and students (peer and self-evaluations were employed) were able to apply performance criteria in the assessment of professional competencies, benefited from the team approach to active learning, and appreciated the opportunity to integrate and apply concepts from a variety of courses and clerkships. The participating faculty strongly endorsed further expansions of the pilot projects and advocated for expanded faculty development in teaching and evaluation training within this context.

FIGURE 4-9

Testing the validity of the collective big assumptions

Consolidated institutional big assumptions	Strategy to test the big assumptions
LIMITATIONS OF STUDENTS Our students are unable to cope with and optimally learn in a less structured, multidisciplinary learning environment that requires a self-assessment and self-directed learning. Our students' acquisition of core factual information will be compromised by new teaching and evaluation methods, new material, and increased emphasis on professional competencies throughout the curriculum. Our students will be threatened by performance evaluation.	Modestly reduce contact hours of traditional curriculum (eliminate redundancy and improve coordination among core courses/clerkships) to accommodate time needed for pilot case discussion course and independent student research time. Develop broad learning objectives and performance expectations for student learning/faculty teaching to be emphasized in curriculum reform pilot projects. Monitor student performance in traditional curriculum and licensure exams as pilot changes are introduced. Track and address student frustration with curriculum changes as they arise. Work closely with faculty teaching concomitantly with pilot case discussion course to assess its impact on their course or clerkships.
LIMITATIONS OF FACULTY The faculty are not interested in or capable of using new teaching methods, utilizing reliable performance evaluation criteria, providing supportive feedback to students, or learning from other disciplines. Our faculty cannot be released from their obligations to staff small, interdisciplinary discussion groups, participate in faculty development programs, or help coordinate the curriculum.	Develop stage-appropriate performance criteria for professional behaviors; train faculty in their application; test reliability and validity. Recruit and train cofacilitators for interdisciplinary discussion course; match cofacilitators' experience and expertise to broaden discussion groups' perspectives. Incorporate essential concepts for case discussion from relevant disciplines in facilitator training to update faculty in areas outside of their expertise. Solicit observations and evaluations from faculty and students participating in pilot projects, acknowledging that teaching and learning "enjoyment" is an acceptable parameter to be included. Publicly recognize faculty and departments supporting the curriculum reform pilots.

FIGURE 4-9 (CONTINUED)

LIMITATIONS OF DEPARTMENTS	Dean/faculty senate chairman to secure the support of department chairs for curriculum reform projects.
Departments are too preoccupied with their discipline-specific learning goals to contribute to overall educational objectives.	Develop department educational plans that more clearly delineate their contribution to overall training objectives as well as their discipline-specific learning goals for students.
Departmental budgets cannot support faculty effort on interdisciplinary projects if their remunerative activities will be compromised.	Broaden the department chair's recognition of the opportunities provided by interdisciplinary, longitudinal projects for further extension of concepts from their discipline throughout the curriculum.
Department chairs will protest centralization of resources for education.	Secure school of medicine support for interdisciplinary endeavors.
	Publicly acknowledge department contributions to new projects.
LIMITATIONS OF OUR INSTITUTION	Design reporting criteria for teaching activities that recognize coordination and planning effort as well as faculty participation on interdisciplinary pilots.
Institutional resources and mechanisms to recognize and reward faculty teaching effort are unavailable to support interdisciplinary projects requiring increased faculty planning and participation.	Ensure that teaching effort (including faculty training, group facilitation, and student evaluation time) is fully acknowledged in the promotion process.
The administration is unable to substantively shift power and resources from departments to support broader educational goals.	Develop a system for peer assessment of teaching.
	Document faculty effort and teaching performance; inform department chairmen as well as the dean for academic affairs.
	Request partial institutional support for faculty leaders directing implementation of curriculum reform pilot projects.

- The pilot projects effectively tested the validity of institutional big assumptions and allayed undue fears and foreboding before implementing desired changes. In many instances, they actually disproved the legitimacy of festering concerns that could ultimately limit the impact of attempted changes.

Persistently dissident factions tended to be isolated by their peers because their objections were founded on preexisting opinions rather than evolving data.[11]

As they collectively began to overcome this institutional immunity to change, the faculty's actions shifted from testing their big assumptions to effecting lasting change:

Following the first pilot year, the faculty-at-large voted to cut back curriculum time for traditional courses and clerkships to promote more independent student learning. The allotted time and requirements for the interdisciplinary, longitudinal course were expanded throughout the first 3 years and the mentored clinical experience was extended into the second year. As the pilot projects became formalized curriculum components, several additional projects were initiated to integrate material within and across the pre-clinical training program, coordinate clinical skills teaching and to develop an interdisciplinary ambulatory clinical experience within the third year. All of these curricular endeavors are now supported by a new executive vicedean for medical education whose educational philosophy resonates with the faculty's goals for the institution's future.[12]

The use of the immunity-to-change process, Bowe and her colleagues conclude:

significantly impacted this institution's educational culture and general acceptance of alternative educational approaches. Both of these factors have sustained the original reforms and fostered additional faculty-initiated advances in inter-disciplinary teaching, active learning and integration in keeping with the guiding educational commitments [in column 1]. Perhaps most importantly, the solidarity of core faculty resolve proved to be especially important as the administrative leadership successively changed, a situation considered to be a huge risk factor for failure in curriculum reforms.[13]

Most of these collective success stories received a big assist from the fact that key participants had also diagnosed—and were working to overcome—their *individual* immunities to change. What does that work actually look like? In the chapters that follow, we examine in detail the overcoming-immunities process for two individuals, each one in the throes of a personal challenge that we think will resonate for many of you. We then turn to what might be the most powerful design for overcoming immunities: taking on several individual change challenges at once in the context of an intact group's efforts to enhance its performance. When you finish this part of the book, we hope you will have an affirmative answer to the question that betrays one of our culture's most constraining big assumptions: is there any new evidence that should cause me to rethink my basic belief that people "are who they are," and that by the time they are in their thirties or forties *they really cannot change?*

[5]

DAVID DOESN'T DELEGATE

Overcoming an Individual's Immunity to Change

A s any experienced manager will tell us, being an effective delegator is crucial to using everyone's time, skills, and knowledge appropriately. Skillful delegation gives everyone a greater chance to grow, and the quality of the work reflects the many talents that have been drawn into its production along the way. Without it, today's talents go underdeployed, tomorrow's talents go undeveloped, and some people—especially ineffective delegators themselves—get overused and burned out. A mere peek into the management literature would give us the impression that all a person needs in order to develop the capacity to share work effectively is a good road map and a can-do spirit.

Many practical guides, such as Robert Heller's *How to Delegate* and Gerard Blair's *Starting to Manage: The Essential Skills*, offer excellent advice—excellent, that is, if learning to delegate is, for you, a technical challenge. For most people, however, we suspect that it's more of an adaptive or developmental challenge, of the kind we described in chapter 2.[1]

This was certainly true for David, one of the rising talents in a worldwide engineering company, who had been trying, unsuccessfully, to delegate since he was recently promoted to a senior management position. Let's take a closer look into David's experience in his new role, especially his experience with delegation.

DAVID'S IMMUNITY TO DELEGATING

In his midthirties, David had been promoted to general manager, reporting directly to the company's CEO, six months before we met him. Overall, things were going very well: he was excited about his work, and people throughout the company respected him and were pleased to have him in this new role. Nonetheless, he felt relentlessly overwhelmed for the first time in his career. He had no difficulty naming an improvement goal that met all our criteria, including that it was "very important" to him to make progress on it.

His first cut describing his goal was "to better focus on a few critical things," something he had been working on explicitly for the past months via a time management approach. He saw progress, but still felt in over his head and knew that better delegation was part of his solution. He was quite specific about what he wanted to do differently, including getting better at clarifying for others the outcomes he desired, accepting people's different approaches to the work, challenging people's thought processes and logic, and finally, supporting small failures as learning opportunities. Clearly, this was not the first time David had thought about how to delegate.

We've chosen David as one of our cases in part because the goal he identifies is a version of one of the most common we see. Whether someone says he or she wants to get better at "holding others accountable," "leading from behind," "empowering others," "shifting from 'hero on the field' to 'coach on the sidelines,'" or "letting more people lead," the thread that runs through all of these aspirations has to do with delegation.

But as David's column 2 entries in figure 5-1 reveal, delegating is not always easy. He had no problem identifying ways he acted inconsistently with his intent to better focus on a few critical things. He listed these three behaviors:

- I let new opportunities distract me, adding to my list.

- I accept more tasks and sacrifice non-work-related things (sleep, family, hobbies).

- I don't consistently balance time commitment regarding urgent and important rankings.

His counterbehavior to his intent to delegate was straightforward: "I don't ask people to help me."

Having done a good job filling in column 2, identifying what he did and didn't do that worked *against* his column 1 commitment, he was ready to consider what all those behaviors worked *for*. He could easily see how those same behaviors were very effective when it came to his hidden commitments (see his column 3, including his fears). Adding new opportunities to his list, accepting more tasks, and not asking people to help him were clever ways to make sure he could stay "independent," "capable of anything," and "selfless." He was clear how costly the flip side would be; that is, if he didn't do those things, then he would pay a price, such as being dependent on others and feeling selfish.

You can see from his big assumptions that he assumed these would be costly—he would lose self respect, become superficial and trivial (exactly what he dislikes in others), and stop being valuable.

Figure 5-1 was David's first map. As often happens when rereading a first draft a few days later, he had a new thought: he realized that his three hidden commitments were all expressions of what it meant to him to be a "real" worker, not just someone who puts in time and "is overhead." He added the following to his map: "(I worry I'll abandon my values of what it means to be a worker.) I'm committed to being loyal to my blue-collar roots." This turned out to be a crucial insight because we can see, looking at even his earliest version of his map, that underneath his words is an as-yet-unrecognized view of "delegating" as "getting other people to do your work." With this definition of delegating, how could it ever seem like

FIGURE 5-1

David's initial immunity map

Commitment	Doing/not doing instead	Hidden competing commitments	Big assumptions
To better focus on a few critical things: • Delegate • Clarify outcomes desired • Accept different approaches • Support small failures as learning • Challenge the thought process and logic	I let new opportunities distract me, adding to my list. I accept more tasks and sacrifice non-work-related things. I don't consistently balance time commitment to urgent and important rankings. I don't ask people to help me.	(I fear missing a good opportunity. Falling behind.) I'm committed to being independent and capable of anything. (I fear letting my team down. If I put myself first I feel guilty and selfish.) I'm committed to being selfless. (I dislike leaving boxes unchecked—it's harder to drop something than just to do it.) I'm committed to always finding a way to get it done.	If I am dependent on others and unable to do many things well, I lose my self-respect. If I put myself first I'll become what I dislike in others—superficial and trivial. If I don't find a way to get things done, I'll stop being valuable.

anything but laziness or selfishness? Uncovering the source of this definition proved key for David's eventual bigger learning.

Looking at his column 4 assumptions in light of this "aha" about his loyalty to his blue-collar roots, David realized that he had folded his beliefs about being an effective worker into a tacit, powerful theory—one that no doubt he had absorbed from the people he admired in his family and community—about what made a good leader. Foremost was the distinction he saw between blue- and white-collar workers: in a nutshell, blue-collar workers get their hands dirty (literally and figuratively), whereas white-collar workers are dispensable, air-filled sources of overhead who tend to act (unjustifiably) superior. Embedded in this distinction, he saw, was his apparent belief that hands-on work is more important and valuable than thinking. He added an assumption to his fourth column: "If I don't add value by myself directly doing jobs that involve the guts of the business, I will not be a contributor, and I will be overhead."

His summary big assumption statement was this: "I believe that leadership without *doing* is 'overhead' and worthless. I'd walk away from my roots if I was not doing the work itself. I would be selfish, lazy, and spoiled, and lose my self-respect." It's understandable—given this belief system—why David behaves as he does, and notice that how he feels about himself is at the heart of his struggle to be a better delegator. The behaviors of his immune system successfully protect him from feeling selfish, lazy, or spoiled; they protect him from the apostasy of defecting to the "other side" and becoming all that he and his people loathe; they enable him to feel like a self-respecting, hard-working guy who pulls his own weight, and can look squarely in the eyes of any blue-collar worker even as he assumes a different role.

His challenge is an adaptive one because *it clearly implicates his very self-identity.* Becoming a better delegator is not (as it might be experienced by someone else) primarily about learning a new set of skills or techniques for assigning work. This is why, as you can imagine, it would be impossible for him to make progress by taking advice from delegation experts. Practical tips don't address the essence of why David, an exceptionally bright and motivated new leader, does not delegate.

As he goes on to observe himself further, David (and we) learns just how central not delegating is to his self-image and self-esteem. He realizes that he gets enormous benefits from feeling "important and valuable by doing individual tasks myself. It connects me to people. And I'm doing a kick-ass job. I feel good about being a star." He also sees he gets a great deal from how *others* regard him when he is the "doer": "They see me as smart and a good problem solver. I get their respect for that."

These are rich additions for his column 3 commitments to protect the self he wants to be—that is, important, valuable, and a star, especially perhaps in the eyes of a critical reference group, the worker on the floor level with whom he has the strongest identification.

We now have a fuller picture of David's "problem" (the kind of problem which is also a developmental opportunity): right now he is stuck between seeing the need to delegate and not being able to do so because that means abandoning aspects of his identity and many of the ways he feels good about himself. His mental frame for understanding who he is—his values, beliefs, likes, and dislikes—is inconsistent with being a delegator. This frame creates an impossible forced choice: he can solve this problem either by giving up on his wish to delegate or by giving up on his loyalty to his roots.

Another solution—a more *adaptive* one—would be to create a bigger frame on *who he is* that *includes* delegation; that is, to undertake a developmental shift that makes delegating consistent with his self-definition. This more inclusive frame asks, "Is it possible for David to respect and feel good about himself, be true to his roots *and* be a good delegator?" While David initially tells us through his map that this is absolutely *not* possible, in less than a year his way of leading and his own words end up answering this question with a resounding "yes!"

DAVID OVERCOMES HIS IMMUNITY

Before we turn to *how* David became a better delegator, let's focus on what his changes looked like. His success can be summed up, using David's own words, as a move from "being a 'tradesman' to an 'architect' and 'developer.'" This shift captures a whole new way of working with his team, of which being a successful delegator, it turns out, is just one element. As an "architect," David now spends the majority of his time building the business, having redefined the "right" work as focusing on strategy, people, and resources.

This has had profound implications for how he works with his team. His way of interacting has changed to ensure that there are open and honest exchanges and a shared ownership of the work at each appropriate level. He now spends considerable time communicating about the team's direction, and doing so in ways that allow everyone to "get *what* they are doing and *why* so that they can make decisions to keep us going in the right direction." He makes a point of open communications "so people will be honest with me about how things are really going so that I can 'know' without doing everything myself." Delegating is woven into the way he works, prompted by questions like, "Who is the best to do this piece of the work and what do they need from me?" He has figured out how to both accept different approaches and still uphold his standards for excellence.

The consequences of these different ways of working are huge: "Challenging people's thought processes, and being open to them pushing me, has enabled everyone to produce quality results." His team members also have excelled at becoming better delegators themselves. In addition, he noted: "Individuals are able to make quality decisions themselves consistent with our direction and generate ideas for moving ahead . . . Best of all, people are coming to me to tell me ideas about how we could move ahead differently. That's been very fulfilling, much more so than getting an individual task done myself."

Whereas being a "tradesman" had led David to focus on his own performance only, being an "architect" has meant attending to other people's development and their capacity to deliver on the business's mission. This wasn't an easy transition for him. As he got better at building other people's capacity, he said, "I love that I can get more out of my team, but it is a little bit of a blow—when you give people a chance to shine, they do it better. So my assumption that I would do it better isn't correct." This statement bespeaks a core move in David's development: he is no longer subject to his prior way of being a star to feel good about himself, but has developed a new way to shine, one that allows other people to shine. This has become a new part of his identity and satisfaction.

He can now shine at doing what he calls the "right work." Key to his transformation is this redefinition of what actually *is* his own work. So long as he continued to see what he might delegate as essentially "his," delegating would always seem to him an act of getting others to do his work—an ethically indefensible (even shameful) act, raising the unavoidable specter of selfishness, laziness, being a useless "suit," and, most of all, violating a deep-felt kinship with his fellow laborers. Viewed this way, delegating could only be an exercise in class betrayal, letting oneself be lured into the heresy that moving away from the direct means of production is a desirable advance.

And yet today, reflecting on where the overturning immunities work got him, there is no longer any sense that the work he is giving others to do is a way of getting out of doing it himself. The work he gives them to do is now theirs, not his, and his work is about helping them develop in the process of taking on new goals and challenges. "I feel important and valuable by spending my time finding ways to help my people be more effective. I find myself looking more at what my people are accomplishing."

Self-respect is still essential to him, but he has a different understanding of what he respects about himself because he has redefined how he wants to lead. He now feels self-respect for being a leader who is able to direct the work and to optimize resources, people, and finances to do it. He says, "I have a clearer and more satisfying leadership practice, where I see that I don't have to *do* in order to know what's going on, but that I do need to *know* what's going on in order to direct the work" (our emphases). "This is because I now believe that the biggest single impact isn't from doing details," he explains. "It's from doing lots of thinking and planning on my part, while having a real picture of what's going on, and finding the best way to bring all my resources to bear."

This last sentence captures David's reformulation of his original big assumptions, that he had to be able to do things himself or he would lose his self-respect, his connection to his roots and his sense of being valuable. He has discovered that he can add value by knowing *differently* how to get the work done. His revised assumption is this: "It's not that I need to do it, but I need to know it. I need to understand how the parts fit together in order to do the big-picture work effectively. Maybe it's not even having the skill to do the work, but it's having the detailed information."

David's newly earned self-respect and sense of added value come from a more complex mindset. He has not abandoned his roots and the value they place on getting things done, being capable of anything, and being selfless. But he has reauthored these core value themes into a bigger, roomier story that allows him to be both a good delegator *and* a good leader. In the original story that "authored him," his understanding of "leader" equated with "white-collar," "overhead," "useless," "not doing," and "blowing hot air." "Blue-collar" automatically connected with all good things, including his family of origin, being a "doer," and being important and valuable. Deep down, however sophisticated and smart he was, he still held on to a black-and-white, either-or construction of these sets of ideas. Or, to put things a little more rigorously, these ideas "held on to him."

But through the course of overturning his immunity, David goes far beyond merely getting better at delegating. He takes up the pen and gradually rewrites the self-narrative that had previously authored him. He remakes his mindset by moving the blue-collar family ethos from something that holds him (i.e., he is subject to it) to something he can hold (i.e., he doesn't lose it, but he moves it to an "object" of his attention, putting him in a position to work out a new relationship to it). The worlds of leader and doer move from "either-or" to "and-also" in his mind.

Notice how David's success exceeded his initial aspiration. Yes, David learned how to delegate, even how to take joy in doing so. But his biggest learning might be that he changed his relationship to his own labor without violating his love of, and loyalty to, hard-working family members and heroes who inevitably served as models for what it meant to do a good day's work. This is often the case when a person overturns his immune system: his grasp ends up exceeding his reach. What is actually accomplished goes far beyond the "improvement goal" that, like a Trojan horse, initially tempts him out of the fortress of his established habit of mind.

When we last talked with David, he had just received word from his boss that his plans for an especially ambitious new project had been accepted, and David would be getting all the money he asked for. One of his final comments to us was, "We're going gangbusters!" He added, "And that followed from lots of thinking and planning on my part."

TOOLS AND TURNING POINTS IN DAVID'S IMMUNITY WORK

How was David able to make a change of this magnitude? We turn now to highlight a few of his critical turning points during the months we worked with him. The starting point for his inner change was, most likely, stepping into a new leadership role. This position posed more challenging demands than those he had met in the past, and David saw very quickly that he couldn't handle his workload in his accustomed player-coach fashion. From there, David's own view was that the two most influential steps he took were understanding his immunity to change ("that was the biggest leap") and acting on that understanding by telling people what he personally wanted to change. About the latter, he says, "Once I started to explain to people what I needed to work on, I gave them permission to step in and tell me when they saw me not delegating properly. I told them to tell me when I'm doing something that you think you can do better."

David used two overturning-immunities tools to increase people's understanding of his goal. (You'll find a summary of all the tools in chapter 10.) He started by completing what we call a continuum of progress, as shown in figure 5-2.

FIGURE 5-2

David's continuum of progress

Commitment	First steps forward	Significant progress	Success
I want to be better at increasing the number of things I delegate to people in order to have fewer things on my plate.	Meet with my team and let them know what behavior I'm trying to change, why and how. Role-play through some examples, integrating them into what types of tasks or responsibilities should go to whom and how they'd like it to happen. Prioritize items based on ease, importance, and ability and then start doing them. Review at monthly staff meetings how I did and how they did. Adjust our plan as appropriate. Review in six months to evaluate the longer-term impact on my performance and role in leadership vs. our expectations.	My team would notice the change in the work I do personally and their shift in workload. They would likely have to empower their people more, passing on the next level of work so they could absorb what I give them. I believe they would feel more important and more trusted. My team would see my contribution toward longer-term planning increase, giving them more confidence that we have a direction and are paying attention to staying on course.	I would be able to clearly identify every item that comes up as something I should do or, if it should be delegated, to whom it should go and how. My team would become so comfortable taking on larger responsibilities that the work would start going directly to them, releasing me from the need to delegate at all. I would have at my fingertips the pulse of the market, our plan of attack, and our performance at a market level at any moment.

This exercise begins with the column 1 commitment, and lists the specific initial steps a person plans to take toward fulfilling it. It goes on to establish the kinds of indicators that would show significant progress and, finally, full success. Notice how David's "first steps forward" focus entirely on his relationship with his team (communicating with them, planning activities that increased the likelihood that they could help him, and involving them in his and their success).

A few weeks later, David used another tool, the overturning-immunity survey, which he sent to all his team members. As most people who use the survey do, he identified a small group of "witnesses" (usually six to eight) at the start of his work. These are typically people from within and outside your work life who would be in a position to notice real changes around your improvement goal if you made them. The surveys are short, simple, and anonymous. (You can see David's survey in figure 5-3.)

The coachee usually receives an anonymous, scrambled aggregate of respondents' rankings and comments on two occasions—after the first survey, at the start of the work, and again after a follow-up survey several months later, as part of the end of the work. The survey responses provide a kind of external change metric—a way of gauging your progress toward your improvement goal. The first survey also serves as a reality check on whether you've identified the best or most valuable goal for yourself. The second survey also serves as a safeguard against self-deception.

At more subliminal levels, the surveys create an internal and external "audience" for your progress. Sharing your commitment to change and knowing that others will comment on your progress make you much more likely to stick with your personal program. At the organizational level, the surveys signal throughout the system that senior leaders are working on their issues. In our experience, survey respondents often get intrigued by the process and become interested in participating themselves or undertaking a similar process within their teams. It has consistently impressed us how willing people have been, across a wide variety of organizations, to produce rich and thoughtful feedback.

As sometimes occurs, David's first survey didn't go out until he had already begun his overcoming-immunities process; as a result, he

FIGURE 5-3

David's survey form

David's Baseline Survey

The area David has chosen to work on is to be a better delegator. There are ways that David's hands-on involvement can be a real strength, of course, but he wants to reduce ways in which it can be problematic.

This is a confidential survey. You were chosen by David to be one of his survey respondents. It is his hope you will answer as frankly as possible. Obviously, David's own self-assessment on the following questions at the present time would be rather low.

Responses will not be identified by respondents. David will receive an anonymous profile of the results of six to eight surveys like this one. On his behalf, thank you for the benefit of your thinking and about fifteen minutes of your time—now, and again in about six months.

1. The area David has chosen to work on is to be a better delegator. How well does David delegate to you?

   1 2 3 4 5 6 7 8 9 10

   1 = Poorly   10 = Extremely well

2. From your perspective, how well does David delegate *to others?*

   1 2 3 4 5 6 7 8 9 10

   1 = Poorly   10 = Extremely well

3. Comments: Please take a minute to expand on this quick take. For example, any further thoughts, explaining what you mean, giving examples, will be helpful.

4. As you think about just this aspect of David's functioning, *how important do you consider his making significant improvement?*

   1 2 3 4 5 6 7 8 9 10

   1 = Not at all   10 = Very important/valuable

5. Why do you say so? In what ways would it matter/not matter? (We know these take a moment, but they are extremely helpful to David and his coach.) The more particular you can be, the better.

   THANK YOU for you time and your thoughts!

---

learned that some of his initial efforts, including those in his "first steps forward" column, were paying off, and that he should continue working on his new strategies. He also had an important insight: "I see myself having made progress on accepting different approaches. And as I think about what I've been doing differently with my staff, two of those things are both referenced here—my giving starting and end points, and making sure to give them the context. I think part of the reason I struggled in the past is that I didn't share the context.

I look back and think that if I didn't give super good directions, then I can look smart! I could like the respect of being a problem solver!"

We often say that the immunity-to-change technology allows us to overcome blind spots, helps us see formerly invisible ways we are undermining ourselves. Here David sees that he may have been "stacking the deck" by deliberately (if unconsciously) preparing people inadequately, thus setting the stage for his heroic intervention. He could not give us a better example here of what it means to move third-column commitments from subject to object. When the third-column commitments are fully in force, they are like internal thieves running unfettered, stealing at will from the first-column commitment. When they become visible, we are then in a position to clamp down on them, to stop them in their tracks, as David did when he literally stopped preparing his people for failure and began preparing them for success.

In taking stock of his progress six weeks into the overturning-immunity process, he said:

> My initial big assumption was around a couple of thoughts—one, that if I don't directly add value I'll stop really contributing to my team—in essence become pure "overhead." Wrapped up in that is a feeling that I need to be willing—and able—to do almost any job that could come up within my team, this being linked to a view of leadership needing to really have their hands in the guts of the business in order to be a good leader. The result of this big assumption was poor delegating and sometimes poor communication when I did delegate. I've done a lot of things to change my behavior— and in viewing my continuum of progress feel good that I've actually done the things on that list and I am now between the first step and "significant progress" in most areas. I believe that was reflected in the survey—with higher than expected results due to people seeing the change. I'm doing a better job delegating—better in quality rather than quantity, and I continue to focus on identification of more elements of my day-to-day job that can be delegated to others.

David was now well on his way toward better understanding the limits of his current mindset, including finding aspects about it that he did not respect. Following an assignment to focus on what he *feels* when he delegates, David had a mixed report. He said:

> It's slippery. Maybe I do things myself because I can feel good about being a star. My current learning is a double whammy—delusion number 1: the only way is if I do it myself; number 2: I will do it best. Actually, this guy's getting it better than I would have done! I'm doing a kick-ass job, yet they came up with a spin that's even better! Love-hate: love that I can get more out of my team, but it is a little bit of a blow. When you give people a chance to shine, they do it better. So my assumption that I would do it better isn't correct.

He also discovered gaps in his own leadership philosophy that he had never noticed before. About the latter he realized:

> In my leadership philosophy, I say I ought to be able to do anything I ask individuals or the team to do. Yet, if I am actually following other aspects of my leadership philosophy—that I should be selecting/hiring people with potential and supporting their development—then I won't be adding value by being their equal! If I select people who become the best, I have to be willing to have them outstrip me. I *shouldn't* be able to do everything they can do!

On the other hand, he was feeling very excited about what he was learning about being a better delegator. One of his first breakthroughs was discovering that he had been limiting his own effectiveness by using one way of delegating, based on his own strengths, not the other person's strength. David asked all thirty-six people on his team to take a "strengths-based" inventory and then asked how they thought they could get their job done given their strengths: "If I were to give you an assignment, what are the five things you'd want to know?" Here's what happened when he did this:

> This got a huge response. Everyone identified different needs. Susan, outstanding with customers, has "context" strength—if

she can see everything she's doing within the context, she gets great work done. She needs to know how it will be used, etc., the "why." I was delegating "10 phones by tomorrow" and she wasn't getting it done. And I wondered whether she was lazy. Now she can do ten phones by 3:00!

David's take-away?

The first mountain was my willingness to delegate. Now I see the next mountain, which is, "Does the delegating really have an impact?" The impact was inconsistent. Now I see that was about my being a novice at delegating. I've learned that I need to communicate in a way that fits the way the person hears. Successful delegating is individualistic. Even though I can get better at delegating, I need to do that in a way that fits the individual/team.

Generalizing over his many instances of more effective delegating, David began to alter his mindset regarding what makes a leader valuable:

I add the most value when the boundaries are most unclear. When you delegate you need to be clear what your expectations are. That requires that I know the "box," including the constraints. I met with my team about going through next year's plan. And there's a way to do that—like blue sky thinking about the business, or "here's a hundred things, you decide"—that sends them spinning. But when I gave them enough clarity, they went with it! I also realize that when I delegate to more than one person, the box has to be especially clear, as in dark, black ink. I can see my value coming in giving the lines, more than the delegation.

FROM DELEGATION TO LEADERSHIP: NEW BEHAVIORS AND A NEW MINDSET

As a consequence of his successes giving people clearer ownership over the work, David now sees "there is a point where they turn to me and ask 'what do you want us to do?' Not in an autocratic way, but to make a judgment call about direction. I see this as further differentiating my role as leader." Asked what the implications are for his leadership, he is clear that there are three "right" activities for him:

- Attract and grow talent—then we can achieve big. Should I get hit by a bus, there should be two people who can step in. If not, I'm not doing my job well.

- Provide direction.

- Fight for resources.

David has been pursuing these three leadership challenges along-side delegating. Remember his column 1 commitment (in figure 5-2) to better focus on a few critical things? Indeed, he is now enacting it. Notice that the new behaviors do not wait until the mindset completely transforms. The ancient question, "Do changes of mind lead to changes of behavior or do changes in behavior lead to changes of mind?" is, in our view, a poorly constructed inquiry. The relationship is far more dialectical. The immunity-to-change process creates just the sort of behavior meant to usefully trouble the existing mindset. David's behavior, which is getting him good results from the perspective of performance improvement, is also informing a process of gradually reworking his mindset, one that can only author a new definition of "being a good worker" by wrestling with internalized models and deep-running loyalties. This takes time, and isn't easy. Asked how it feels when he engages in the activities he now sees as appropriate leadership behaviors, David is honest about the inner conflict it creates: "Intellectually, I know those are absolutely the right things for me to work on. But it doesn't feel big enough. It's not *personal* enough. I have a sense of *separateness*. In my gut, I still have this sense that I need to be pulling the wagon. It's deeply ingrained."

Our goal with David over the next few weeks was to create as many opportunities as possible for him to see whether he could feel fully good about his three new categories of leadership behavior. His next assignment was to pay attention to what happens in his gut when he engages in these three leadership behaviors. We also asked him to review his calendar (current and over the past six months) using the three "right" activities as a filter, and to circle everything that didn't fit. From there, he could answer questions like, "What's the ratio of 'right' to 'wrong' time? What's the trajectory over time? Is there any theme to the 'wrong' behaviors? What purpose might those behaviors serve? What do I get out of those?"

Doing the calendar assignment turned out to be another turning point for David. For starters, he concluded that a solid 75 percent of his time was devoted to these three areas, and he felt very good about spending so much time on strategy and people issues. Here are his notes on the mix of activities he discovered:

- Strategy/business planning—25 percent, but about half was in "coordinating viewpoints"—basically not really focused on solving problems but gaining agreement across a bunch of different people.

- People—25 percent. I've spent a large amount of time working with everyone in my group one-on-one for their personal development plans. Also included in this is team planning— looking at the strengths of our team and the individuals involved and allocating resources (people) against our business plan. I feel really good that this was the right thing to be working on.

- Tasks—25 percent. This includes my individual work/analysis time as well as specific things given to me such as drafting presentations for our leadership conference or meeting with customer groups—doing sales work, etc. Overall pretty rich content—and it has gotten dramatically more focused in the past six months as I've delegated more of the busy work.

- Wasted—25 percent. I still do tasks that others could do better, or others could just do and free me up for more of the above priority areas. I can get sidetracked by an exciting idea that wasn't part of our plan and end up wasting time—meaning that while I enjoyed it, we weren't probably ever going to use it or benefit from the idea or concept. Other waste is rework—fixing things that I or someone on my team forgot, did wrong, etc. I've started a list of these and will be working to identify root causes just as we do with product quality.

Just as important, David was able to work on his deeply ingrained assumptions, to step back and observe his changed behaviors and his newly emerging mindset in order to better see and feel his added value, including being more connected with people:

I began to see that much of what I put under planning and strategy was working through communications—getting people to agree. That was a surprise—how much time it takes. We don't have a mechanism to communicate broadly the direction of change. I made a point of meeting with people individually to see what their goals were. I'm grabbing people more informally. I think that's incredibly valuable. That's a means for my connecting to my people. I work with my assistant to purposely make time to connect with folks—check out how things are going. Yes, it's still business, but it's also personal. One of the biggest things I'm working on is open communication—so people will be honest with me about how things are really going. One is buy-in, I need you to trust me on this, and the other is to have enough trust that people will tell me what's going on.

It was at this time that David redefined his value as a leader. Listen to the way his own enhanced self-authorship leads him to support the self-determination of his people:

If everyone in my team is not in their head getting what they're doing and why, then they can't make decisions to keep us going in the right direction. So spending this time up front . . . I'm adding more value than when I did everything myself. In positive ways, I'm hearing from people that they're very appreciative about knowing what's going on. I've been telling them you need to make the call, the decision, don't ask for permission, and after you do, you let me know that you have and we can look at it. I'm hearing, 'I know why you're trying to get there, it makes sense. It's great you're letting us make decisions ourselves. In the past we just waited to hear.' Best, people are just starting to come to me and tell me ideas about how we could move ahead differently! That's been very fulfilling. More so than getting an individual task done by myself.

Once again David responds to the question, "How does it feel when you engage in the "right" work?" but this time he says, "I feel like that balloon [of assumptions] has popped. It's like looking at a picture. You stare at it and try to see it. Once you see it, boom, there it is and that's what's happened for me." David has stepped out of his own picture. He can *look at* it, rather than merely playing his part *within* it.

David's story reminds us that immune systems can be constructed to save us from many forms of personal danger, including the danger of doing damage to the memory of those we love. In meeting the challenge of delegating adaptively, he shows us that we may need to move beyond the "compositions" we inherit, while retaining their cherished elements. Composing one's own mindset is never a bloodless, merely cognitive affair, and David shows us that at first it can feel like putting at risk bonds of faithfulness and loyalty that form the ligaments of our soul.

But notice that his journey is not one that ultimately moves him farther from his roots, but one that enables him to form an even stronger relationship to them. He moves from being captive to his roots to learning to cherish them and incorporate them into his evolving mindset. He goes from seeing leadership as inevitably partaking in the "pretend work" of the "enemy" (and seeing the leader as overhead in an empty suit) to viewing leadership as an opportunity to pay the respect to blue-collar workers his forebears deserved. The most frequent complaint about ordinary leadership by the worker on the line, after all, is "Nobody listens." This is at once a claim about the untapped value in the perspective of those closest to the work, and a sad or angry expression of feeling discounted. But David is no longer an ordinary leader. David is listening.

[6]

CATHY CAN'T CONTAIN
HERSELF

Overcoming an Individual's Immunity to Change

C ATHY LOVES HER WORK. She is a gifted, energetic, and highly successful marketer for one of the world's leading pharmaceutical companies. She also tends to be impatient and stressed—or, as she sometimes puts it, high-strung and emotional—when problems or obstacles arise. Her colleagues think she's a terrific asset to the team, but they also wish the price they had to pay for the asset were not so high. Her boss thinks she could well become a star, but believes Cathy first needs to get a better grip on "self-management."

Cathy's change challenge is also widely represented, like David's, among the thousands of men and women whose immunity X-rays we have seen. However the goal is expressed—"to better handle my emotions," "to be less transparent," "to take things less personally," "to get more perspective," "to better manage my passions and enthusiasms," "not to overreact," "to achieve a better balance between my emotional and intellectual sides," "to get better at maintaining a more professional emotional distance," or "to stop wearing my emotions on my sleeve"—the overarching issue has to do with self-management and emotional self-regulation.

Cathy worked on her personal changes within the context of a team-based intervention, which we'll describe in the next chapter. As we'll see, addressing one's individual change challenge within the context of a group's efforts to improve may provide the strongest source of motivation and support to successfully complete the work. But let's begin by learning how Cathy came to understand that she both created and was captive to high levels of stress in her work life.

CATHY'S IMMUNITY TO MANAGING HER EMOTIONS

Cathy's first draft of her column 1 commitment went like this: "When problems emerge in one project or with one person, I am committed to containing my upset to that situation. I will then try to deal directly with the problem, and not let my upset spill into other interactions with others or to other projects. This will help me to better manage my own emotional state and well-being, which will contribute to team balance as well."

This was a significant problem for her, especially since she knew that even when her upset was not visible to others, she felt overwhelmed frequently and stressed most of the time. She knew her upset was taking a toll on her physically (she got run down and tired) and mentally (she became unable to think clearly). She worried about burning out and the price she would pay personally. And she worried that her burnout would bring down the team's performance, just as they were developing a high-stakes marketing strategy for a multi-million-dollar product launch.

Because Cathy's immunity-to-change work was being done in the context of the team's development, an additional criterion for a column 1 commitment was that it clearly link to the team's collective improvement goal, which was to improve the quality of their relationships with each other. Cathy imagined that her tendency to overreact periodically was also a problem for her colleagues, but she wanted to know whether others saw this too, and even if they did, would they agree this was the most important improvement goal for her to tackle?

Like David, Cathy took advantage of our survey tool in the over-turning-immunities coaching cycle. (The full cycle is explained in chapter 10.) Because she was working on her changes within her team, Cathy asked fellow team members to be her respondents, and they all agreed. In this way, she could get a reality check on whether she had identified the most valuable, relevant goal for herself relative to the team's needs; and she could get a baseline as to people's current assessment of her regarding this goal.

The results certainly confirmed Cathy's self-assessment, while also celebrating the positive sides of her emotional energy. Let's listen to their input:

> "Overall, Cathy manages these situations well, yet there are enough times when it is evident that the situation has gotten to her, and when this occurs, it seems to take over her mood and persona for a period of time—not in a positive way. Her reason for being emotional/upset/concerned in these instances is often justified, yet because her reaction is outward and visible and sometimes seemingly uncontrolled, it does become a noticeable trait to her colleagues."

> "Team members would feel more comfortable having discussions and debates about the business with her, knowing that she will not react emotionally and carry this emotion to other work; team members would focus more on *what* she is saying and thinking versus *how*; team members and colleagues beyond the team would recognize her as one of the more experienced/capable marketers without question. I also think Cathy's potential for advancement would expand. Again, I want to reiterate that Cathy's positive emotion and reactions must be maintained, as this is part of her unique character and valuable contributions to our team."

> "I feel this is particularly relevant. Cathy does a tremendous amount of work, and her results are always of high quality. She, through experience, has proven her capabilities and completion

of projects. While others appreciate it when she takes on the work of others, by doing so, she is not helping herself in the balance, or developing others around the projects she leads. Hence, I feel she should continue to clearly communicate to others what she needs or expects from them, in projects she leads, and be candid in her feelings about what she receives from these requests. This takes time in the short term, but will save time in the long term."

"Cathy has a lot of passion for her work and her team and I think it is important to note that this is a really positive quality. It brings a sense of fun and motivation to the group and it can positively impact others she interacts with beyond our team. So I think it is really important that as she works to better manage her emotional reactions, she should focus on the situations where her emotional reactions have negative impact on her or her colleagues. When her emotions have positive impact, she must keep this alive as it is one of her strongest assets."

Cathy appreciated (and agreed with) her colleagues' view that her targeted area of growth was also one of her strengths, and heard (and agreed with) additional examples of how she was not as approachable as she wanted to be. She concluded that a useful summary of her improvement goal was "to better manage my emotional state and my expression of my emotions." Figure 6-1 shows her full immunity map.

We don't know about you, but we found ourselves a little exhausted just reading Cathy's map. It looks like she might put 150 percent into *everything* she does!

To understand what makes Cathy's goal an adaptive one, let's review her map. We'll start with column 2 to learn what she does and doesn't do that works against her column 1 goal of managing her emotional state. We can group her column 2 list into themes: one is about being emotional (that she feels a lot and reacts intensely and fast, without first being aware of how she's feeling); another is about taking on too much (she doesn't ask for help, doesn't say no, does everything she thinks needs doing); and a third is about her standards (she does everything at high quality, whether it's critical or not). Her

FIGURE 6-1

Cathy's immunity map

1 Commitment	2 Doing/not doing instead	3 Hidden competing commitments	4 Big assumptions
I am committed to better managing my emotional state and my expression of my emotions, including: When problems emerge in one project or with one person, I am committed to containing my upset to that situation. I will then try to deal directly with the problem, and not let my upset spill into other interactions with others or to other projects. This will help me to better manage my own emotional state and well-being, which will contribute to team balance as well.	I let myself feel all the emotion. I react emotionally (intense and fast). I'm not checking in with myself . . . how am I feeling? I'm not aware in a next situation, until my emotions come out, that I'm spilling my emotions. I don't ask for help. I don't say "no." I do everything I see that needs to be done. I push myself to do each of these things at 110% quality. I don't differentiate between critical/essential and less. I let myself operate in overdrive (frequently and for long durations).	I am committed to giving my best to everything— anything less is a let down to my team and to myself—at any cost. I am committed to being seen as the go-to person, the teammate people can count on to get it done and done right—even if that is unrealistic and at a huge expense to me personally, which ultimately will burn me out and bring down the performance of the team. I am committed to not showing my cards or having a discussion with someone else that may be difficult (in my case, saying "no" or having to ask for help or having to say "I just can't do it," etc.). All of these hidden commitments combined with an intense passion to deliver the perfect end-product can put me into a high-strung state. This state can be controlled until it takes its toll on me physically (I get run down and tired) and mentally (I can't process anything more—my performance suffers) and I express the burnout emotionally.	If I were to let my team down, then I jeopardize their view of me as a team-mate that is dependable and up to the team's bar of a good team member. If I were to let myself down, then I would feel like I'm not giving as much as I should be giving. I assume that a good team mem-ber—for everyone—is giving 110%. I assume all my team members hold the same standard. I assume a good me is 150%. I assume that it's worth the risk for me to burn out than to not go the 110%. If I'm not the go-to person, I would risk losing my status on the team. I assume that my team status depends on my being a top-rate go-to person. Saying "no" once to a team member is below my standard. I assume that I ought to be able to control my emotional state no matter what, even when I am in a high-strung state.

last item, "I let myself operate in overdrive (frequently and for long durations)" is consistent with the last two themes. Now, step back from the list and ask yourself whether you see how these items work against her ability to manage her emotional state and expression of her emotions. If that's not yet clear, reread Cathy's hidden commitments in column 3, as she explicitly states the connection there.

One feature of a good column 3 statement is that it is self-protective. Cathy is saying that she is committed to never letting herself or a team down, no matter what, even if it means getting overstressed. Never letting anyone down means, for her, giving her best to everything, being the go-to person and not doing anything that might suggest otherwise (e.g., saying no). Some of you may be wondering how this is self-protective, since Cathy's jeopardizing her health and performance sounds like it is, on the contrary, *insufficiently* self-protective.

There's no doubt that she could take better care of herself. But the kind of self-protection we are looking for here is less about self-care than it is about protecting or defending the self we want others to see, or the way we want to see ourselves, even when that self may be costly. Cathy makes very clear what those costs are to her in the last sentence in column 3. She does a very good job of putting together her various hidden commitments to show how they collectively lead to her outbursts. At the same time, she shows us a perfect picture of an immune system—how she is committed both to better managing her emotional state *and* to always living up to standards of perfection that guarantee she will eventually get into a high-strung emotional state.

A good column 3 entry also shows how column 2 behaviors productively accomplish some form of self-protection (while simultaneously working against the initial commitment). Cathy's column 3 commitments seem to explain well the themes of taking on too much and insisting on high standards, while it is less clear how they explain the first theme of being emotional. (Her coach explored this with Cathy, wondering whether she feared she might inadvertently lose her "edge" or gift in being productive and successful in her work if she were less emotional, or worried that she would abandon herself or someone close to her. But Cathy couldn't identify any fear, at first, and believed that portion of her column 2 was best explained by her strong personal preference for structure and decisive action, particularly in challenging assignments.) Overall, Cathy felt that her column 3 was very powerful.

Let's turn to her big assumptions in column 4 to explore the mental model that keeps her immune system intact. You'll notice that some of these assumptions follow from the formula, "If (opposite of col. 3), then _____," whereas others are straightforward assumptions. Two of the latter seem especially important in understanding what makes her goal an adaptive challenge: her assumption about standards of effort, especially that *a good Cathy delivers 150 percent* (even more than the standard for everyone else), and that *it's worth the risk for her to burn out rather than to give less than 110 percent.* It doesn't take much to imagine how a belief in this level of personal effort leads to extremely high stress (self-imposed though it may be), which increases the likelihood of becoming emotionally overwhelmed. Everything is high stakes when your performance expectations are so high.

Understanding how Cathy's goal to better manage her emotions is an adaptive (rather than technical) one has implications for helping her succeed. Methods that focus on stress reduction alone, such as exercise, breathing techniques, or yoga, are not likely to change Cathy. Our prediction is that she would engage in those activities 150 percent too! For her to improve, she needs to revise her limiting beliefs and assumptions. When taking on an adaptive challenge, it's impossible to know exactly which aspects of one's mindset will change and to what extent. But Cathy's four-column map shows that the territory she needs to explore connects to the very standards she applies to herself or the risks she runs in living by these standards.

AN IMPRESSIVE PROGRESS REPORT

So what happened with Cathy? Let's fast-forward six months and show you what she was able to accomplish. Listen to what her team members said on their second round of surveys about Cathy's progress with her goal:

> "She has reached a new level in managing her emotions which is very noticeable to me and I also believe to her other teammates.

This was demonstrated in many situations yet one of the best examples is during her terrific management of the RollOut project under very difficult circumstances that were mostly out of her control due to operating plan factors. With very few exceptions, she managed her emotions very well and was always ready for plan B, plan C, etc.—whatever was required due to the circumstances. I was able to personally see her working on her commitment during this time. It was noticeable and her effort, commendable. When she needed to let go of her emotions, she chose the right setting to do so—in one-on-one interactions with trusted colleagues. Another good example of Cathy's great management of her emotions is in her new role as RollOut captain. In this situation, she sees many things taking place and these definitely stir her emotions. She has managed this extremely well, keeping her cool and utilizing an effective 'question posing and wait approach' to help manage difficult situations versus just letting out her thoughts. This has helped Cathy's impression across the group and has simultaneously led to effective business outcomes that are quite important to the team."

"Cathy has shown clear development in this area. Others' negative behavior still bothers her but she is able to let that go and still be productive and positive. She was able to lead an excellent project, despite one of the team member's absence from many planning meetings. Even her feedback on that person, though very specific about how he let her down on a number of occasions, was filled with positive feedback for him on the things he did well, showing her ability to 'compartmentalize' her emotions."

"Cathy and I worked through a stressful situation. Her vision of RollOut was clear; however, her desired components were at times moving targets—both in her expressed desire as well as my interpretation of what was expressed. This situation would be ripe for conflict, with the firm deadline. However, Cathy and I were able to maintain our composure, and speak frankly about the situation, and work towards alignment. The result was a workshop that addressed Cathy's vision, and further enhanced our mutual respect."

And what is Cathy's own perspective? She found herself able to make changes that go far beyond the specific goals her survey respondents were asked to address. Yes, she saw herself making big improvements in self-management: "I'm not so emotionally drained, even during the worst of weeks." "I am better attuned to what sends me down the path to becoming high-strung, and I can interrupt it once it starts." But beyond this she experiences a transformation in her overall outlook on herself and the world: "I am no longer living in fear." "A whole weight has been lifted from me."

TOOLS AND TURNING POINTS IN CATHY'S IMMUNITY WORK

Now let's back up and explore just how Cathy made these changes. After her colleagues confirmed that her improvement goal was on target, she began to develop her continuum of progress (see figure 6-2) by envisioning the first steps forward as well as indicators of success. (She didn't actually complete this exercise. It got interrupted by what she called the "Houston event," which you will soon hear more about.)

Cathy enacted one of her first steps forward by telling colleagues her commitment and giving them explicit permission to inform her when they thought she was reacting too emotionally to them or others. She couldn't have anticipated that within the week she would give her colleagues all the possible data they could need to give Cathy the "sign" that she was being high-strung, and in spades.

The Houston Event

Cathy inadvertently tested her big assumptions in a fashion completely different from the safe, modest first experiment we advise people to design. Instead, the Houston event served as a dramatic, full-blown test for Cathy's assumptions. She and her teammates had to present their marketing proposal in Houston to a group of top

FIGURE 6-2

Cathy's continuum of progress

Commitment	First steps forward	Significant progress	Success
I am committed to better managing my emotional state and my expression of my emotions: When problems emerge in one project or with one person, I am committed to containing my emotion to that situation. I will then try to deal directly with the problem, and not let my feelings spill over into interactions with others or to other projects. This will help me to better manage my emotional state, which will contribute to positive team balance as well.	I will share my commitment and my map with others on the team. I hope this will help them to understand me better. I will ask them to give me a kind of signal that I can hear and use. Pay attention to how I end up feeling high-strung. Unpack what actually happens for me— what are the steps along the way? As I better understand the road I get on to being in a high-strung state, I let people know how they can help me interrupt the cycle. I seek explicit feedback on my emotional state. Develop a repertoire of "mantras" to test.		I am better attuned to when I'm on the path to becoming high-strung. And I can interrupt the cycle. I have a robust set of effective ways of interrupting the cycle, using physical (e.g., breathing deeply, de-stress balls), emotional (e.g., mantra), and cognitive devices (e.g., what are some things I can do to feel calmer about this?). When I feel high-strung emotionally, I take a breath both internally and externally to reflect before acting. When others are present who know about my commitment, they will use a code or a signal to indicate that I've entered into a high-strung state. I will be able to pick up that signal and go with it (back to using my effective devices).

decision makers. Even if all the materials had been fully developed, the meeting would have been stressful, since this same audience had outright rejected the team's prior proposal six months earlier. But a week before the presentation the materials weren't yet in shape and several mishaps occurred, adding further stress to the approaching deadline. Just prior to the meeting date, Cathy found herself in Houston working nonstop for two days straight, taking cat naps and quick breaks to keep going.

Everything finally came together. During the morning of the day she was to present the team's proposal, as she and her team were putting finishing touches on the presentation, Cathy passed out. In the minutes it took to revive her, someone called an ambulance. On the way to the hospital, Cathy protested needing to go. While she had no recall of this later, the person accompanying her in the ambulance told her she kept repeating, "We're going to be late for the meeting."

She did, however, remember thinking things that, in retrospect, she saw as evidence of the extraordinary hold her big assumptions had on her. Here is her recollection: "I kept thinking I should be there giving the presentation. In not being able to deliver all of what we created, I felt I would be letting down my teammates in some very fundamental way. It's hard to believe that value could be so strong in light of all that was happening, being hospitalized and all! It felt that everything was slipping away from me. Somehow I felt that if I couldn't go to this one meeting, then everything would slip away from me."

She adds, "Even as people were later sending me e-mails, I felt so badly they were spending their time that way. I didn't want to go to the emergency room, and everyone, especially Teresa, who stepped in to do the meeting, had to deal with the repercussions."

A close colleague tried to challenge her: "I know you would think this was 'crazy talk' if anyone else was saying this. And that you know it doesn't make sense for yourself." What suspended that line of thought, at least momentarily, was when this same person asked her, "What are you afraid of?" Pausing, Cathy said, "I'm afraid that I'm going to fail and that Chet [Cathy's boss] will regret his decision for me to be on the team, let alone the lead." In later retelling this, Cathy says, "Of course, on a thinking plane, I knew it made no sense. But it's deep down, like somehow I'm not capable, that I'm going to be exposed. But what I am thinking is I know that I am competent. I believe Chet does value me, and that he sees my capability."

Up to this point, we would say that Cathy is reporting on a self-observation of her big assumptions working unchecked, and overtime.

She can plainly see, and she talks about this, that her big assumptions have *her*, even when she is getting clear information from her body that she is burning out. But by the time Cathy was briefing her coach on these traumatic events, her observation had turned into a test of her big assumptions. How so?

For one, she actually did—though certainly not purposefully—exactly what her big assumptions tell her she should *never* do, which is to do less than 110 percent. And from her perspective, being unable to present the proposal that day meant that she had let her team down, another no-no in her mindset. Of course, these actions in themselves aren't a test. That occurs only when the person also attends to *what happens as a consequence* of those actions, and *what those consequences suggest about the validity of the assumptions.*

What happened is this: the presentation went extremely well; the proposal was accepted; and Cathy learned from debriefing with her team members and one of the top executives that the framework she had created for the proposal was a key factor in the decision to accept it. (Cathy was discharged from the hospital two days later after being treated for exhaustion.) She concluded, now weeks later, that she didn't have to be at the presentation at all, that the team had worked together on developing the proposal within her frame and they could speak to the logic and merits of the whole idea as well as she could. She concluded that she hadn't let her team down. She got clear feedback from her team members that she continued to be a top-rate contributor, and that was made clearer when her boss later put her in charge of yet another key project. Perhaps most significant, she had concrete data that she was hurting herself by taking on so much, and she confidently concluded that it was *not* worth the risk for her to burn out.

While typically no single test is sufficient to overturn a person's immunity to change, this experience had a profound impact on Cathy because it enabled her to see additional pieces of the puzzle that had also kept her locked into her immunity. Whereas thinking earlier about the history of her big assumptions had generated nothing compelling, Cathy now had an insight that brought her to tears when she tried to answer whether there was anything her boss could have said that would have convincingly communicated his high regard for her work. Realizing that there was nothing anyone could have said, she spontaneously flashed back to her devastation at being rejected from medical school more than ten years before.

Cathy's Most Hidden Commitment

At that moment, Cathy understood how deeply she had been affected by that blow:

> I never tried very hard when I was little, in contrast to my brother who always worked very hard. Even in high school, I had a 3.0 without exerting any effort. There was nothing that really grabbed me, and my parents' nudging wasn't enough. Then I gradually started working hard when I thought I wanted to go to medical school. I chose the college I did because they have a preferred admission program for medical school. And I did programs that you weren't supposed to be able to do there; I got internships, I basically dedicated an entire four to six years of my life to getting into medical school. I worked like a demon. People said to me, "I don't know why you are such a worry-wart." I applied to the one place where I saw myself. And then I got rejected—to the amazement of everyone and myself. It was so traumatic to me—all of what I gave up in college—that I never dealt with it.

A few weeks later, Cathy thought back on the power of unearthing what she calls "the medical school thing":

> I had buried that for ten years, and it's like someone died and you never acknowledged it. The act of saying it aloud allowed me to deal with it—how painful, embarrassing, horrible, devas-tating, and hard for me it had been. Because I felt at the time that it was not a big deal. Just to say to someone out loud, a piece of me died . . . It wasn't that my dream was taken away from me, it was that I invested that amount of myself in some-thing and then didn't reach the goal. It's the embarrassment part. It was how much I had at stake, not the actual thing itself. And everyone knew—families, friends, schoolmates all knew

I had been working so hard . . . a.k.a. "what's wrong with you?" Like it was all a reflection on me.

What Cathy took from her rejection experience was self-doubt. Until this current traumatic hospitalization, Cathy hadn't realized the fear she was carrying around, how burdened she was by it, and how that fear kept her in a mode where she had to continuously prove her value to others and herself. In her words, "I was afraid to have what I love taken away from me." Cathy's second powerful "aha," which followed from realizing the toll of her earlier rejection, was that she had assumed the way to prove her value was to say "yes" all the time, and thereby make herself indispensable to others.

As is so often the case, which we saw with David as well, the exploration of our immunities brings us to our developmental core. It appears that Cathy's hold on the self-authoring plateau had been relatively tenuous. Rather than feeling free to apply her capacities for personal direction and invention wherever she might, it now seems clear that she had been using these talents to ward off being vulnerable again to the devastating verdicts of others—that is, to keep from sliding back to a socialized mind. Her need to be perfect, her refusal to ask for help, her vigilance that she not "expose herself" all suggest an overdetermined effort—a hidden commitment—that others see her, and that she regard herself, as valuable *despite her deep and lasting flaw*. Unlocking her immunity meant reconstructing this basic self-evaluation.

The unfolding consequences of the Houston event enabled her to see that her true and unique value lay not so much in her doing as in her thinking, including how she thought about issues, framed problems, and opportunities. This emerging view of herself as a person who had a great deal to bring to the team became the new proposition she explored even before returning to work after her hospitalization. First, Cathy tried this idea on internally, trying to reconcile her pre-Houston self with this emerging self. In the process, she began to see the silver lining in getting rejected from medical school:

It [not getting into medical school] happened for a reason and I'm glad it did. I wouldn't have traded any of those experiences—it's the reason why I'm the way I am, who I am, and why you should want me on your team. I now appreciate that I have a base of scientific knowledge that most people don't have or remember. I never realized how much of an asset having a photographic memory is to how I approach my current work and how I operate.

Even while working from home the next few weeks on a scaled-back schedule, Cathy saw more of this new self. In fact, her part-time participation on a project allowed her to better judge what she was bringing to the team's work. Rather than being caught up in the day-to-day execution mode, Cathy joined only during the feedback loop. Having read the materials in advance, she says, "I had this clear vision about what we needed to do." During the phone meeting, Cathy expressed her views and the immediate response was, "Wow, this is good, you are right." When she returned to work, Cathy was asked to captain that project.

Cathy describes how she felt upon returning: "It was a sense of clarity. When I came back I was clear about what I needed to do and how to do it. I belong here, and I can see things that should happen that I never noticed before."

This is exactly what we mean when we say that unlocking immunities allows people to access more of their potential. The "energy" released from no longer expending oneself in two countervailing directions shows up not only behaviorally (e.g., the ability to work harder and longer), not only emotionally (e.g., feeling freer, less burdened, less exhausted, less restricted), but intellectually, as well: when we develop we are able to use our intelligence in ways that most people would call being smarter. Just as acute anxiety impairs momentary performance (studies show for example, that highly anxious test takers appear to lose IQ points in comparison to how they perform when they are not), *chronic* anxiety requires *continually* diverting our intelligence to our own self-protection. When we do not have to apply our genius as much to our self-preservation, we are free to see more in the world beyond our own skin. The experience is sometimes akin to the lifting of a fog, a fog we did not even know we were in. As Cathy says, "If you're operating within a sense of fear, as I was but didn't even know, that's not a productive place to be. Emotionally, it's exhausting. Now, I'm totally freed up from feeling that way."

Her clarity about what needs to be done shows up, for example, when she talks with one of her senior colleagues about "eight creative projects that I think we should consider. And I explained why this other person ought to include me in a current project." Inside, she feels confident of what she is bringing to her setting. She compares now and then: "In the past, I would have shared those creative ideas, but with subtle cues that I wasn't sure. And now I see my knowledge, my perspective that comes from knowing the data and seeing it in a different way from other marketers. It's that difference that adds value, not what I do." Cathy says she also now understands a long-ago, puzzling comment her boss made to her: "Chet had told me once before—'why can't you be more confident?' I thought it was a weird comment, because I'd always had the feedback that I'm cocky. And I've never been afraid to share my opinion. But now I get what he meant." Cockiness is not the same as confidence, just as working overtime at maintaining one's self-governance is not the same as securely inhabiting the self-authoring plateau.

Still, an important data point was yet to be collected—whether the Houston event would negatively impact Cathy's upcoming evaluation. The outcome was unambiguous. There was no negative impact and, moreover, her boss's positive review included comments about Cathy's value, saying, "Your value isn't tied to what you do. It's your special insights. Your value is you. It's the way you are present in what you do."

Let's pause here, approximately two months after Cathy was hospitalized for exhaustion, to first summarize and then see where she is in the process of unlocking her immunity. First, the event and its aftermath consumed Cathy: her mindset had been significantly challenged, her typical way of operating at work had been disrupted, she powerfully accessed her buried past and productively began to put it to rest, and she was well on her way to using her newfound energy and self-confidence to prioritize and to focus on strategy and planning. As for the big assumptions she had tested, she concluded none was valid. Asked what the outcomes of her various observations and tests (unplanned and planned) meant for her assumptions, she says a number of telling things. Notice how much less she is vigilantly looking over her shoulder at what others might decide about her, and how much more she is looking to her own internal governance:

> My definition of "letting down" is now different. Before it was about doing, and now it's about being—like if I didn't speak up, or share my insights. Now it's the act of having the insights. I would be letting myself down if I no longer had the insights or didn't believe that they are of value.
>
> Another of my original big assumptions was "I assume that a good team member—for everyone—is giving 110 percent." I still believe it. What's changed is that percent is not about checking off tasks and making sure everything is perfect. Perfection isn't about crossing every *t*. It's about perfect in concept, intent, and in thinking about it.
>
> Another original assumption was "I assume a good me is 150 percent." I still think that's true. It's just defined differently. Even if it's three minutes, it's a sense that I determined the necessary energy and time that was appropriate. It's the amount of time and quality of thinking that makes for excellence.
>
> My biggest big assumption was: "I assume that it's worth the risk for me to burn out than to not go the 110 percent." That's simply not true now.

Cathy's process up to this point was more dramatic and compressed than most (surely, you don't need to be hospitalized to overturn an immunity!). Her mindset changed very quickly, which perhaps is a silver lining of her Houston incident. This was her view: "I'm glad that this hospitalization happened. I otherwise wouldn't have had to listen to myself." But had the test of her big assumptions not been thrust upon her so dramatically, our view is that she could just as surely, if more slowly, have come to the same realizations through the more methodical, less dramatic process of successively running a series of graduated experiments, as we have now seen many, many people do.

PUTTING HER NEW INSIGHTS TO WORK

Perhaps because she unlocked her immune system so abruptly, Cathy worried some about her ability to hold on to her new understandings when she returned to the office. She knew that although she had altered many of her big assumptions, she would have plenty of opportunities to "lose it" emotionally (several people still pushed her buttons, and the project she was leading would have the usual deadline demands and pressure points, to name just two). She also knew she needed to translate into action her revised definitions of letting down, adding value, and being perfect, which meant changing how she interacted with people as well as exploring new ways of dealing with time, her calendar, and appointments. There was still room for improvement on her column 1 commitment.

Before returning to the office, Cathy worked out a new schedule that included firm limits on her work hours, especially in the evening, and time to exercise. Working backward from her original column 2 behaviors that led to too much on her plate, Cathy thought through what she believed she could do differently now, such as whom she could ask for help and what she could let go of. She kept sticky notes on her desk and on her computer with the question, "How important is this?" to remind herself that her unexamined sense that everything was urgent contributed to her overly emotional state. She also returned to her continuum of progress and started to systematically engage all of her first steps forward.

Reducing her overall stress also required that Cathy continue to feel confident about the quality of her work. She continued the overturning-immunities process by enacting new behaviors, *then asking herself what she was learning about her new mindset as a consequence of what happened when she acted differently.* For example, Cathy needed to test whether she could both contain her scheduling and continue to feel that she was adding value. This led her to monitor whether she was using time as she intended and to ask what she was contributing. Her assessment several weeks later was this: "I've done very well with my scheduling and my leaving. I've been able to adapt my processes. And I still feel confident that I'm contributing."

Along the way she noticed new ways she added value. For example, Cathy's marketing team was getting mixed communications from various sources about what they could and couldn't say, and as the captain of RollOut, Cathy needed to address this increasingly hostile and entrenched standoff between the medical and legal groups. Developing a marketing message is a complex task, not only because it needs to be consumer-centered, but also because it requires reconciling such differences between groups and getting the requisite sign-offs from people outside of marketing. And beyond the varied points of view, personalities often get in the way of a timely or good decision.

To everyone's relief, Cathy did address the standoff. She realized that the process would still be stuck if it were not for her ability to facilitate the conversation: "I see that I had to bring my negotiation skills a million times to accomplish this. I needed to bring all the right players to the table, and then create a process for them to have an effective conversation, including the ability to diagnose what was getting in the way of people agreeing on a message."

Appreciating her role in clearing this hurdle, Cathy also sees how this could have been one of those situations that would have sent her over the top in the past. From the beginning, everyone's emotions were running high, and much was at stake. For Cathy's team in particular the stakes were enormous because marketing messages are rolled out to the sales force only a few designated times throughout the year. Missing one of these events is unthinkable. It was the perfect-storm scenario for Cathy, where she could have been furious with one person, let that spill over into her interactions with others, and also gone into overdrive to ensure that the work got done. But she didn't do any of those things. And this is especially noteworthy because Cathy and her team actually were *not* able to deliver the product on time—which, from her previous mindset, could well have triggered another meltdown.

Asked what enabled her to stay calm amid the high uncertainty and stressful conditions, Cathy explained that she kept asking herself what she had control over and made her decisions accordingly. Two of the many microdecisions she made give a sense of how Cathy newly thought about and acted on what she could control. The first example is with her team, and took place after they finally received approval for a general message and then had to produce the specifics: "I made sure not to lose sight of what I believed was right. After I heard the latest version, I said to myself, 'This sucks.' I brought us all together and said, 'I want to scrutinize all of the data. Then I want us to take a moment for everyone to think quietly about this, and does it tell a compelling story.' Everyone thought, 'This sucks.' Collectively, we came up with the story that we have today."

A second example relates to how she managed her time and deadlines differently. Here, she recalls her reaction to an email she received:

> I was saying to myself, "This guy is telling me we need to turn this all into a presentation for the next day and it's now 9:00 at night." I then started to write a scathing response. But I stopped myself and asked, "What's in my control here?" In just that second I thought to myself, "He probably doesn't know what's happening." So I explained to him, "I don't have a visual aid or a message approved yet, and I will not have one until next Friday at the earliest. I know I was supposed to have this done. Can I have a new date?" He responded very favorably.

Cathy's new sense of control can best be conveyed at this point by her responses to a final overturning-immunities exercise, where she crystallizes her new learnings, the situations most likely to hook her back into her old immunity, and the means to release herself if that should occur:

> Overall, I am more self-aware and more self-regulating. I am better attuned to what sends me down the path to becoming high-strung, and also when I'm on the path. Here's what I do to interrupt the cycle before it even starts or to interrupt it once it starts before I become overly emotional.
>
> • I use my mantra "I am calm."
>
> • I use de-stress balls.
>
> • When I feel high-strung emotionally, I take a breath both internally and externally to reflect before acting.

- When I am in a situation where someone is saying something that gets me agitated, I tell myself, "Be respectful and calm. This is not the end of the world. You are in control of this situation. You can listen respectfully and then politely disagree."

- When I felt/feel something is wrong, I ask myself, "Is it me? Or is it something in the environment?"

- When I am aware that I'm getting stressed, I ask myself, "What is in my control here and what isn't?" And then look to make choices based on what's in my control.

- I ask myself: "Is this important enough to get hospitalized?"

- I make more choices about what I can and can't do with my time.

- When I have a timeline, I will tell the person that I don't think I can meet the deadline, or I tell them what I think I can and can't have done by that time. Or I will ask them about whether there is any flex in the timeline given what is on my plate and other commitments I have agreed to meet.

- I'll say to myself, "This is what I can and can't make happen in order to get my priority item taken care of."

- Around deadlines, I ask myself, "What will have to give in order for me to meet this deadline?"

- I conduct a process check re: my calendar. I make myself go home by a certain hour on most days and keep that promise to myself. When there are back-to-back meetings, I ask myself, "Is it important to me to attend all of these?"

- When I broke my rule of going home by a certain hour, I would call my boss and say that I wasn't going to be in the next day. He was fine about that.

- I ask, "Is this so important that I should jeopardize my health?"

- I pay attention to the value I am adding and what I'm contributing. (And I continue to see my value as not about the product.)

- I pay attention to my feelings of confidence that have emerged through this process (letting go of the fear has helped me see what value I am adding).

Cathy reveals another kind of control and choice when she explains what enabled her to make these changes. You can hear how these are not changes that somehow happened to her, but that she herself engineered:

Most importantly, I realized that my original big assumptions came out of my operating from a sense of fear. I was afraid that something I loved would be taken away from me, and I felt like I had to keep proving over and over to everyone that I was good at this so they should know not to take it away. My "aha" about how my not getting accepted to medical school has kept me worried and afraid all these years was also very important. I realized I believed my not getting in was a reflection on me, that something was wrong with me. And I never voiced that belief; I just kept "doing" things to make sure that would never again happen to me. It's been a huge relief to unburden myself of that. Emotionally, it's exhausting to have carried that around. Now, I'm freed up from feeling that way.

I continue to see my value as not about the product, and that was the biggest surprise. I proved to myself that my value is more than marketing. This whole experience helped me to see that I actually am very good at what I do, and not only because of what I do, but because of who I am and the unique perspectives I bring to the work. And I recognized that others see that in me too.

The Houston event was the catalyst for my understanding this about myself. That Teresa succeeded was a test of my not having to "do" and a confirmation of my value as someone with the particular skills, knowledge, and views I hold. Teresa succeeded because I had set it up as I did, and because I did write the objectives so clearly. My unique value was in the planning process. That newfound confidence was an enormous boost to my change.

I'm very scientific—without proof I don't believe it. It was a forced experiment—Teresa succeeding—my goals and vision were able to be realized without me doing it!

NEW WAYS OF MAKING MEANING

We wanted you to meet Cathy and David (in chapter 5) not because we think they are remarkable exceptions, but because we think there is no limit to the number of people, in any organization, who have the potential to make changes of a similar magnitude. We hope you will see their stories as a kind of "proof by existence" should you be skeptical about the possibility of achieving deep-seated change for yourself and your colleagues. Over the last several years we have witnessed many, many "Cathy" and "David" stories, here in the United States and far from our shores; as frequently in one sector as another; featuring men and women at the beginning, middle, and later years of their careers. At the same time, we want to reemphasize that these changes don't happen automatically. Learning environments need to provide a good fit with the developmental nature of these goals. We are bound to be disappointed (and disillusioned) if we expect our conventional learning methods and means—which generally address only technical challenges—to support truly adaptive changes.

Both David's and Cathy's stories suggest that any bigger investments made in providing such supports are likely to return very handsome dividends, since what each of them accomplishes far exceeds their original aspirations. A hallmark of adaptive change is that one's grasp exceeds one's reach. "Good problems," we say, "solve us": They bring into being, or strengthen our purchase on, a whole new developmental plateau, a new self-paradigm. Columbus was only looking to solve a navigational problem; instead his discovery led to reimagining the world.

Cathy wanted to learn to better manage her emotions. She did, of course, and in the process she learned how to be a better delegator too, letting others take on more of the work. But her new capacities amount to much more than just a longer list of superior business attributes. The immunity-to-change technology enables the development of a more complex self, which, as we described in chapter 1, is always a matter of being able to look *at* something that, before, we could only look *through*. We overcome a kind of blind spot by getting some distance, or perspective, on a way of making meaning to which we had been captive.

Cathy was helped to grow more fully into her self-authoring self. She seems to have already had a well-worked-out personal standard (albeit a very tough one). She clearly seems to have built a personal frame or filter with which to organize her experience. But in the course of the immunity-to-change work, she learned that she had founded this self-system on a core belief that she was defective. Although it never quite makes it into her fourth column, this is clearly her biggest big assumption: "There is some flaw in me, and I must do my self-authoring the way I do—I must do my world-regulating the way I do—to protect myself, to keep the world from discovering this flaw and taking away what is precious to me."

Cathy's change is an enormous one ("a whole weight lifted from me," "no longer living in fear," an ability "to see things [in my work] I would have missed before," "to see the forest and not just the trees") precisely because she has been able to make this subject-to-object move, an altering of her core way of knowing. She is now authoring a far more spacious, less defensive, more open self, one that is based on a firmer sense of an intrinsic worth that frees her up in a host of ways within her work and beyond. If you don't need to *do everything* in order to establish your worth, you can really begin to delegate, ask for help, and let others shine. If you do not need to stand a continuous post in your own personal watchtower—to insure that the world does not discover your shameful secret—then you can scan the world for more promising possibilities and bring to your own living a deep restfulness that you may never before have known.

$$\begin{bmatrix} 7 \end{bmatrix}$$

THE CASE OF NASCENT
PHARMACEUTICALS

Overcoming Individual Immunities
to Help a Team Succeed

I N CHAPTER 4 WE LOOKED at overcoming collective immunities, and in chapters 5 and 6 at overcoming individual immunities. We mentioned at the beginning of chapter 6 that Cathy's individual change challenge emerged as part of a groupwide initiative with her whole marketing team. By taking a fuller look now at this collective endeavor, we can examine a single design that may be the most effective way to deliver on two fronts at once—facilitating individual adaptive change in the context of an intact group's desire to improve its collective performance.

Cathy's boss, Chet, was chosen to lead a newly merged senior marketing team at one of the world's leading drug companies—we'll call it Nascent Pharmaceuticals. Chet knew he had to pull the group together fast to succeed on its high-stakes mandate after the previous team had failed. The task was to produce a clear and compelling marketing plan for a new drug that figured prominently in Nascent's strategic growth agenda.

Chet's strong track record as an energetic, hands-on manager led his bosses to put him in charge of the effort. Like Cathy, he and the others were all determined to succeed. But when we first met them, they did not look like the best of bets, however talented and experienced they were as individuals.

Half of the people were old hands from Chet's group, but the others came from a group with a distinctively different approach to the work—although the extent of the differences wasn't immediately apparent to any of them. Chet was highly involved and directive, and the other subgroup was accustomed to the charismatic, low-intervention style of their former leader, who was not part of the merger—a woman who was also highly regarded within the organization. Both subgroups brought valuable qualities to the team. Still, there seemed to be a chasm between the two factions. How would they work together?

Chet recognized that, like most mergers, this one would be difficult—even though there were only a total of eight people on the new team. But time was short, and the marketing program was mission-critical for Nascent. He decided to offer the team the opportunity to choose an outside facilitator to help them coalesce.

That's when we came in, as one of the groups Chet invited to outline a potential team-building process for them to consider.[1] We first spent time with Chet to understand his intentions and wishes, and then met with the entire team to discuss what we learned from Chet and to offer a proposal for how we could work with them.

We described an intensive, team-based program that would help them overcome their individual and collective immunities to change, with each process informing the other. Over a six-month period, we would meet with the whole team for a two-day workshop followed by two more full-day sessions, with individual coaching in the interims. As we went along, we would customize our activities to meet emerging issues and challenges. We proposed taking qualitative and quantitative before-and-after "portraits" to characterize their current interactions and to measure their progress six months later, then reinterviewing each team member three months after that to check on their ongoing experiences and the overall impact of the program. Despite the significant commitment of time and energy this would require, they decided it would be worth the effort—they called it an investment—if they could really learn to work together better as individuals and as a team. So we agreed to take each other on.

THE GROUP'S INITIAL SELF-PORTRAIT

We started with a round of one-to-one interviews and surveys with all the team members, which confirmed that there was a serious lack of trust.[2] In support of Chet's hunch about the reason for this, people's specific comments suggested that the team had divided into two factions along lines of former team membership, and that there was good cheer and trust within each faction, but low trust between them. The frequently evoked term *back-stabbing* captures the level of some people's distrust.

Almost everyone agreed that Chet communicated a clear vision and objectives, and was strategic, practical, and energetic, even driven, to make the product succeed. Chet was also on the right path in suspecting that some team members—those who had been working with the other leader—were having a harder time than others. The most challenging comments came from these new team members, who characterized his style as micromanaging. They saw him as "overly instructive" and "seeking a high level of detail, frequently." They also felt that he was not paying sufficient attention to team morale, to recognition, and to other human elements of teamwork. There was high agreement, even among those who had worked with Chet all along, that he needed to readjust his work/life balance (read that as "get at least *some* balance"), as the pace he set for their work was too intense.

Additionally, on the positive side, people across both factions agreed there was a strong work ethic, dedication to the product, and a great deal of talent, expertise, and valued diversity across one another's skill sets. But within these strengths people named two additional areas for growth, both of which were seriously getting in the way of developing the necessary level of trust: "different working styles" and "communication." About working styles, one person's comment expressed what almost everyone on the team felt: "Differences in approaches to the work are not understood and appreciated."

Everyone in the group recognized that at the heart of every high-performing team is the ability to communicate effectively. They knew that without it their team could not function as anything more than a set of individuals, with each person pursuing his own purpose. When communication is not flowing properly within a team, it is not surprising that someone, often the leader, throws up a red flag. Teams with successful communication experiences can typically handle these bumps themselves, once the problem has been aired. But other times, especially when a team is new and is faltering, as this one was, outside assistance can help—and they recognized this too.

The team's communication needs crossed a wide spectrum, as the following statements suggest:

"I feel like what I say is falling on deaf ears."

"Too much of the time I don't know what to communicate to whom, and what level."

"I read emails from some of my team members and I find it impossible to know the tone—are they mad? Or do they just think I'm at their service?"

A majority described the communication as indirect, where people were not expressing thoughts, ideas, and feelings directly to each other, but instead to and through Chet. Moreover, when there was direct communication, it came in the form of feedback characterized by attributions and assumptions, rather than specific data.

The top three strengths of team communication? There was no agreement here, though everyone stated at least one strength. Here are some examples:

"The team is working at improving communication."

"Use of all available means to communicate, e.g., e-mail, voicemail, meetings."

"Public presentation skills."

"Sharing of information."

There was, however, consensus that the team had two significant assets relevant to improving its communication: "dedication to the product's and team's success" and "a willingness to work on issues." What was the single biggest barrier to improving communication named by everyone? Not surprisingly, "insufficient trust in each other."

Let's pause in our description for one moment. While we are presenting a picture of the team, we have also included data about how individuals within the collective see a particular individual, their team leader. In doing so, we do *not* want to suggest that the ills of the team are *because* of Chet. Our working assumption is that the team is a collection of individuals, and everyone contributes to its current challenges in his or her own way (and not even so much in an additive way, but in a dynamic and systemic fashion).

For example, all the team members (including those who had worked with Chet before, and even Chet himself) described Chet as instructional and seeking detail frequently. However, people interpreted these behaviors very differently, and consequently had different feelings and reactions. The "old hands" were fine, if not pleased with Chet's leadership style. They regarded his "instruction" as helping them to grow and creating a continuous improvement culture. They saw his requests for detail as a signal of his care and involvement in the product's success. That's not how the "newcomers" saw it at all. They had difficulty with Chet's leadership style (this is what they named as his growth area), we suggest, because they read his actions as statements about how he saw them.

It is easy to imagine how their interpretation of Chet's leadership style contributed to less trust. Imagine an internal conversation: "There he goes again, telling me what to do. He must think I don't know what I'm doing. He doesn't trust me to do my work capably. And his constantly asking for details is just one more piece of evidence that he doesn't trust me to perform well. Why else would he need to micromanage?"

These understandably different reactions illustrate the power of individual meaning-making and how perceptions create one's reality. Chet isn't *the* problem.

Does he have a part in it? Yes. And as the team's leader, he is the person who sets the tone for the team and its culture. That being said, we assume that everyone else *also* is a part of the equation. Consistent with this view, we included the following open-ended question in our interview: "What are your contributions, if any, to any communication difficulties the team is currently experiencing?" That question was a precursor to launching each person's four-column improvement exercise.

The group members impressed us with their ability and willingness to identify their own hand in the group's less-than-optimal communication patterns and trust levels:

"I could do a better job by refraining from jumping to conclusions. I haven't taken the time to get to know other members of the team."

"I contribute to the culture of defensiveness by being indirect with several people on the team. I interpret people's defensiveness as arrogance and disrespect."

"I could make sure that I think through more carefully the decisions I make that affect others, e.g., to ask myself 'what impact will this decision have on them?'"

"I need to develop in the area of how to convey information to someone who may need to hear it in a certain way. I am direct and speak my mind and it may be hard to take."

"I don't take the time for giving or receiving feedback. My intensity can be off-putting."

"When I get emails that irritate or anger me, I sometimes react and follow the same pattern. I need to be less reactive."

In addition to every person identifying at least one way he or she contributed to the problem, people commented on behaviors and attitudes that we can well imagine *would* get in the way of good communication. Whether these self-assessments are accurate is another question (which we get to later in the process), but their answers reveal a willingness to consider themselves as part of what needed to change. This boded well for the immunity-to-change work.

The quantitative survey results confirmed exactly what people told us in the interviews. In summary, the team presented itself as strongest on "business" items (vision and direction, strategic focus, goals) and most in need of improving the "soft" side of their work. Their top three learning goals were to build trust, communicate better (including respecting each other's work styles), and improve their team learning. Finally, the team brought noteworthy assets to the work of improving, including people's self-awareness of their contributions to the team's current challenges, a strong work ethic, and dedication to the product as well as a great deal of talent, expertise, and valued diversity across people's skill sets.

With this "before" portrait firmly in mind, we proceeded to the first full-team workshop.

THE FIRST WORKSHOP: GETTING STARTED

Because the initial two-day meeting set the tone and laid the foundation for the whole project, we will describe it in some detail. We will also consider the individual immunity-to-change work, and why we made certain choices. We will briefly describe the two other daylong sessions, in good part because these followed so naturally from the first team meeting and our individual work with people.

We had three explicit intended outcomes for the first session: develop a shared teamwide improvement goal based on the survey and interview data, develop individual improvement goals that were tightly connected to the team's goal, and set dates for both individual coaching and the remaining two meetings we would have with the full team. We also wanted to model good communication, especially good listening, throughout the meeting, and to provide a safe context for people to take a few risks and get to know each other. We were hoping people might even have a laugh or two together.

We first presented all the data to Chet alone, given that it included negative comments on his leadership style. With his consent, we then presented a summary of the interview and survey data to the team. The first outcome of their discussion was a consensus that their number one priority was to improve team communication. They agreed that the top two areas for improving their communication were to have *clear and direct communication with each other* (people agreed that they needed to talk directly with each other and not to and/or through Chet) and to create a *supportive, trusting environment*. The team agreed on what they all needed to do to create greater trust:

- Accept that a person's intent is good

- Accept different working styles

- Believe in each other

- Feel less like one is on "pins and needles"

- Interpret questioning as a positive, not a challenge

They identified specific responsibilities for senders and receivers of information:

- For the sender: Be open, direct, sincere, timely, motivating, and nonassumptive.

- For the receiver: Assume good intentions of sender, listen fully, ask clarifying questions (especially around tone), and maintain openness to learning.

- For both sender and receiver: Be self-aware. What impressions do I evoke in others? Know my strengths and weaknesses, and ask (verbally and nonverbally) how I am hindering communications.

They next decided that it would be useful to make their discussion more concrete by creating a shared picture of what they meant by effective communication and what its purposes were. This led to a second outcome, an actual picture, with team learning and productivity as the core purpose, as shown in figure 7-1.

After the group created this picture we conducted a "consensor check," a quick process that allows everyone to learn how much agreement exists. In this case, we wanted to know two things: Did people regard the picture as adequate for their purposes ("To what

FIGURE 7-1

The pharmaceutical marketing team's picture of effective communication

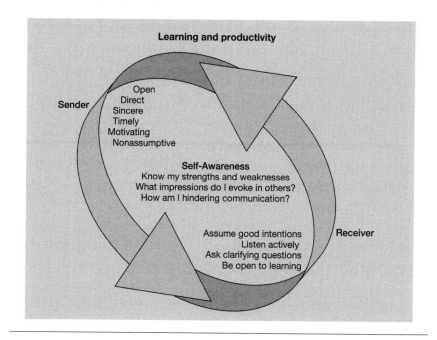

extent do you think the team's learning and productivity would increase if the team could communicate in these ways?"); and were they, as individuals, willing to sign on to it as a blueprint for how they would communicate with team members and expect others to communicate with them? A positive response to our first question was followed by a question about people's degree of personal commitment to the picture (low, medium, or high). Everyone was highly committed.

These two agreements laid the groundwork for the collective and individual work we were to embark on with the team. While there is nothing novel about their picture per se—indeed, it represents many common practices for good communication—what was refreshing for the team was that a common picture emerged and everyone agreed to it. In doing so, the team took its first step toward having an explicit agreement among its members about their mutual expectations around how and why to communicate. This created a shared reference point or norm for what was considered productive, as well as a focus for the team's learning.

Of course, from our point of view, these agreements, important as they are, are closer to first-column commitments than actual principles of operation. That is, we expect the group or many of its members to have difficulty actually keeping these agreements. If there were no hidden commitments waiting to thwart their good intentions, they probably would not need to go to the trouble of discussing and making promises about their communication challenges. If those promises are not to be hollow New Year's resolutions, the team will need to understand its members' immune systems. The value of explicit norms, then, is not, from our perspective, that they will not be broken, but instead that there *is* something that can be broken, and therefore named and discussed. When these agreements are broken, as eventually they certainly will be, the rule-breaking behaviors actually become a kind of second-column entry—that is, things we do and fail to do that *work against* the improvement goal.

Discussion of these behaviors (in an exploratory rather than recriminatory fashion) can help uncover the important phenomena of the hidden competing commitments in column 3, the forces that make the rule-breaking behavior sensible. For example, I may discover that, yes, I am committed to "trusting that others have good intentions" but I am *also* committed to "maintaining solidarity with my buddies from the former disbanded team," and out of this commitment I might sometimes be overly protective of my closer friends and suspicious toward those I am not so close to.

As valuable as it is for a group to come to a shared agreement, from our point of view it is equally important to keep in mind that each individual will have his or her own particular challenge in keeping that agreement. A skill one person has already mastered might be easy for another to develop but an adaptive challenge for someone else. Our intent, therefore, was to invite all team members to identify their most challenging personal change goal as it related to the team's commitment to effective communication.

Toward this end, we asked each person to look at himself in relation to the team's picture of ideal communication and ask himself what he needed and wanted to improve in order to be an even better team communicator. This, you will now recognize, is a version of our standard prompt for helping people to generate an individual column 1 improvement goal. What differs here is that we asked the question within the context of the team's aspiration to become more effective at communicating. We gave people quiet time to answer this question on their own and had them record their responses in the warm-up column of a four-column worksheet.

We conducted the conversation from this point on much like we do every immunity-to-change exercise, with a few important differences. As usual, we started by laying the groundwork for the exercise, emphasizing confidentiality, asking each person to choose a partner with no supervisory relationship, and explaining the roles of listener and speaker. We then asked them to check in with their partner and share their initial column 1 entries.[3] As we listened in on the pair-share, we heard people talking quite freely. Judging that they were up to it, we asked each individual to share with the whole group a first draft of his or her column 1 commitment. In this way, group members would have a chance to hear directly what each other saw as his or her personal responsibility toward improving team communication.

We upped the ante once more (again, first having considered the cost-to-benefit ratio) by invoking the "knock-knock" rule for commenting on one another's improvement goals. Under this rule, the person "knocking" to offer feedback must do so in the spirit of an inquiry, not a certainty, and the person whose door is being knocked on must feel perfectly free to say "no thanks, I'm not inviting you in." After all, around the table were the very people each person was seeking to better communicate with, and who better to provide input on one another's improvement goals? A guiding question for everyone was this: "If your colleague were to make progress on the specific goal he or she identified today, do you see how that would significantly improve team communications and increase team learning and productivity?"

This turned out to be a very lively and productive work session. In between teasing and laughs, people made genuine suggestions to each other. Chet was the first to volunteer, and in doing so he modeled openness to people's direct feedback and the value of transparency. Not everyone offered input or asked questions of others, but everyone received input and everyone else heard the suggestions, and the receiver's responses. The level of team discourse was the most honest it had been to date, including, for example, one person's expression of appreciation for Chet's specific goal choice.

Let's take a look at the various column 1 commitments that emerged that day. As each person took a turn, his or her goal was written on a large piece of newsprint and revised according to the input he or she accepted. To give you a feel for the conversation, the level of self-disclosure, and degree of team engagement, following are examples of two people's revised goals.

One person, Anton, started with this:

> To understanding and changing how I interact with others in a way that leads them to see me as arrogant and closed to their feedback.

Someone wanted to better understand why Anton chose this goal, asking what he hoped would be different if he could change his interactions. After Anton responded and a few others commented, he changed his goal:

> To being a more effective team collaborator. This includes (1) taking responsibility for how I contribute to misperceptions (i.e., how others see me and how I see others) and proactively working to alter these; (2) seeking out, finding value in, and applying the feedback I receive. (This will involve my dealing with my own sensitivity to negative feedback.)

Another person, Neil, started with this goal:

> I am committed to listening well and utilizing my colleagues' insights and experiences, especially in the area of marketing. I am committed to letting go of the mental model that I created by my sales experience.

Neil ended with this goal after getting responses and suggestions:

> I am committed to communicating clearly and concisely, listening well, and appropriately adapting the amount of communication and style for the intended recipients. I am committed to utilizing my colleagues' insights and experiences, especially in the area of marketing.

Here are two more team members' goals. The first will be familiar because it is Cathy's, from chapter 6; the one that follows hers is Chet's:

> When problems emerge in one project or with one person, I am committed to containing my emotion to that situation. I will then try to deal directly with the problem, and not let my feelings spill over into interactions with others or to other projects. This will help me to better manage my emotional state, which will contribute to positive team balance as well.

> I am committed to not reacting immediately, rather to inquire into people's thinking first and to listen actively. I will then provide feedback tactfully. Tactful feedback means using active listening and inquiry to respond empathically. Simultaneously and when appropriate, I will seize those moments as coaching opportunities, e.g., helping the individual to explore barriers to their effective action.

Once people firmed up a self-improvement goal connected to the team's picture of improved communication, we continued the four-column exercise as we typically do, giving directions and examples of each next column, and giving people individual think time, then pair-share time. After completing the maps, someone suggested that people share their immunity maps with the whole group. This wasn't a step we had planned, given the team's low trust self-assessment.

Why not? As you know from reading the earlier cases, each column entry gets progressively "closer to the bone." Sharing column 1 self-improvement goals had already crossed a threshold of increased self-disclosure within the team, and we weren't clear how to assess people's readiness for a next level of intimacy. Also, we were at the close of the day and there would be little time to address any potential unintended negative outcomes. We raised these thoughts for discussion with the group, and this led to a collective decision that each individual should decide for himself or herself, an agreement that there was no intended group pressure to participate, and an explicit statement by Chet that he would not draw on anything from the day's work in any formal evaluation.

What happened next is that, almost without a pause, everyone chose to share his or her map. It's to be expected that as more people moved toward this new level of openness, the remaining people would feel pressure to open their kimonos too. This may have happened. But what also happened is that in their closing comments, people—including those who were among the last to share their maps—said they felt little doubt and great certainty that the team would indeed succeed. People were moved to hear each other's honesty in their named struggles, and were pleased that every person was taking the work seriously.

Our final agenda was to review the path and timeline ahead, including the individual immunity coaching and two additional teamwide meetings. We headlined the individual work as a four-month process involving approximately ten sessions by phone or in person, each following a structured exercise aimed at making progress on the person's column 1 goal. The team meetings would be occasions to take stock of both team and individual progress and to address emerging learning needs.

So what did we accomplish in our first session? The team collectively set its priority goal; they successfully created group norms; individuals identified personal improvement goals within that context and understood the next steps for individual coaching. But more than that, people took risks in revealing themselves: They shared the increasingly disclosing depths of their full 4 column immunity map and said things that in their earlier interviews with us they asked to keep confidential. They even laughed together. They genuinely talked and listened to each other, and in the process, experienced greater respect for one another, a foundational ingredient to building trust.

What explains the team's sudden productivity? Here are our hunches about the several factors that may have enabled its success:

- The team had options as to whether they would work with us (remember, they interviewed other consultants before choosing us).

- The team accepted our initial invitation to address its needs via a two-pronged approach of both team and individual improvement (again, the team was not required to comply with a top-down requirement, and could instead commit to a process of its choice, a trust-building opportunity).

- The needs assessment (or "before" portrait) followed this frame by asking about team strengths and weaknesses along with questions about each respondent's personal contribution to those team qualities; the data review echoed this frame (this reinforces the idea that each person is responsible).

- Chet was a champion for the team's development, and continued to be nondefensive and a learner when reviewing the team survey data, including how people perceived his leadership.

- The team's improvement focus was anchored to business results (its improvement goals were determined by an analysis of strengths and gaps in the context of work the team had to do).

- Finally, we knew from our interviews with each member that people were highly motivated to succeed as a team. No one was willing to settle for less than making their product the hit it was supposed to be. They knew that everyone needed to be involved if the team was to meet its sales objectives. They embodied the stance and reality of a true team: "If one of us fails, we all fail."

THE INTERIM WORK

Our intent, following this session, was to capitalize on the team's momentum and good spirits through working with individuals on their improvement goals. Our main work during the next four to five months focused on coaching people to overturn their immunities. Our earlier description of Cathy's process and progress (see chapter 6) is representative of the work we did with each team member. This included a baseline "witness" survey (which, you may recall, asks the person's selected respondents only for input on the column 1 commitment; see David's survey in chapter 5 for a sample), a continuum of progress, the biography of the big assumption, designing and running tests of the big assumption, a follow-up survey, and finally, hooks and releases. (The whole "coaching arc" is described more generally in chapter 10.)

You may wonder why we did the individual baseline surveys, since everyone had already been invited to ask questions and make suggestions about each other's communication goals at the team workshop. We opted for a survey for several reasons:

- Because the individual work was such a time-rich dimension of the intervention, we wanted people's goals to be as powerful and relevant as possible, and there was always the possibility that fellow team members did not feel they could speak freely during the group session.[4]

- The survey would provide a baseline assessment of the person's starting point, a public record of his or her focus, examples describing relevant behaviors the person might be unaware of, and other people's thinking about how progress on this goal mattered to the team's success.

- Because measurement is part of this organization's culture, the survey signaled that people's individual development work mattered, and combined with the follow-up survey, indicated a belief that people would improve.

These provisions, we believed, would create additional sources of motivation for each person to stay the course of his immunity work.

Team members took their respondent role seriously, as evidenced by a very high response rate and many rich examples and commentary. (This was the case despite the fact that each person was a respondent for every other fellow member's goals). A few individuals slightly altered their commitments as a consequence of the input, but the main value was the confirmation that they were working on a high-leverage communication goal.

Our biggest take-away from survey input across the team was that a wide range existed in people's preferences for how they approached their work and what they needed from each other. In other words, we could see an enactment of the comment made during our initial data collection that "differences in approaches to the work are not understood and appreciated." For instance, recall people's negative interpretations of Chet's leadership style. Another example: some people clearly sought positive feedback and lamented that they never heard any, while others were unaware of this need and had not considered that a lack of positive feedback could be interpreted as negative.

THE SECOND WORKSHOP: NEW TOOLS FOR EMERGING CHALLENGES

We made the assumption that the team members could increase the level of trust if they better understood their different working styles. Understanding preferences—one's own, that of other individuals on the team, and the team's—became the focus of our next daylong session with the whole team. What follows here is a brief description of the prework for that workshop, the workshop itself, and the thinking behind both.

We chose the Myers-Briggs Type Indicator inventory (MBTI) as a way to help the team understand differences.[5] This tool, based on psychologist Carl Jung's ideas, produces a snapshot of people's mental preferences, which have implications for different communication styles. It is important to know that the MBTI is a *nonjudgmental* way of describing these preferences; no one set of preferences is superior to another, and each preference type has its strengths and limitations. This nonprescriptive frame makes it easier for us to nondefensively look at ourselves and, just as important, to not judge others for their preferences.

When we understand these natural differences, we have a more generous interpretation of how miscommunication occurs (that is, it's not my "fault" or the other person's, but rather an outgrowth of our differing needs and values). We become aware of our own "cultural" biases, so to speak, and are therefore in a position to take responsibility for not imposing our local preference. Instead, we can respect the other person's culture and bridge the natural gap in our meanings by actively taking that person's preference perspective. In a nutshell, the MBTI can be used to increase our self-understanding, increase our ability to send and receive communications, and inform us about how to adapt our style and become more sensitive to teammates' communication styles, including their information-processing preferences.

For all these purposes, we asked every team member to complete the MBTI profile as part of the prework for the second team workshop.[6] We also introduced the ladder of inference (shown in figure 7-2) as another tool for understanding how misunderstandings between people occur.[7] Combined with understanding one's own MBTI preference, the ladder of inference is a very practical device for getting outside of one's personal preferences and into considering another way to see things. The ladder shows how we automatically tend to be evaluative, create inaccurate beliefs, and draw untested conclusions about other people, and then easily end up reinforcing these misguided meanings by attending to and interpreting the data that fits them.

Used on one's own, the ladder helps a person to slow this process so he can catch and correct himself from jumping to conclusions too quickly. Used collectively, the ladder has even greater power to improve communication. In addition to the value of showing that it is a normal human tendency to be inaccurate meaning-makers (which we all are at least some of the time), the tool offers norms and concrete suggestions for how to test for understanding and correct misinterpretations.

Another objective was for people to connect what they were learning about their style preferences to their immunity work. A majority of this second full-day team workshop centered on helping people make sense of their own type, understand its implications for

FIGURE 7-2

The ladder of inference illustrates our tendency to adopt inaccurate beliefs based on selective observations, false assumptions, and misguided conclusions

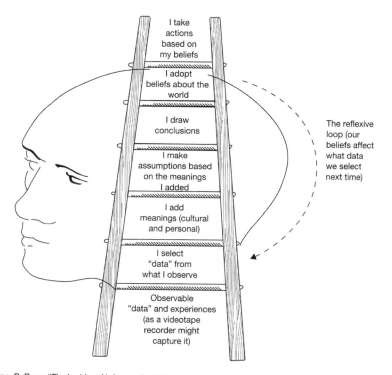

Source: R. Ross, "The Ladder of Inference" in P. Senge, A. Kleiner, et al., *The Fifth Discipline Fieldbook* (New York: Doubleday, 1994), 243.

communication, and practice thinking and talking in ways that were compatible with other type preferences. People also updated each other on their immunities work, including their continuum of progress (which could be revised based on the day's work on communication across people's preferences). High interest and high energy persisted throughout the day, despite the full agenda. People were as excited to hear about their colleagues' MBTI profiles as they were to understand their own, and showed a great deal of appreciation for people's progress with their column 1 goals.

To illustrate, let's return to Cathy from chapter 6. Remember that her column 1 improvement goal was "to better manage my emotional state and my expression of my emotions: when problems emerge in one project or with one person, I am committed to containing my emotion to that situation. I will then try to deal directly with the problem, and not let my feelings spill over into interactions with others or to other projects." Once she understood her own MBTI preference profile, Cathy quickly saw the implication that she was primed to overreact to people with different preferences, especially along the "judging-perceiving" dimension of the instrument. This preference pair—demarking two poles of a continuum—describes the person's orientation to the outer world, and captures the tendency to prefer a more structured and predictable lifestyle (judging) or a more flexible and adaptable lifestyle (perceiving).

As you might guess from reading chapter 6, Cathy had a clear and strong "judging" preference, leading her to feel most comfortable and productive working in a planful, structured manner. When she learned that the teammate who pushed her buttons fastest and most frequently (whom she saw as "unreliable" and "taking forever to get anything done") had a "perceiving" preference, it didn't take long for her to say to this person, "No wonder I get so upset with you. I'm just the opposite!" You can imagine how Cathy's colleague welcomed such a comment!

After this session, Cathy would go on to use this information about the two of them when she started to become agitated or feel high-strung. If you read her case, you know that asking herself what she could and could not control became one of Cathy's critical tools for creating a less stressful environment and interrupting her stress once she began experiencing it. Understanding her own and others' MBTI preferences, as well as how quickly and easily she could generate negative attributions of people (illuminated by using the ladder of inference), gave Cathy more handles on what she could control.

THE THIRD WORKSHOP:
TAKING STOCK AND MOVING ON

Our final session with the team was a time to take stock of and discuss where they saw themselves as a team and as individuals relative to their initial goals, to celebrate progress, and to identify and make plans to address the next phase of their work. In this way, the session was less about ending than about transferring ownership of the learning process to the team and getting members started on their next chapter.

In preparation for this meeting, we sent everyone the results of their second round of personal immunity-to-change survey data and debriefed it with them. (Despite having to complete a survey for each of their team members, again everyone replied with extended, thoughtful responses. As we saw in chapter 6 with Cathy's second survey, the overall feedback tended to be very positive. The "after" survey, in contrast to the "before" survey, reflected team members' judgments that their colleagues had changed, in most cases in significant ways.) In addition, a week before the workshop, everyone completed the eighteen-item "after" team survey assessment, the same quantitative instrument we had used to support the "before" assessment. We compiled the data to build a portrait of their progress and a starting point for discussing the implications for their upcoming work.

The team self-portrait that emerged after our first several months of work looks very different from the "before" portrait. Figure 7-3 compares the before and after ratings on all eighteen items, which appear in the table as column headings. The team members used a 5-point scale to record their impression of the group's performance on each item. We combined their individual responses to produce the groupwide before and after profiles.

The initial results showed below-average ratings (below 3 on the 1–5 scale) for more than half of the eighteen items. Effective communication came in dead last, at 1.93, followed by overall trust, team building, and organizational learning, tied at 2.21. Though still below average, personal trust was higher than overall trust (2.71), suggesting that individuals' own trust exceeded the trust they perceived other team members had (except for one respondent, who rated overall trust higher than his personal trust). The highest averaged score was in strategic focus (3.86), with clear and definable goals next (3.71) and compelling vision and purpose right behind (3.57).

As we noted earlier, this data confirmed the qualitative observations that the team was strongest on "business skills" and needed to work on the "soft items" as well as on team learning.

FIGURE 7-3

Before and after self-assessment ratings of team performance on 1–5 scale

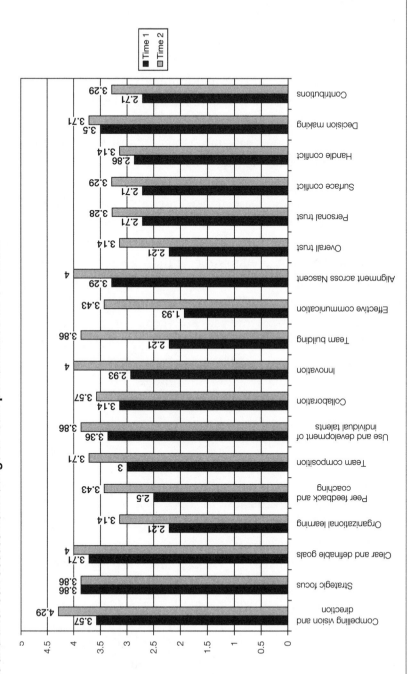

The "after" survey shows improvement in all but one area, strategic focus, which was the team's highest baseline score. Second, the greatest gains were in exactly the areas the team most needed to improve: effective communication, overall trust, and team building. Third, all eighteen items were now rated above average (fourteen items above 3, and 4 items equal to or above 4).

That data is useful for what it tells us about people's revised perceptions of the team. While the results don't show precisely where the team is in its learning curve, we can get a quick sense of whether people believe the team has moved in the right direction or not. Clearly, the numbers suggest that people collectively see the team as taking many forward steps, as reflected in their comments during the final workshop:

"The biggest jumps are in areas we set out to accomplish. I'm very happy about accomplishing what we did!"

"Overall, our vision and strategy focus was always there. Team building has helped and led to improved innovation and communication. We're moving in the right direction."

"We made a lot of progress in overall trust. And we're still just above average. Looking at individual numbers, there's a mix of high and low scores, which means that there are a couple of people who still don't feel we're there. We can't move to the next level without everyone feeling trust."

"Strong vision . . . but we need more time to reflect and learn, both at the individual (e.g., learn from our work) and team levels (e.g., how might we "slice and dice" our way of organizing to work smarter given we can't work harder!?)"

Having absorbed these before and after self-portraits on the morning of the last workshop, the team moved on to flesh out the new demands of their current and short-term work. Six months had passed since the initial goal setting, and the business context had shifted. Once the team agreed on the most significant context changes, they discussed the implications of these for how they needed to function differently. They then identified their team's development needs for its next work phase.

We then used this updated picture of the developmental needs to help frame the subsequent round of individual improvement goals. All team members reported on what pleased them most about their own progress, shared one of their most significant learning experiences, made a public commitment about their continued personal learning goals relative to the team's needs, and asked for the support they needed from the team to continue their individual development.

We'll start with Chet, the team leader:

> "I'm committed to creating a motivating environment so that we can accomplish what we set out to. To me, that means creating a balance of empowering people and also keeping to timelines. That's a challenge. I want you to understand what I have to face every day—do I say something? Let it go? It's a delicate balance. In terms of creating an empowering environment, I want to continue to work on my commitment to be a listener, asking questions rather than making assumptions. I also want to have retreats, and do days like this on a continual basis. I'm working to provide praise on a real-time basis, even if it has to be on e-mail or v-mail. What I need from you is to be open to receiving feedback from me that is direct. I know it may need more patience on your side to swallow, but I ask that you listen to what I say knowing that my feedback comes from a good place. If you have suggestions for how I might give direct feedback in ways that would work better for you, please tell me. I will be open to hearing that."

Now, let's listen to a few others:

> "I'm committed to continue with my commitment (to communicate more based on my colleagues' styles). I want to be more focused in the moment and more consistent with my tone and the way I communicate with my colleagues in every scenario (1:1 or group settings). I have the hardest time in our team settings. I think that's because if I see us going in circles, I want to provide structure. That may come across authoritative. My intention is to help, but what comes out is that I want it done

my way. I'd prefer to ask questions, like 'Is this working for everyone?' And then let the team decide rather than me jumping in all the time. I don't have to run everything. When I'm in the 'authoritative zone' can we just pause, and will you let me know that I'm in the zone. I need some way to stop the snowball from going down the hill and not having people feel bad for the signal. I don't want to put people on the spot. For me personally, anyone can let me know. If I'm in the zone, it's because I don't realize it."

"I overcommunicate. I give too much detail. And over cc in my e-mails. I need to think through who to send what to, and if I'm uncomfortable with what to do, I ask someone. If you receive something from me that you don't need or want, please tell me that. And I know I need to be more concise in my communications, leave something in the well, so there's something to draw on! You can give me feedback—if I'm not clear, tell me, 'can you say that in ten words or less?' "

By the end of this part of the session, each person spoke and had made a personalized pact with the team about what he or she needed. People understood that the purpose of these agreements was to take a *next* step of getting direct, immediate, and relevant feedback from one another. A number of people had already had such conversations with individual team members, so the idea was not new. But this was an explicit way we were moving everyone into the next phase of the work: We had gone through a full cycle of individual goal setting and input gathering, and now it was their turn to take full ownership of their individual agendas and of being supports to each other's learning.

We also asked each person to identify one team member who would serve as his or her partner moving forward. We would be sending each person a personal "learning contract" based on the day's session, and we suggested how the document could be useful in working as partners. Each person had one last individual coaching session to schedule, we reminded them, and added that this could be a time for people to finalize how they wanted to transition from working with us to working with their partner and the team, more generally. People then reflected on the day's session and the overall project.

That was the last time we met with the team. But the data from our impact interviews with people three months later revealed that the team had maintained and deepened its progress.

THE FOLLOW-UP INTERVIEWS

We intentionally scheduled final individual coaching meetings and impact interviews to follow this last workshop with the team. The interviews focused on how the process had changed both the individual and the team. These took place three months after the project concluded so that we could learn what "stuck." They were conducted by a third party to allow people to talk candidly. Together they revealed significant progress on the team's learning goals and each person's individual improvement goal.

Specific comments confirmed the team's new and improved self-image and brought color and detail to the picture. Here is a sampling:

> "This work accelerated the gelling of our team. We were so broken and busy that had we not had this process, we wouldn't have come together. Everyone had the willingness to change— that was already there and this work got us there incredibly quickly. Once people got into it they all knew what they needed to do."

> "Our group meetings got better and better. It was good to see how people were changing in their reactions, and making new connections. In the end, I see openness, discussing issues, candor, thinking out loud with each other, real openness to helping one another, and people fessing up with their issues, like when one of our team members realized openly that his missing meetings was having a negative impact on us."

> "My teammates now have my confidence, we're more reflective, we've had better dialogue, and we have more credibility outside the team."

Every person saw important changes within himself or herself too:

"I've changed in so many ways. I'm a lot more conscious of interactions and how I impact people. I manage myself better now and have better interactions. I think about my style, what works and what doesn't in different situations. I'm a lot more conscious. Even when I fail to meet my commitment, I notice that. The hard part is it's more gut wrenching, looking at myself in a reflective way. I'm self-critical and this process forces me to look in the mirror and see whether you are being honest with yourself, where you're making progress and where you're not."

"I'm aware of when I'm entering into a danger zone. The awareness is the biggest, most helpful thing. My commitment was being more open to people's suggestions. For example, there were a few people who weren't pulling their weight. We'd have weekly meetings, and I used to be really impatient and wouldn't hear them through my irritation. Now I'm more open to situations to allow others to present themselves. There was one person in particular who was a challenge, and through this, I found myself liking him more—I couldn't stand to be in a room with him before. As the months went by I found myself seeing a different side of him. He may still come in not as well prepared as I'd like, but I'm already on guard that I shouldn't shoot him down."

"It's not only self awareness, it's more insight into how people might react to something that I might think is benign, and that's very important. I now think through things before I say or do and am more sensitive to all types of audiences. It was a marginal change but it was very important; I didn't go from 0 to 10, it's more like I went from an 8 to 10, and the 2 point gain was significant."

Which isn't to suggest that some people weren't worried about continuing or sustaining their growth:

"I have become more self-aware, including that I was looking at things through my lenses only, so it made transparent other people's issues that I didn't see before. I still struggle with it because it's good to be self-aware, but when things get busy I go on autopilot and fall back into my old patterns."

"I am more self-conscious about interactions with others. I think about my people skills now and use my knowledge of what my weaknesses are to see how they show up in my daily projects. I'm trying to change, but it's stressful—keeping it at the top of my mind is always difficult to do."

Many saw a clear connection between their personal development and the team's progress:

"I feel very good about my performance *and* my team and the dynamics . . . I gained a lot professionally and saw the team gain a lot. The two together made it powerful—now I see my responsibility as helping the team and not just myself; I feel that much more now. This team came from a tough place. I always recognized that, but I think I became very focused on helping the team (while still helping myself)."

"People come to me as they did before, but we have more productive conversations now, and they're more confident in their own work; they're growing and are happier. Someone came to me for advice the other day and the way I engaged her was different—I was more collaborative instead of directive. This forces them to think through their own solutions. I'm not giving answers anymore, so they're not shutting down."

"We are so focused on doing our tasks at hand that we don't really realize half the battle of being effective is working with other people. I never had to investigate my team working style. This was interesting because it's obvious that one has to be self-aware, but this process made us stop and take time to do it. I'm a stronger communicator and manager of people. This all helped me to break the ice. It helped me with a reason to take time out with team members to say, 'This is what I'm working on.'"

So now you have an end-to-end picture of our work with the group, and an idea of their ongoing commitments. You already know, from Cathy's story in the prior chapter, that the team produced a successful high-stakes plan where the previous group had failed. The team-level immunity-to-change work created valuable improvements in six months, and we believe these improvements were significantly related to the team's ultimately succeeding in its company mandate. But what made the process successful?

WHAT WE LEARNED ABOUT WHY IT WORKED

Our starting place is the issue of trust, one of the team's core issues. You might even say insufficient trust was *the* core issue, since it prevented people from communicating effectively with each other and it got in the way of people accepting their different work styles.

It helps to understand (or at least to have a working theory about) what generates trust. Our working model, drawn from research on trust in organizations, identifies at least four elements:[8]

- Respect for the importance of the other person's role in producing high-quality outcomes

- Belief in the other's ability (competence) and willingness to fulfill his or her formal role responsibilities

- Care about the other professionally and personally

- Consistency between what people say and what they do

All of these elements were important for the Nascent Pharmaceuticals team. We start with Chet because, as team leader, he played a crucial role in the team's emerging trust.

The role of the leader is key.

Within the first few weeks of forming his new team, Chet heard people's need for team building and acted on it by bringing in potential resources and asking the team to decide whom they wanted to work with. Such listening is an act of respect. The less happy team members could have seen Chet's swift and responsive actions as acts of leadership competence: He was not allowing his team to sink. Being asked to decide on a consultant could enhance the team's trust in Chet and the process, since whoever this was would not be *his* agent. Moreover, being decision makers at the outset gave team members immediate ownership of the outcomes.

Chet furthered the development of trust during the first team session with his up-front decision to discuss the survey and interview data about his leadership weaknesses with the team, and his nondefensive listening throughout that conversation. He expressed his understanding that many of them thought he was pushing too hard, through micromanaging and giving excessive direction without any appreciative comments. He made himself vulnerable, again, when he shared his personal commitment not to react to people immediately, but instead to inquire into their thinking and to listen actively. Only then would he give feedback or directions.

How did this build trust? Fundamentally, Chet's listening to the team's feedback was another form of respect, and in his choice to follow their feedback, he was acknowledging the value of their ideas. He was also "walking the talk" right then and there by listening and understanding their point of view, before reacting. At a more pragmatic level, expressing his intent to act on their specific feedback also meant he was willing to address one of the key reasons for lack of trust—differences in work style.

While a long-term aspiration is for everyone to understand and appreciate one another's different approaches to the work, including Chet's, this goal is more apt to be reached if, as leader, he can honor others' needs. His public commitment has immediate symbolic value: As the leader, he is including himself as someone who needs to better appreciate others' work styles (and understand that success for the team isn't about everyone accommodating to his style). Additionally, people could feel hope that Chet would build his competence as leader and manager in a needed area.

After the first workshop, Chet continued to build people's trust by pursuing his commitment to listen and understand before reacting. This had very practical payoffs for building trust. For one, being more inquiry-oriented allowed him to learn what people were thinking, which furthered his belief in their ability and the quality of their thinking. Additionally, as he listened more to what people had to say, he opened to them and their ideas and he found himself caring more about them as people. People felt his personal regard for them.

Throughout the months of this work, Chet also kept his promise *never to use in any evaluative way (formal or informal) what people shared about their personal learning challenges* in that first workshop and thereafter. Consistency between what one says and does couldn't be more important than in honoring this particular promise. (A contrasting picture captures the cost of inconsistency: Imagine how much and how quickly trust would be lost if Chet had not kept his word on this assurance.)

We don't have the sense that it was hard for Chet to remain true to his word here. Looking back, it seems that he was simply being consistent with his belief that people could and would succeed with their individual goals if given the opportunity, and documenting that work would not add value but instead possibly interfere. In any case, by not drawing on people's personal learning challenges in his evaluations of their work, Chet continuously affirmed the team's shared values around personal development and professional safety.

While the role of the leader is key in building trust, he or she cannot, alone, make a team successful. That requires everyone's engagement. We identified six additional elements that explain the team's development:

- The teamwide goal was a high-leverage one for the team's development.

- Individuals continually worked on improvement goals that fit with the team's goal.

- People brought relevant "personal business" into the team's business.

- There was a strong collective commitment and motivation to improve.

- Individual learning was enhanced by the social fabric of the group.

- The learning structure was appropriate to the learning needs.

*The teamwide goal was a high-leverage one
for the team's development.*

The team's decision to work on communication was well suited to where they were in their early formation, especially since it provided a reason to address the issue of trust. Developing an explicit agreement about what good communication would look like provided an early bonding experience for the team. Despite a history that included episodes when some people felt hurt or unappreciated, everyone liked the communication picture they created together. As one of the first products the team agreed on, this picture offered a safe and productive way for people to name the perceived sources of their prior bad feelings.

Just as important was that the team defined quality communication for themselves, giving them greater ownership of where they wanted to go and how to get there. Their description gave explicit dos and don'ts consistent with developing interpersonal trust, and they had a shared expectation that everyone would follow these guidelines. Recall, for instance, their directions to be "open, direct, sincere, timely, motivating, and nonassumptive" as a speaker, and to "assume good intentions of sender, listen fully, ask clarifying questions (especially around tone), and be open to learning" as a receiver. Their picture reminded them to be aware of their personal contributions to hindering team communication, and it turned out that individuals were willing and able to do this.

*Individuals worked throughout on personal improvement
goals that fit with the team's goal.*

When we asked (in the impact interview) whether people experienced working on their individual development goals as connected to the team's overall critical needs, everyone said there was a clear connection, and many commented on how important that was for them:

> "Each of our commitments was about making the team
> stronger, caring more about each other and our work; my

commitment affected the overall team dynamic so they fed into one another."

"It's really good to identify the needs and strengths and weaknesses of the team in general; that can only further your own goal and that will help that team dynamic. It's good to look at inner self—as individuals, we are adding or detracting from the team overall and we ought to be aware of that."

"The way I see it, team needs come from the individuals on the team. If there are enough weaknesses in certain areas, it impacts the team. Our team communication needed to be improved overall. Individuals needed to work on it. When we started working on it, I didn't feel like I forced my own issue to fit the team need—they were very connected. I think it's the only way you should do it. If you have a team goal without individual ownership of that goal, I don't know how you would do it."

Because everyone was working on being more effective in communicating, we were able to introduce tools applicable to everyone's individual learning needs in one of our sessions with the whole team. The MBTI preference work in the second workshop led people to see others (especially those who pushed their buttons) in a new, more generous light. The MBTI, along with the ladder of inference, helped people to understand their role in creating misguided interpretations of other people's communications, which led everyone to feel less self-righteous and better equipped to expand their interpersonal repertoire. Comments like, "It never occurred to me that I was being hard on people because they didn't do what I needed them to do" are representative of the way people deepened their personal understanding of the role they personally played in not trusting other people. This individual learning, in turn, served the team's goal.

People brought relevant personal business into the team's business.

People's "personal business" was tightly tied to "business" so there was a clear reason why it was being shared, and there was a clear framework for defining what was appropriate. A spotlight on the self started in the first workshop and continued throughout our meetings with the team. To begin with, people publicly stated their personal improvement goals and, in doing so, were vulnerable with each other. This allowed people to see and be seen by their teammates as humans who had foibles, like themselves. People then went on to share entire immunity maps, including countercommitments and big assumptions, which revealed ever more personal, more self-protective needs.

This had enormous and immediate benefits for building team trust as people began to see unexpected reasons why they and their teammates were less than ideal communicators. That not only helped people to feel less put off, but led them to feel softer and more caring toward each other. Sharing the personal dimension of this work also deepened trust within the group over time as individuals witnessed others using this privileged information appropriately: They heard comments in which people noticed or appreciated their greater effectiveness, and, conversely, they heard no one abuse what they learned about each other.

We also think that bringing relevant personal business into the team's business, testing big assumptions, and overturning individual immunities led all team members to succeed with their personal improvement communication goals. Without getting to the heart of what was preventing each person from accomplishing his or her particular communications goal we don't think we would have seen as much progress for individuals or the group. A crucial ingredient to appropriately bringing the personal into the professional realm is the ability to be self-reflective. Every person on the team was able to look in the mirror and be honest about what he or she saw. You know from chapter 6 the kind of work Cathy did in overturning her own immunity, in coming to understand how her own hidden commitments produced her stressed-out state. Now imagine every member of that team undertaking the same level of work, having opportunities within the team to reveal their immunity to the others, to run tests of their big assumptions, and to have their resultant changes recognized and appreciated. This forms a very powerful crucible for personal learning tightly tied to business needs.

*There was a strong collective commitment
and motivation to improve.*

This builds on our earlier point that the team embodied the stance, "If one of us fails, we all fail." Every person was on board with the need to improve and the team's specific learning goal. First, they knew that they needed to improve communication and felt some urgency about addressing this need. Second, by defining the goal, they owned it. They did not act out of compliance; building trust and improving communication was not anything Chet asked or required them to do. Instead, they saw themselves as the agents of change. Chet, alone, could not have created greater team cohesiveness.

*Individual learning was enhanced by the
social fabric of the group.*

The team's collective intent and motivation provided crucial conditions for individuals to stick with this work. A predictable and typical pattern in change work is for people to start off strong and then trail off, especially when there has been enough progress that the emerging reality is tolerable. "Not enough time," is the standard refrain. By contrast, everyone on this team continued to work on both team goals and individual goals, even when work demands and the accompanying time pressures spiked.[9] Chet explains, looking back, why he thinks people kept at this work:

> The most important thing is that you ensure in your team somehow that everyone feels they need something, can get something out of this. When we started working on building our team, there was a sigh of relief. We needed to be fixed. We liked having someone from the outside helping us along, but then we realized it was a lot of work on top of the other work going on. Everyone is busy. It was very important that the team articulated why it needed this and what they wanted to get out of it to keep the energy going.

People can overturn their immunities without the social fabric of their work team. But having a group of people who know what we are working on, who themselves have an investment in our making progress on that improvement goal, and who interact with us frequently and so can give us direct and timely feedback (both when we seem to be in the hold of our big assumption and when we are acting in new and more productive ways) goes a very long way towards increasing our individual ability to stick with it. We want others to see us as personally responsible and effective. We are inclined to take a stance like, "We said we were going to change and that's what we are going to do!"

The team's collective motivation to improve led individuals to feel accountable to each other. People's individual goals weren't simply something they could take or leave, since everyone around the table was counting on and rooting for one another. Not only that, each person knew everyone was well informed about his or her personal goals. Knowing each other's goals enabled people to give each other relevant feedback spontaneously. This pressure and encouragement from others was another source of motivation for people to continue working on their goals.

One of the team member's final reflections touches on this point: "I honestly feel our learning can't be in isolation; you need to do it with a team. I think the individual coaching experience by itself might be too isolated for self-improvement, without having measures of whether changes are happening. Learning from the team is more effective because your behavior matters to others and you can get feedback."

The learning structure was appropriate to the learning needs.

Different learning needs require different amounts of time, quality of space, and types of materials and resources. Conceptualizing and planning the nuts and bolts of time, place, and materials paid off here.

From the start, Chet and the team knew that their problem (whatever it was) was not something they were going to solve by themselves. They brought in a resource (us). They also knew their problem was not going to be solved in a day or even two, but they were prepared to take the necessary time, despite the extraordinary pressures they felt to deliver on their product.

They scheduled that time, and made their team sessions with us sacrosanct (as you can imagine, scheduling daylong workshops is very challenging with so many people, all with very full schedules). In addition to the obvious sheltered time for learning, scheduling multiple sessions created a timeline of expectations for progress. If you've ever taken music lessons, you probably know the feeling of wanting to be prepared for your next session. Knowing when they were going to meet with us over the six months helped people to stay focused and ready to participate at the next level.

We sought to make every meeting—whether with the team or in individual coaching sessions—sufficiently safe and sufficiently risky. Support and challenge, the research tells us, are the tandem features most facilitative of development. We modeled practices people could use outside our meetings to better understand and appreciate each other, and the tools we chose were intended to support that same goal. The data we gathered and shared throughout the process enhanced their ability to see where and how they could further their team and individual goals.

The Nascent team reflects a design for improving capabilities that may be at once the most ambitious and the most cost-effective. The nonartificial, nontemporary nature of intact work groups under pressure to perform creates powerful supports and incentives for people to stay with their individual improvement work. At the same time, when they do, the payoffs include the higher performance of the team as a whole.

Over these last several chapters you have met a variety of people and places, each taking up the "immunities work" in their own fashion. It's possible you've begun to think about trying this for yourself or your team. In the third and last part of this book we want to share with you our understanding of the ingredients crucial to success in overcoming immunities, and then support you to diagnose and overcome your own.

PART THREE

OVER TO YOU

Diagnosing and Overcoming Immunities
in Yourself and Your Organization

$$\left[\begin{array}{c} 8 \end{array}\right]$$

UNLOCKING POTENTIAL

Three Necessary Ingredients

PEOPLE OFTEN ASK US, "Do you find that some people are better suited than others to make progress using your method?"
Often this question comes with some tentative (or not so tentative)
hypotheses—"I'll bet this is much more likely to work with women,"
they'll say (or "people from the United States and Europe rather than
Asia," or "people in the social sector"). As we hope our examples
throughout this book have made clear, all of these hypotheses are
wonderfully unsupported.

But we have noticed that some people *are* better suited to overcoming their immunities. The body of evidence suggests that the
more people are connected to three ingredients—which for shorthand purposes we'll designate as "gut," "head and heart," and
"hand"—the more significant their changes will be. We'll look at
each of these metaphors in turn.

INGREDIENT #1: THE GUT—A VITAL SOURCE OF MOTIVATION FOR CHANGE

To start and stay the course of doing genuinely developmental work, a person must really, *really* want to accomplish his or her first-column goal. It is almost never enough to have a goal that just "makes sense," not even one with compelling, logical reasons behind it. Reasons can help fuel our motivation to change, but they aren't enough to help us cross the critical thresholds. Reasons tap into the "ought" and "should" realm of inner talk. We must also experience sufficient need or desire, visceral feelings—which is why we say they come from the gut.

We have seen people who described their self-improvement goals in column 1 as "important" or "extremely important" to them to accomplish (a 4 or 5 on a 1–5 scale), yet they end up deciding not to pursue them. Why? They probably wouldn't say it this way, but it is almost as if they didn't have the stomach to endure what they imagine will be the unpleasantness of changing. These people were so alarmed when they saw (via their immunity map) that accomplishing their goal depended on altering their self-protective countercommitment, that they immediately reassessed the importance of their goal. A goal that felt, just an hour ago, like it was a 4 or 5 in importance to achieve, suddenly was no longer as critical. This is one way people resolve the dissonance. The way to countering it comes from a powerful enough gut feeling that the *cost* of this self-protection—the impossibility of making progress on a deeply desired goal—has just become too big a price to continue paying.

David and Cathy, whose success stories we explored in part 2, experienced their goals as more than "very important" to accomplish; they felt it was *absolutely necessary* to address them. Putting it the other way, they came to feel it was no longer tolerable *not* to address the goal. Relenting was not a viable option. They had reached some sort of limit as to how much they could bear. They were aware of and loaded down by the high price they were paying for the status quo.

A prime source of this fire in the belly comes from feeling that if we don't change, we are putting someone we love or something we care about at risk. As we write this book, we are working with a successful business leader who created a four-column map initially for professional purposes alone, starting with the improvement goal to be a better listener. But when he realized, weeks later, that his poor listening was harming his daughter and their relationship, it transformed his motivation to overturn his immunity. It broke his heart to hear his daughter's therapist suggest that her acting-out behavior could be related to him and his emotional unavailability. Seeing for the first time how he was failing his daughter, he tapped into a bigger reservoir of desire to deal with his immunity to change.

So a gut-level urgency to lessen distress—one's own or another person's—is one common driving force for individual change. Self-efficacy, including having a notion of what we can do to accomplish our desired change, is another. We may have a goal we care about (be it to stretch ourselves, follow a passion, address a shortcoming, or build our competencies), but if we don't feel in our gut we can do anything about it, or we aren't sure what we can do that will make enough of a difference, we don't act on it. For some people, seeing a picture of their immune system in front of them gives them exactly this direction and hope for what they can do to accomplish their goal.

For these people, readiness to change is often triggered by a sudden inspirational understanding of a truth about themselves. As they uncover their immune system, a door they did not see before opens and reveals how they have been holding themselves back. Even if their initial reaction is to be upset, many also feel a promise and opportunity in finally understanding the source of their undermining behaviors.

That was exactly how a woman we worked with described the turning point for success in meeting her change challenge. A tenured faculty member and associate chair of her department, Anna responded this way when we asked her to reflect on her process:

> The mapping session helped me liberate myself from doing other people's work so I could do my own. I had been on too many committees, taking on roles with responsibility and little authority,

picking up the pieces that my colleagues always seemed to be dropping, being pressured into research collaborations peripheral to my own interests. The four-column exercise provided the spark—an epiphany, really—for me to step out into relatively uncharted waters, on my own. This meant having the confidence to set, and work toward achieving, my own goals. When I think back on the session, it opened my eyes and it empowered me. I got permission from myself to pursue a different path.

Anna's epiphany about how she was inadvertently making herself miserable by doing everyone else's work happened, not surprisingly, when she thought about her hidden commitments. Here's how she talked about her self-discovery:

It started when I got to the third column. I wrote down my fears—that my work might not be good enough, that I'm fallible and imperfect—and when I actually said it aloud, I said to myself "Oh my god," and I got this sinking feeling. These worries were real! I knew I would have to put my own work up for scrutiny. Peer review is the whole world here. You have to go into a peer-review situation either naive, and you do that only once, or you have to have a shield of armor built. I think people think of me as tough, resistant, and unstoppable. But I don't see myself that way.

So here I was, on the one hand saying I was frustrated with work because I was giving too much of myself up to others when I had all these things I wanted to do, and then seeing that the real reason I serve on so many committees and say "yes" to everyone is that it's easier to do their work than my own! And that's because I'm afraid mine isn't good enough!

Drawing on her new insight, Anna had already worked out a plan before she left the mapping session for how she would tackle her goal of pursuing her own work: "At the close of that session, I decided I needed to be more confident. I needed to create more time and mechanisms to do my work to get it out there. I figured that if I can make the time and do the work, I will gain more validation that it is good."

It's hard for us to resist telling you what her results were—so here they are:

> I am this year in [a prestigious fellows program]. I am negotiating a book contract with a major textbook publisher for innovative learning materials in genetics. I have submitted a National Science Foundation grant related to this project, and the grant reviewed well so I am optimistic regarding its success; and I am writing several papers about this new method and its consequences for understanding genetics. If you knew me even a few years ago you'd understand this is a complete turnaround. Instead of being miserable and grumpy all the time, I am excited. And it has a positive impact on the rest of my life. I eat better, I exercise. Everything has fallen into place.

So gut feelings can prepare us to take action either because the cost of the status quo (to ourselves or others) has become intolerably high, or because we've experienced a burst of hope from seeing a way forward that was never clear before. A third source of gut motivation can be the personal experience of deep discrepancy.

In these cases, people feel the need to resolve a glaring gap they see in themselves. The gap can be cognitive, affective, and/or behavioral. It can be a mismatch that leads one person to feel badly about herself (e.g., "I want to stop smoking but I am smoking as much as ever") and another to feel excited about becoming more of the person he aspires to be (like the Welsh cell-phone salesman, Paul Potts, who clung to his dream of being an opera singer and ended up performing for the queen). The column 1 goal might be to correct a deficit ("becoming a better delegator") or to realize a fuller self-expansion (we worked with a highly accomplished senior executive nearing retirement who nonetheless, for his own fulfillment, deeply wanted to get better at mentoring and "leading from behind").

In either case, for many people, seeing themselves operate so contradictorily—a foot on the gas, a foot on the brake—activates the gut. As the psychologist William Perry observed, "Organisms *organize*. Human organisms organize *reality*." When you put before people a

stark picture of highly discrepant self-organization, it is often a powerful recruiter of their attention.

Our gut is the source of what moves us—our deepest appetites
give us the motivation and energy—to take on adaptive change challenges. Once people have taken the first step of committing to
change, they still need resources to sustain the journey. These come
from the next two ingredients, and are generated as we begin to experience the rewards of the change itself.

INGREDIENT #2—HEAD AND HEART: THE WORK MUST SIMULTANEOUSLY ENGAGE THINKING AND FEELING

In every adaptive challenge, the problem space lies above *and* below
our necks. Because an immunity to change expresses the thinking and
feeling dimensions of a given level of mental complexity, we need to
work on both dimensions to achieve real, adaptive change (as illustrated in "Engaging Feelings and Thinking Together"). No amount
of thinking or effort alone will be sufficient to solve an adaptive
problem, since how we feel is inherent in the problem itself. And
because how we feel is intricately tied to how we know, we cannot
feel differently if we don't know differently. We need a bigger emotional and cognitive space, one in which we experience that the internal conflicts and inconsistencies of our adaptive challenge are not
inevitable and intractable.

Engaging Feelings and Thinking Together

REMEMBER DAVID, from chapter 5? His goal was "to become a better
delegator and to better focus on a few critical things." On the face of
it, this goal seems relatively straightforward and nonemotional. Nonetheless, in looking at his immunity map, we can see that David's goal was an

adaptive one essentially because delegating was tied to his identity and his beliefs about effective leadership. Recall his big assumption: "I believe that leadership without doing is 'overhead' and worthless. I'd walk away from my roots if I was not doing the work itself. I would be selfish, lazy, and spoiled, and lose my self respect."

Becoming consciously released from this assumption required David to redefine effective leadership—not just intellectually, but in his heart—so that he could continue to respect and feel good about himself, be true to his roots, and be a good delegator.

Put another way, for David to change his mindset regarding leadership, he had to deal with the feelings—in this case of disloyalty and self-contempt—that immediately emerged when he even thought about walking away from the picture of good leadership with which he had long identified.

The mindset reflected in an immunity to change is not simply a cognitive phenomenon. As we have said, it is also a brilliant anxiety-management system. Tampering with it means tampering with a well-tuned, highly serviceable, long-possessed instrument for keeping dangerous dread at bay. We said earlier that every immune system is an intelligent force that seeks to protect you, even to save your life as you know it. You can hear in that definition how the head and heart are furiously working in tandem.

When people see their own X-ray, they are inevitably looking at two realities at once—the benefits of the way they have come to take care of themselves, and the costs they are paying for doing so in exactly this way. Working through an adaptive challenge is a head-and-heart consideration of an alternative cost-benefit equation. Learning whether it is possible to think and feel that we can still be safe while pursuing a change is the essential change challenge. This is what we mean by working through anxiety: We come out on the other side with a new understanding that the world works differently than we had imagined, that we can still be safe—and even experience more expansive benefits—doing things we never thought possible before. We discover not only that we can survive, but thrive. This discovery—a kind of recalculating of our risks and benefits—entails a simultaneous "thinking about our feelings" and "feeling our way into new ways of thinking."

To make this more concrete, let's see how Cathy (from chapter 6) experienced this shift. Figure 8-1 shows the benefits Cathy got from

FIGURE 8-1

Cathy's benefits: Before and after

Benefits	When captive of her immunity	When released from her immunity
What Cathy gets from others	I get to be seen as the go-to person, the teammate people can count on to get it done and done right all the time. I am viewed by my teammates as dependable. I get to be seen by others as up to the team's bar of a good team member (110% effort and making sure everything is perfect).	I continue to be seen as dependable by my teammates. I am respected not so much for what I "do" as for who I "am." I get ongoing feedback about when they think I may be heading toward a high-strung state. I get frequent and specific feedback about my work and an appreciation for my contributions to the team.
What Cathy gets from herself	I avoid feeling that I may not be capable, and keep others from taking away the work I love. I know that I can deliver the perfect end product. I know that I am always giving my absolute best and therefore can't or won't let down my team of myself. I successfully hide from others the truth of my defectiveness.	I have confidence. The satisfaction of really understanding my value added. No longer living the possibility that something precious can be taken. No longer feeling that the deep-down truth is that I am inadequate. Feeling that my worth is more intrinsic than extrinsic. (Before I was always "doing" things, and now it's about "being" myself, trusting and using my unique insights, given my experiences and education, in order to produce an excellent end product.) I have the satisfaction of being able to take care of myself by acting on my understanding to make good decisions about what work I should do and how to do it. I don't worry about burning out. I ask myself, "What is in my control here and what isn't?" and make choices based on what's in my control.

others and herself when she was unconsciously captive to her intact immune system ("before"), and when she overturned it to be consciously released ("after"). In both cases she benefits, but a critical difference is that the latter gains are *not* keeping her from being able to deliver on her aspiration to better control her emotions. These descriptions parallel Cathy's shift from reacting emotionally, not asking for help, not saying no, and operating in overdrive, on the one hand, to effectively managing her emotions, prioritizing and pacing her work, and saying no to herself and others, on the other.

Let's look at the shifts in David's experience of risks and benefits. Recall that David initially felt rewarded by being a "doer" and not asking people for help. Over time, though, he discovered greater benefits from doing things selectively and focusing on core priorities. He learned that he could actively enjoy and feel good about himself operating in a world he had formerly dismissed. Figure 8-2 offers a snapshot of his shift.

As people experience the emergence of options where before there were none, they begin to feel new energy and hope. Tasting the possibility of living in a no-less-safe, but significantly larger space is intoxicating and a source of continued motivation to stay in the work and carry it through. New ways of thinking permit new ways of feeling, and new ways of feeling encourage and validate new ways of thinking. Energy that had been trapped in the immune system is now released and can be redirected to feeling increasing competence and control in our lives. New energy leads to new action, and a particular kind of action furthers the process of adaptation. This brings us to the third ingredient of successful change.

INGREDIENT #3: HAND—THE WORK IS SIMULTANEOUSLY ABOUT MINDSET AND BEHAVIOR

We can't merely think or feel our way out of an immune system no matter how high our motivation is to accomplish our goal. Kant said "perception without conception is blind," and we don't disagree: the mindset does create what we see. But it is also true that conception

FIGURE 8-2

David's benefits: Before and after

Benefits	When captive of his immunity	When released from his immunity
What David gets from others	They see me as smart and a good problem solver, someone who can do what they do better than they do it. I get their respect for that.	People appreciate knowing what's going on—what our direction is and that they understand why we're trying to get there. They also think it's great that I'm letting them make decisions themselves. Best, people are coming to me to tell me ideas about how we could move ahead differently. That's been very fulfilling. More so than getting an individual task done myself.
What David gets from himself	I avoid feeling selfish, lazy, spoiled, and like overhead. I feel important and valuable by doing individual tasks myself, which makes me highly productive. It connects me to people. And I'm doing a "kick-ass" job. I feel good about being a star. I feel aligned with my working-class roots, continuing as a guy who can get his hands dirty (and do the job on the ground better than anyone else) even if I am also now the boss in the "suit."	I feel important and valuable by spending my time finding ways to help my people be more effective. (I find myself looking more at what my people are accomplishing.) I have a new conception of productivity that keeps me feeling still loyal to my roots. (I'm not being selfish, but am helping others.) I have deeper self-respect for being a leader who is able to direct the work and optimize resources for doing it (people and $). I have a clearer and more satisfying leadership practice, where I see that I don't have to do in order to know what's going on, but that I do need to know what's going on in order to direct the work. I don't have to be better than the people I hire, and, in fact, if I am, I am not doing my job well.

without inception is paralysis. We must set out. We must begin to take new action. Success follows from taking intentional, specific actions—the reaching hand—that are *inconsistent* with our immunity so that we can test our mindset.

We start this work with what may seem the most modest sort of action. At first, we simply observe the behaviors listed in our column 2, Doing and Not Doing (behaviors that work against our improvement goal). These observations lead us to see our hidden commitments and big assumptions in real time, which can expand access to additional facets of our mindset. Such observations can also lead us to see additional realms in which our big assumptions operate, which can in turn further motivate us to change as we see greater costs than we first realized. David's earliest self-observations did just this, as we see in "Observing One's Big Assumption in Action."

The next "doing" step involves enacting new behaviors—ones that our big assumptions would tell us *not* to do—in order to get information about the validity of our mindset. We need to be as purposeful about which actions we will take as we are about what information we will collect. Testing our mindset through intentional

Observing One's Big Assumption in Action

RECALL THAT DAVID began by consciously observing himself as he continued to accept more tasks and refrain from asking people to help him. These behaviors clearly ran counter to his intent to better delegate so that he could focus on what was most critical. By being alert to when he said yes and didn't ask for help, he recognized that he got more goodies from doing so than he realized when drafting his first immunity map. Watching his behavior and then tuning in to his internal experience, he was able to know that he felt "important and valuable by doing individual tasks myself. It connects me to people. And I'm doing a kick-ass job. I feel good about being a star." He also gained his team's positive regard: "They see me as smart and a good problem solver. I get their respect for that." These were rich additions to his column 3 commitments to protect the self he wanted to be—that is, important, valuable, and a star.

Self-observations also led David to see that not delegating was a big issue in his personal life as well. Beyond seeing how not delegating at work meant carving into his home time, he realized that he never hired anyone to do household chores either. He told us, laughingly, "I have trouble delegating mowing the lawn!" He also told us he didn't feel okay about asking someone to do his ironing.

action, data collecting, and interpreting the data are the core means we use to mine the gap between our intentions and current ability to deliver on them.

Our entire purpose in acting differently is to generate relevant data to test our big assumptions. Our immediate purpose is *not* to improve or get better, but to get information. In doing so, we are again working within the sweet spot of an adaptive challenge, discovering whether it is possible to replace the safety born of limiting ourselves with a safety informed by learning that the expected bad outcomes don't materialize when we suspend self-imposed limits. Not only that, we may discover the benefits of an increased repertoire of behavioral options and the sense of excitement, accomplishment, and mastery that comes from making progress on our change goal. This is precisely what David learned, as described in "Running a Test of One's Big Assumption."

Keeping both mindset and behavior on the change agenda is not easy. Two common tendencies—to favor change on only one or the other dimension—highlight the difficulty. Let's look at the action tendency first. Some people find it difficult to keep clear on the purpose of enacting new behaviors. We have seen people act for a host of

Running a Test of One's Big Assumption

LET'S RETURN TO DAVID to see how his adaptive work combined mindset and behavior. A few weeks into the follow-up process, David chose to stop doing some of the tasks he had always done himself and instead asked others on his team to handle them. Before asking for this help, David used his knowledge of people's strengths and preferences to decide whom to ask; in doing so, he increased the likelihood that people would succeed with the task.

Recall that a key reason David wanted to delegate better was so he could focus on select, critical issues. He clarified his top three priorities and started to work on them.

So far, David's change work has been behavioral. Without a next step, his new behaviors would constitute a technical solution to his adaptive challenge—that is, actions taken "to get better" versus "to get information." But when he uses new behaviors to test his mindset, gathering data about himself as a leader and his ability to still add value when he stops trying to do all tasks and instead pursues his priorities, he shifts into adaptively working on his goals. For this to be a good test, he can't know, in advance, how he will feel. The data he gathers may reinforce his conception of the problem and his continued need to protect himself, or it may begin to lead him to reformulate the problem and reduce or dissolve its either/or quality.

He collects a variety of data by surveying his team and observing what happens over time when he delegates: When he gives people a chance to shine, they complete tasks better than he would have; he has mixed feelings about their success (loving that people are flourishing but also feeling a "bit of a blow" himself); people appreciate his intention to be more open to others' ways of doing things; he feels proud that he has figured out that giving starting and end points and providing context enable people to succeed; and he sees himself adding value by "giving the lines."

He simultaneously collects data about what happens when he works on his priorities over time: He feels that his work is not big enough or personal enough at first, but then discovers new and deeper ways to connect to people, more energy and better outcomes. All of these fuel his excitement and belief in the even greater value he now adds by letting go of "doing the details" and instead thinking and planning around the right work.

His initial assumption was this: "I believe that leadership without doing is 'overhead' and worthless. I'd walk away from my roots if I was not doing the work itself. I would be selfish, lazy, and spoiled, and lose my self respect." After testing this mindset with new behaviors and collecting data about the outcomes of these behaviors, his revised assumption was this: "It's not that I need to do it, but I need to know it. I need to understand how the parts fit together in order to do the big-picture work effectively. Maybe it's not even having the skill to do the work, but it's having the detailed information."

other reasons, including wanting to prove to themselves that they could do "it" (whatever their behavior challenge was), to get something done, or to be brave and get "it" over with. Problem solved. (This happens even for people who understand and accept the premise of the four-column map—that behavior is symptomatic of a system, and any lasting change will require the *system* to change.) Like a patient who prematurely discontinues a course of penicillin because the painful symptoms have been eliminated, many people confuse short-term alteration of specific behaviors with the actual accomplishment of their goal.

It's a completely understandable confusion. If you have wanted to lose ten pounds for ten years and a diet finally helps you do it, you might well assume you have accomplished your goal. But your goal actually isn't to lose ten pounds. Many people (even you?) have lost ten pounds *many times*! The goal is to lose ten pounds *and keep the weight off*. Dieting doesn't lead to weight loss that endures. For this we must join a change in behavior with a change in the way we think and feel—and in order to change the way we think and feel, we need to change our mindsets. When we are working on truly adaptive goals—ones that require us to *develop* our mindsets—we must continually convert what we learn from behavioral changes into changes in our mindsets.

Nor is the work accomplished by just seeking "insights," as empowering or clarifying as those insights might feel. This is the other common tendency we see: People are struck by the self-understanding their 4-column map affords, but then they get mired in their thinking, analyzing and reflecting, with little inclination to act. Those who take this route may be operating on their personal, often tacit, theory of change, which champions self-awareness of one's internal world. The presumption might be that understanding more and more deeply what motivates us is the means to change, or that untangling our thinking is key. But reflection without action is ultimately as unproductive as action without reflection.

Interestingly, as diametrically opposite as the two unproductive approaches are, they share an identically flawed theory of action. "If I can just accomplish *one more* (one more behavior, or one more insight), it will finally unlock the key to why I cannot change."

ACHIEVING ADAPTIVE CHANGE:
THE COMMON THREADS

Our discussion so far has focused on what a David or a Cathy needs from within—guts, head and heart, and hand—to work adaptively. But in both their cases, it is not coincidental that the social milieu also plays an important role. We are not just referring to the relationship each had with a coach, either. More importantly, we are flagging the contributions of people who were a seamless part of each person's change narrative, be they team members, a spouse, a best friend, or a colleague.

Without such an environment, it is very difficult to see ourselves fully. Inevitably, we are limited by our own perspectives. In one of our favorite cartoons, Gary Larson shows us an earnest artist at work. His model sits before him in perfect repose, but on the canvas her likeness is obliterated by a giant insect. It can take us a while to make sense of the cartoon—until we see a tiny fly on one lens of the artist's glasses. If he never shows anyone his work, the artist can be quite pleased with his rendition of reality! At the same time, he is missing any predictable outside source for challenging his flawed world view. Without such a challenge, it becomes too easy for him to drift out of the zone for transformation, and stay stuck in his current mindset.

It is easier to stay in the zone and make progress when there is a social dimension to our learning. We let someone know we are working on becoming, for example, a better listener (maybe we ask them to be a survey respondent). Once they know our intent, we can turn to them at any point to ask for input. Or they may spontaneously tell us how much they appreciated our listening to them during yesterday's meeting. They might even be so bold as to let us know what we did or did not do concerning our intent to be better listeners. Sometimes just seeing someone in the hall or hearing another's voice on the phone reminds us what we are working on. These cues can quickly and effectively get us back into the zone. Additionally, simply knowing that others know what we are working on can provide a form of social accountability; in this way, we count on others to help hold us to our own goals.

What we have described so far are the key features of working adaptively: working from the gut, linking head to heart, and taking a specific kind of action (the hand), all within a social context. When we see all these ingredients in place, we see people change. What is common across all the people we have helped to accomplish adaptive challenges?

- They all succeed at changing both their mindset (the meaning-making system that shapes thoughts and feelings) *and* their behavior; rather than changing only mindset *or* behavior, and hoping the other will eventually follow.

- They all become keen and focused observers of their own thoughts, emotions, and behaviors, and they learn to use these as information. They see the agenda that is driving them, not just the agenda they are driving.

- Changes to their mindsets are always in the direction of seeing and feeling more possibilities: Spaces people had previously thought they could not or should not enter (because they were out of reach or too dangerous) are now fully accessible.

- They take focused risks and build a new set of muscles and metrics around assumptions based on actual, rather than imagined, data about the consequences of their new actions. Their anxiety around the initial adaptive challenge is reduced, if not eliminated, while their experiences of pleasure significantly increase.

- They experience increased mastery, more options, wider control, and greater degrees of freedom. They make progress on, or even accomplish, their column 1 commitment, and, more often than not, their accomplishments extend considerably beyond the initial aspiration. Because they have developed new mental capabilities—not just a new solution to a single problem—they can bring these capabilities to other challenges and other venues, in their work and in their personal lives.

Are you ready to start unlocking potential in yourself, your colleagues, your work group, or your organization? Are you interested in seeing what happens, for you or others, when once-countervailing energies are made available for other purposes? If so, what might be your own best next step? Our recommendation is that you have a first-hand experience of your own immunity-to-change. What would your own X-ray look like? What does an improvement goal of your own become when you convert it into what we would call a "good problem"? What would it really mean for you personally to work on your own "good problem" by letting it first "solve you"? If any of these questions are of interest to you we invite you to turn to the chapters that follow.

[9]

DIAGNOSING YOUR OWN
IMMUNITY TO CHANGE

I N THE YEARS SINCE *How the Way We Talk Can Change the Way We Work* was published, we have guided literally thousands of professionals through the process of constructing their own X-ray, or immunity map, and trained more than a hundred practitioners to guide others through the process. We noticed early in the work that while most people reported having a powerful experience, as many as 30 to 40 percent did not. Many of these people said it was "interesting" or even "worthwhile," but they clearly had not had as valuable a learning experience as their colleagues.

So we set out to identify and strengthen those places in the process where some people's maps lost compression. As a result of these revisions, we have greatly reduced our "failure rate." It is not uncommon now for nearly everyone who undertakes the process to develop an immunity map that feels powerful or intriguing (a 4 or 5 on a scale of 1–5).

If you have never gone through the process of constructing your own immunity map, you are about to be the beneficiary of these enhancements. If you read *How the Way We Talk Can Change the Way We Work* and went through the map-making process described there, we strongly encourage you *not* to skip this chapter. We believe you are likely to create a more powerful version this time through, as we help you to avoid the most common pitfalls along the way.

GETTING STARTED

We can't emphasize enough the importance of defining a good column 1 improvement goal. As an example, let us tell you the two different ways we got people started when we worked with Peter Donovan's senior team, which we introduced in chapter 2. The first way led to a perfectly interesting three-hour experience with absolutely no impact. The second method initiated a process that, over time, as you heard from Peter, positively altered the DNA of the leadership team of the company.

On the first occasion, we were given an afternoon of a three-day leadership retreat for the executive staff (eighteen members, including all the C-level leaders and their direct reports). The first time any of these people considered a first-column improvement goal was the very moment we stood in front of them at the offsite. We gave them a few minutes to think about three or four of the most important and challenging aspects of their job, and then we asked, "What would be most important for you to get better at—in order to perform any or all of these aspects *significantly better?*"

Each person easily came up with something, and each then proceeded gradually to build an X-ray showing how and why they systematically were preventing themselves from accomplishing this very thing. Many people found the experience of creating the map an especially intriguing way of spending a few reflective hours together. They remarked, as people often do, that they "couldn't see it coming," and appreciated the surprise of being "hit in the face" with something they hadn't seen in themselves. They thought the whole concept of an immunity to change was stimulating and illuminating. Peter thanked us for a productive session and assured us he thought the work would be valuable for the team.

But it wasn't.

We talked with Peter a year later and he concluded that what we had done had had absolutely no effect on anyone or anything in the company. His interpretation was something we have since heard from many leaders who have gotten involved with our process:

> It's one thing if the purpose of the exercise is just to demonstrate the immunity to change as an interesting concept. Having people use their own experience is a clever way of getting them personally involved with a set of ideas. But if the purpose is really to bring about significant change in individuals—and, in our case, if the goal is to bring about significant change in a whole team— then *everything depends* on what people put in that first column! After all, even if you carry on the work after the diagnostic [the subject of our next chapter], it ends up being an investment in dramatic change only *along the lines of whatever is in that first column,* and if what is in that first column is not the absolutely optimal goal, then no matter how good the technology, it is being applied to the wrong thing!
>
> You can't just let people choose all by themselves what they put in that first column. We all need input. One of the big messages of your work is that we fool ourselves, right? So, since this is true, how can any of us be expected to be the best source of information on what it is we should really work at improving?

Peter and his two top lieutenants were intrigued enough to try again with a different approach. They saw that, like many organizations, they spent a lot of time evaluating their personnel, giving people feedback, identifying improvement goals—and then, a year later, they didn't notice much change. They had two thoughts:

- Perhaps the immunity-to-change process can "unstick" this familiar story, and ratchet up the ROI on all this assessment and feedback.

- People come out of our evaluation sessions with too many personal improvement goals. What if we identify just "one big thing" and focus all our attention relentlessly on that?

So energetically did they then draw people into the process of identifying their improvement goals that the term "one-big-thing," as you saw in chapter 3, became a lasting part of the lexicon of the company. Every executive was asked to identify a single goal that "would excite you personally if you were able to make big gains on this goal" and "would clearly enable you to add more value to the company." The goal should not be something technical that you could accomplish by learning some new skill. Rather it should clearly involve your own growth as a person. At the same time, the goal should not be something that would require a complete personality transplant.

Before the next executive team retreat, every member got one-on-one feedback from several sources:

- The person to whom they report: "Here's the improvement goal that is going to make the biggest difference to me in evaluating you this year for bonus [or promotion, or whatever]."

- Peers: "Here's the thing I think would make you a better team member."

- At least one person who reported to them: "Here's what would enable me to serve you better."

The top leaders shared with each other what particular one-big-thing was shaping up for each of their direct reports, and then they pushed each other: "Are we each honestly excited about each person's goal? Do we all feel that each of these one-big-things would make a big difference for the company?" They also challenged each other regarding *their own* one-big-thing. In addition to each other, they consulted their executive coaches and, in some cases, they asked ownership and people from ownership's office, to make sure they had good improvement goals themselves. And they didn't stop with purely in-office canvassing. As Peter has described, they went home and checked to see whether family members also felt they would see big benefits were the person to make real improvement on the chosen goal.

A colleague of ours—an expert on research methodology—says, "You can't solve by brilliant analysis later on what you screwed up at the start in the original design." So how can we help you not to screw up your original design? Our first tip is this: don't expect to complete this chapter in a single sitting. You will need to get a little external input even before you make your first-column entry. Talk to the people around you, at work and at home, and find out if the prospect of achieving your proposed goal brings a shine to their eyes. Ask them if they have an alternative goal to propose, something they think would be even more valuable for you; something they personally would be even happier to see. Don't enter your first-column goal until you are certain its accomplishment would be a big deal not just to you, but to people around you.

COLUMN 1: YOUR IMPROVEMENT GOAL

Once you have completed this prework, start to create your map using the template shown in figure 9-1. To help us guide you through your own X-ray, we are going to introduce Fred, a real executive, whose unfolding map will provide examples for your own. (Fred is the fellow we referred to in chapter 8, whose goal to be a better listener was made more urgent when he learned of its importance to his relationship with his daughter.)

FIGURE 9-1

Create your own immunity X-ray

1 Commitment (improvement goal)	2 Doing/not doing instead	3 Hidden competing commitments	4 Big assumptions
		Worry box:	

So you've gotten some internal input and you have now entered your own first-column goal, right? (Okay, we know you haven't! You're just reading on from the prior pages. But c'mon! Your whole understanding of what the immunity to change really is will be much deeper if you have a direct experience of it as it applies to *you*! Take your time. Do your homework; then, and only then, enter your first draft of an improvement goal, your commitment, in column 1.)

Figure 9-2 shows Fred's original first-column entry. Fred was able to affirm all of the following about his goal, and, as you look at yours, you should be able to do the same:

- It's important to him. It would be a big deal for him if he could get dramatically better at this. He very much *wants* to get better at it; he even feels some urgency about getting better at it. It's not just that it would be *nice* if he could; he feels the *need* to, for whatever reason.

- It's important to someone around him. He knows that others would value it highly if he could get better at this.

FIGURE 9-2

Fred's first-draft column 1 improvement goals

1 Commitment (improvement goal)	2 Doing /not doing instead	3 Hidden compet-ing commitments	4 Big assumptions
To be a better listener (to not let my mind wander), to not get so impatient		Worry box:	

- He is clear that accomplishing this goal primarily implicates *him*. His focus for improvement in this area is on *himself,* changes *he* will have to make. (After all, it is possible for someone with his goal to feel otherwise, as in, "If only people didn't waste my time with boring or insignificant communications I would in fact *be* a much better listener.")

If your current draft of your first-column entry falls short in any of these respects, don't worry. That is a common shortcoming with first drafts of this exercise. However, if it *does* fall short, you should not just continue to your second column. That is another common mistake. The power and utility of your ultimate map will be maximized if you take the time to revise your entry until it meets all of the above criteria.

Although Fred's entry may meet all these criteria, we can see another that it does not meet, and this will give us a chance to illustrate what we mean by revising your first draft. He tends to elaborate on his goal in the negative—by saying what he does *not* want to do ("to not let my attention wander, to not get so impatient"). We have found that people tend to end up with maps they experience as more powerful when they start out by saying affirmatively what they want to *become* rather than what they want to *stop* being. Accordingly, Fred revised his first-column entry as shown in figure 9-3, and if you notice this tendency in your own entry, we suggest you do the same.

COLUMN 2: THE FEARLESS INVENTORY

From the sample X-rays you have seen throughout the book, you know that the next step is to take a fearless inventory of all the things you are doing (or not doing) that work *against* your first-column goal.

We will turn you loose to make these entries in your own second column in a moment, but first, some further clarification:

- The more concrete behaviors you can list (what you actually do or fail to do), the better. Fred, for example, initially wrote in his second column, "I get impatient." Similarly, someone

FIGURE 9-3

Fred's revised column 1 improvement goals

1 Commitment (improvement goal)	2 Doing /not doing instead	3 Hidden competing commitments	4 Big assumptions
To be a better listener (especially better at staying in the present, staying focused, being more patient)		Worry box:	

whose goal is to be better with difficult conversations might have initially entered, "I am uncomfortable with conflict." Neither of these are optimal entries because these are states of mind, not external behaviors. We would ask that person, "But what do you actually *do* or *fail to do* as a result of your impatience, discomfort, or other unpleasant feelings?" Before you create your own list, have a look at Fred's second-column entries in figure 9-4.

- The more items you enter here, and the more honest you are, the greater the eventual diagnostic power of your map will be. Keep in mind that no one need ever see what you enter, so take a deep dive, and tell on yourself. The purpose is not to shame or embarrass you, or assign fault. You will see shortly that the richer you make this column, the bigger the eventual payoff.

- Make sure that *everything* you enter provides a picture of you working *against* your own goal in column 1. (No doubt you are also doing things *on behalf of* your column 1 goal. Good for you, but that is not the nature of the column 2 assignment. We aren't looking for balance here. The best information for revealing your immunity will eventually be found in the things you do, or fail to do, that have the unintentional effect of *undermining* your improvement goal.)

- You should also be clear we are not asking *why* you are doing these things, or for ideas or plans about how you can stop doing these things and get better. The urge to explain our own ineffectiveness and/or to devise strategies to cure ourselves of our wicked ways is often very strong at this point in the process. It's understandable, since for many of us it is uncomfortable to look at a list of our foibles staring back at us in black and white, and we want to do something to make this go away. Try to resist these impulses. For now, you are just trying to go for descriptive depth and honesty. Just the behaviors themselves in all their embarrassing glory.

If you need further clarity or inspiration look at Fred's entries in figure 9-4.

If you get regular feedback, supervision, or evaluation, you may want to consider that input as an additional source of column 2 entries. If not, and if for any reason you are unable to create a rich list of your own counterproductive behaviors, we have a final suggestion, if you have the stomach for it: seek out a few people whom you trust and feel are on your side and just ask them if they can identify any behaviors (or avoidances) in your repertoire that tend to work against your goal. We guarantee you, *they have things to add to your list!* Thank them, and enter their observations in your second column.

Okay, over to you.

When you have finished making your entries, take another glance at the four criteria for column 2 entries, and check to see that your list squares with these. Don't read the next section until you have completed your second column and made any necessary revisions.

FIGURE 9-4

Fred's column 2 entries

1 Commitment (improvement goal)	2 Doing/not doing instead	3 Hidden competing commitments	4 Big assumptions
To be a better listener (especially better at staying in the present, staying focused, being more patient)	I allow my attention to wander off. I start looking at my BlackBerry. I make to-do lists in my mind, or even literally on a slip of paper. If I'm trying to listen to a client, I'll often start thinking of what would be an impressive response and stop listening to what he is saying. If it's my daughter, I'll often start thinking of what she should do differently, and stop listening to what she is saying. If it's my wife, I'll often feel "this is not urgent" and my attention will shift to something that I think is urgent.	Worry box:	

COLUMN 3: HIDDEN COMPETING COMMITMENTS

Have you been wondering about the empty square at the top of column 3 in figure 9-1? It's what we call the worry box, and it will help you develop raw material for your column 3 entries.

Step 1: Filling Your Worry Box

When you look at the X-rays throughout this book, it should become obvious that the column 3 commitments produce something unexpected for their authors. It is not until we complete the third column, after all, that we begin to see the hidden dynamic, the immunity to change, emerge. We begin to see a whole different set of competing commitments that live alongside the improvement goals of column 1. In chapter 2, for instance, we understood that Peter genuinely wanted to:

- Be more receptive to new ideas

- Be more flexible in his responses, especially regarding new definitions of roles and responsibilities

- Be more open to delegating and supporting new lines of authority

But when we got to the third column in his map, we learned that he also had commitments (or, more properly, these commitments also *had him*):

- To have things done *my* way!

- To experience myself as having a direct impact

- To feel the pride of ownership; to see my stamp on things

- To preserve my sense of myself as the super problem solver, the one who knows best— yesterday, today, and tomorrow

In looking at the third column of the various X-rays we've shown, you may have wondered, "However did they get people to see these things?" The hard work we hope you have been doing on the first two columns should now help you complete your own third column. The result, across the three columns, should be a picture— you will see in a moment—that intrigues you and can serve as a platform for eventually meeting your own adaptive challenge.

The first step in creating good entries for column 3 is to generate the raw material that will eventually get you there. Have a look at your column 2 list and answer the following question about each of those entries: If I imagine myself trying to do the *opposite* of this, what is the most uncomfortable or worrisome or outright scary feeling that comes up for me?

Peter thought about what would be the most uncomfortable, unpleasant, or scary thing for him if he tried to actually share more of the authority and shaping of the company, and what he got to was, "Eeech. I'd feel less important; I'd *be* less important; I could be displaced, become a marginal player in my own company. Yuk!"

The "Eeech" and the "Yuk" are important. The goal is to locate an actual loathsome *feeling*, not just a thought or an idea about an unpleasant feeling. The goal is to let yourself vicariously experience a little of this feeling, and only then to put that feeling into words.

Go ahead and look at each of your column 2 entries and, in the worry box in column 3, jot down the biggest worry, discomfort, or outright fear that comes up when you think of trying to do the opposite of the behavior you wrote down.

We are at another critical point here, a place where, if you do not take this to sufficient depth, the map you come up with will not have enough power. If you haven't located a genuine "oh, shit" kind of feeling, you are probably not there yet. You have to really reach some fear, and if you haven't gotten there yet, you might ask yourself, "and what would be the worst about *that* for me?" *You need to get to a place where you feel yourself at risk in some way; where you are unprotected from something that feels dangerous to you.*

Many of you have probably gotten to this point all on your own. But since we want to increase the chance that nearly *all* of you will have a powerful map at the end of this chapter, let's take a look at a typical not-yet-there entry, and what you can do about it.

Fred took a first shot at this in his quest to become a better listener:

> If I think of not allowing my attention to wander off, what's the worst feeling that comes up for me? The first thing that comes up is just boredom and the next is impatience. I just hate the feeling of being bored, that what I am doing has no important point. I'm not engaged. It's like the feeling of waiting for a plane

to land. I'm waiting for life to happen, but life is not happening. I'm having to listen to a lot of stuff that frankly doesn't matter, or that I already know, or that I got from the person in the first two minutes and now he is saying it all over again in some slightly different way. I hate that. The boredom often runs quickly into impatience. I haven't time for this. There are a lot of balls in the air, things that need attending to, and I've got to get moving. So, boredom and impatience. Two awful feelings, and those are the feelings that come up.

This is a very common example of not yet going quite deep enough in this step, not yet identifying what is really the anxiety in the wings here. We have learned that some people quickly identify certain kinds of negative feelings that are like valuable "book covers"—they've drawn the right volume from the shelf, but now they need to open the cover and read what is inside.

Boredom is one of these common covers. We get bored because we have disengaged. But often we back off for a very good reason! Often we have disengaged because of something awful we didn't want to feel. Something happened, very quickly, *before* the disengagement that led to the feeling of boredom. What is that awful something? When we asked Fred about this, he quickly got to a deeper place: "If I don't disengage with my teenagers, I'm left feeling like whatever I say, they are going to roll their eyes; I am going to feel humiliated by their disdain. That is actually a very awful feeling for me. If I don't disconnect with my wife, I often have a feeling of helplessness that the situations she is talking about are out of my control. There is nothing I can do about it. I hate that feeling."

Now we are getting to the self really being at risk!

The same is true of impatience. Again, this is a good start; a cover to a valuable book. But what is the text underneath the cover? Am I impatient because I feel I must be somewhere other than where I currently am? How come? What is the danger? Impatience, too, signals some risk to me, but what? Listen again to Fred:

The impatience comes up in a variety of ways. I'll be listening to someone and something they say reminds me of something that needs doing. If I don't allow myself to go there in my mind, I feel terror that one of the balls I am juggling is going to drop. I have a lot going on in my life, and the truth is that I'm not a very well-organized person. If I don't attend to the worry that has come up for me, I could forget about it, and something bad could happen.

Sometimes, with my kids, or with junior people in the company, the impatience has to do with an alarm that *they* are going to screw up. When I think of just continuing to listen, and stifling my urge to start giving my wonderful advice, I worry, for example, that my daughter is going to take a big wrong turn in her life.

So what was originally boredom and impatience we now see is:

- The fear of looking stupid

- The fear of being humiliated

- The fear of helplessness

- The fear of being out of control

- The fear of making a big mistake

- The fear of allowing someone else to make a big mistake (especially someone for whom I am responsible)

This is what went into Fred's worry box in column 3.

Now take a look at what *you* have generated for this step, as you considered doing the opposite of what you wrote in column 2, and see if you have reached this level of fear—feelings of being unprotected in some way against a danger or a risk you absolutely do not want to run.

Step 2: Generating Possible Competing Commitments

The actual entries for column 3, however—the hidden competing commitments—are not these fears in the worry box themselves. The fears, we said, are the raw material for generating third-column commitments. The idea behind the immunity to change is that we do not merely have these fears; we sensibly, even artfully, protect ourselves from them. We create ways of dealing with the anxiety these fears provoke. We are not only afraid; we take action to combat our fears. We defend ourselves from what terrifies us. We are actively (but not necessarily consciously) committed to making sure the things we are afraid of do not happen.

This is the heart of a third-column commitment. It is a commitment to keep the thing we are afraid of from happening. Fred not only fears looking stupid; without his realizing it, he may also have a commitment *to not looking stupid*. (Or, more precisely, a commitment to not looking stupid *has him*.)

He does not merely passively "have a fear" of looking stupid; he actively behaves in ways that very effectively, even brilliantly, protect him from looking stupid to his teenagers. How does he do this? He disengages when they speak, makes himself bored, finds something else that needs doing in his mind. He worries that if he really stays present to them and listens, and tries to respond out of his listening, they are going to be disdainful and roll their eyes, and he is going to feel humiliated, a feeling that is almost unbearable for him. And so, he does a very intelligent thing—he withdraws.

His withdrawing is now perfectly understandable, to us and to him. It is perfectly sensible. On behalf of his commitment to protect himself from humiliation, we could say he should withdraw even more than he currently does! His behavior is highly effective. It just has one drawback: It will prevent him from making any progress on his improvement goal, a goal that is very important for him to accomplish. He can see here an expression of how he systematically prevents progress on his own goal. He is captive of a mental system that is working to protect him, to save his life as he knows it—a perfectly effective immune system.

Fred can now go ahead and convert *each* of the fears he identified into a possible third-column commitment (which he holds alongside the goal to be more present and be a better listener). As he fills in his third column, he will see taking shape the dynamic equilibrium that the arrows stretching across the first three columns are meant to suggest. In figure 9-5 he can see a picture of himself with one foot on the

FIGURE 9-5

Fred's column 3 commitments: The immune system comes to light

1 Commitment (improvement goal)	2 Doing/not doing instead	3 Hidden competing commitments	4 Big assumptions
To be a better listener (especially better at staying in the present, staying focused, being more patient)	I allow my attention to wander off. I start looking at my Blackberry. I make to-do lists in my mind, or even literally on a slip of paper. If I'm trying to listen to a client, I'll often start thinking of what would be an impressive response and stop listening to what he is saying. If it's my daughter, I'll often start thinking of what she should do differently, and stop listening to what he is saying. If it's my wife, I'll often feel "this is not urgent" and my attention will shift to something that I think is urgent.	I worry I will: Look stupid Be humiliated Be helpless Be out of control Make a big mistake Allow someone else to make a big mistake (especially someone for whom I am responsible) To not looking stupid To not being humiliated To not feeling helpless To not feeling or being out of control To not making a big mistake To not allowing someone else to make a big mistake (especially someone for whom I am responsible)	

gas (his genuine, even urgent, interest in being a better listener) and one foot on the brake (all those countercommitments).

We invite you to go ahead and generate some possible third-column commitments of your own. Each of them will be a commitment to *not* having the things you'd fear most (from step 1) occur. If your worry box holds something like "I'm afraid I will lose credibility" or "People will dislike me; see me as one of Them," then you might enter third-column commitments such as, "I am committed to not losing credibility" or "I am committed to not running the risk I will lose credibility"; "I am committed to not having people dislike me, to not having people think I have gone over to the 'dark side.'"

There is no sense in reading further until you have actually entered your third-column commitments. Have you done this? Do you now have a picture of your own version of the phenomenon of the immunity to change? Does your picture intrigue you? Do you find it interesting? Notice the questions we are not asking you. We are not asking if you feel you have solved anything. You should not feel that you have. We are not asking whether you are happy to see this picture. Is it an altogether pleasant experience to see your own immunity? Often it is not.

You will remember Einstein's injunction that it can be as important to see the problem clearly as to see the solution. All we are going for right now is a more adequate grasp of "the problem," the problem of your genuinely wanting to succeed with your first-column goal but not being able to do so. You should see the way you have a foot on the gas and a foot on the brake. And that picture, however temporarily unnerving, should at least feel interesting, should draw you in with the power of seeing something you did not know before. But it is also possible that you have long been aware of the personal issue that appears in your third column (you always knew that pleasing others was too big a thing for you, or that you were a control freak, or that you worried you were not smart enough), yet the new discovery may come from seeing, in a new way, how tightly this familiar issue is tied to your inability to succeed on the goal in your first column.

In whatever way the map, or X-ray, feels powerful, the important thing is that it does. What if it doesn't? Fred's map felt powerful to him after writing his third-column entries because all of the following were true. See if these conditions are true for you, as well:

- Each of Fred's third-column commitments is clearly a commitment to *self-protection*. Each is tightly tied to a particular fear. If he noted in his worry box that he had a fear he would destroy his marriage by overworking, he wouldn't bleach out the self-protection by writing his third-column commitment as, "I am committed to a better work/family balance." We wouldn't see the danger from which he is committed to protecting himself if he framed it that way. Rather, he would write, "I am committed to not having my wife abandon me and my children hate me, and becoming a miserable, lonely workaholic."

- Each commitment makes some (or all) of the obstructive behaviors in column 2 perfectly sensible; he can see how, given X commitment, Y behavior is just exactly what anyone might do.

- He sees exactly why trying to succeed merely by eliminating his second-column behaviors won't work, because those behaviors are serving a very important purpose.

- He feels stuck because he sees that he is moving in two opposite directions at the same time.

We have learned that if your map does not yet feel powerful or intriguing at this point in the process, it is likely because your entries do not match these criteria in some way. Try to revise them so that they do, and see if your picture gets more compelling to you. Remember, the power or intrigue we are going for here is not yet one of solution or even a road to solution. The experience is not yet one of liberation.

So just what kind of power or intrigue are we talking about? This might best be illustrated with a story about a university provost who participated in one of our institutes. The program was expressly for university presidents, provosts, and the like. It was a summer program at Harvard, and, as with all of our summer programs, we tell the participants to dress casually. There are always a few people who do not dress casually on the first day (probably because they are uncertain whether their definition of casual is someone else's definition of being a slob). This particular participant, a middle-aged woman, wore a beautiful power suit the first day and an elegant string of pearls around her neck. Every day, as the others became more and more informal in their dress and demeanor, she sat in the middle of the case conference room, with one lovely business suit after another. She sat with a dignified and erect bearing. And always with the pearls.

When we came to filling out the third column, we explained the criteria and what we were really asking them to go for in their entries. We said something like, "And if you get good entries in your third column, your map should stop looking like a collection of notes in response to a bunch of separate questions. Rather, you should begin to see a single, whole thing, across those three columns. You should begin to see a coherent picture. You should begin to see—"

And before we could finish the sentence, it was obvious that she had already gone ahead and made her third-column entries, and the wholeness, the "singleness," the coherence of her picture had hit her square in the face. This dignified, formal, erect woman with the pearls blurted out, to everyone's surprise and delight, "I can tell you what you'll see, all right. You'll see how you are—how you are *screwed*!!"

That succinctly sums up our aim at this point in the process—namely, that you now see more clearly how your own important goal is "screwed" by your core contradictions. That is, there is no way for you to move forward since every genuine, sincere, earnest step in the right direction is countered by an equal force in the opposite direction.

If your map offers you similar insight, then you have reached a paradoxical place in the process—namely, that it may only be by seeing more deeply how you are systematically preventing your own change that you put yourself in a dramatically better position to bring about that change! You will have succeeded in taking the first big step toward converting your change goal into a *good problem*.

Now what's the next step? You need to create a tool for adaptively (rather than technically) working on your change challenge. This tool is what completes the four-column exercise.

COLUMN 4: THE BIG ASSUMPTIONS

The intent of an immunity map is to support a way to treat adaptive challenges adaptively, rather than technically. This begins, we said in chapter 2, by creating an adaptive formulation, one that shows us how our first-column goal brings us to the current limits of our development.

We said an adaptive formulation will register on both the *thinking* and *feeling* levels. If we have succeeded in helping you make a powerful map so far, you have a glimpse of your own immunity to change as it involves the improvement goal you identified in column 1. You should now be able to see your own change-prevention system (how you systematically generate the very behaviors that prevent progress on your goal) and an anxiety-management system (how generating these behaviors helps to ward off some of your worst fears, which are associated with your actually making the progress you hope for).

One sign that you have come up with an adaptive formulation of your challenge is when you can see clearly why a technical approach—going straight to the obstructive behaviors in column 2 and trying to eliminate or reduce them—is not a winning plan. Given how well these same behaviors serve the commitments of column 3, you would be inclined to keep generating them (or their cousins)—unless you were able to reconstruct the immune system as a whole.

The most reliable route to ultimately disrupting the immune system begins by identifying the core assumptions that sustain it. We use the concept of big assumptions to signal that there are some ways we understand ourselves and the world (and the relationship between the world and ourselves) that we do not see as mental constructions. Rather, we see them as truths, incontrovertible facts, accurate representations of how we and the world *are*.

These constructions of reality are actually assumptions; they may well be true, but they also may not be. When we treat an assumption as if it is a truth, we have made it what we call a big assumption.

Some of our big assumptions are inevitably brittle and necessarily short-lived. There won't be too many more romantic nights for the dinosaurs in figure 9-6.

We are reminded of a Gary Larson cartoon: two airborne pilots are looking out through their windshield. We see an animal ahead of them enshrouded in fog. "Hey," says the pilot to his co-pilot, "what's a mountain goat doing way up here in a cloud bank?!" These pilots won't be able to hold their distorted assumption much longer. Unavoidable countervailing evidence is about to hit them in the face.

Interestingly though, there is a whole other class of distorted assumptions that is much more problematic, because we are so talented at holding the countervailing evidence at bay. In these instances we may be able to keep ignoring the evidence that our assumption is a distortion. We may continue to fly the airplanes of our lives, so to

FIGURE 9-6

Oh, look honey! Make a wish!

speak, with an inaccurate picture of reality. We can use our genius to compensate continuously for all the aerodynamic inefficiencies of our distorted mental model. We are able to keep the plane aloft—but at some cost.

In short, any mindset or way of constructing reality will inevitably contain some blind spot. An adaptive challenge is a *challenge* because of our blind spot, and our *adaptation* will involve some recognition of, and correction of, our blindness.

Thus big assumptions, like competing commitments, normally are out of sight. Making an assumption apparent involves bringing it from "subject" (where we cannot see it because we are so attached to it, so identified with or subject to it) to "object" (where we can now take a perspective on it from outside of ourselves). This is the underlying motion by which *greater complexity* gets created.

Once you have begun to surface some possible big assumptions underlying your own immunity to change, you will be in a much better position to work on your immune system, rather than being captive of it. While this would be very difficult to do "from scratch," the hard work you have already done in creating a picture of your immune system and, in particular, identifying your hidden commitments makes it much less difficult than you might think.

We asked Fred to take a good look at the third-column entries he finally made emerge. Then we asked him to brainstorm all the possible assumptions a person who had such commitments might hold. This was slow going initially, but once he got started, the possible assumptions began to flow. Figure 9-7 shows what he came up with.

In a moment we'll ask you to generate possible big assumptions underlying your own third-column commitments. Before you do, it may be helpful to consider the criteria by which Fred judged the robustness of his entries. All of the following were true for him and his entries, and you should be able to say the same:

- Some of the big assumptions you may regard as true ("What do you mean I *assume* some bad thing will happen? Believe me, some bad thing *will* happen!"); some of them you may see right away are not really true ("I can see that it is clearly not true, but I act and feel as if it *were* true"); and some of

FIGURE 9-7

Fred's full map

1 **Commitment (improvement goal)**	2 **Doing/not doing instead**	3 **Hidden competing commitments**	4 **Big assumptions**
To be a better listener (especially better at staying in the present, staying focused, being more patient)	I allow my attention to wander off. I start looking at my BlackBerry. I make to-do lists in my mind, or even literally on a slip of paper. If I'm trying to listen to a client, I'll often start thinking of what would be an impressive response and stop listening to what he is saying. If it's my daughter, I'll often start thinking of what she should do differently, and stop listening to what he is saying. If it's my wife, I'll often feel "this is not urgent" and my attention will shift to something that I think is urgent.	To not looking stupid To not being humiliated To not feeling helpless To not feeling or being out of control To not making a big mistake To not allowing someone else to make a big mistake (especially someone for whom I am responsible)	I assume there is a limited number of "chances" I get with my teenagers (that if they see me as "stupid" too many times, they will just stop listening to me entirely). I assume there is absolutely nothing positive in an interaction with my kids in which they dismiss and ridicule what I have to say; that such an interaction is clearly worse than no interaction at all. I assume my wife *expects me* to be able to help her solve the difficult problems she shares with me. I assume that "helping" is always a matter of helping someone *take a next step* in the right direction. I assume if I feel helpless there is no way I can be a good listener. I assume if I cannot be in control of the situation things are likely going to get worse.

FIGURE 9-7 (CONTINUED)

Fred's full map

			I assume if I make a big mistake I will not be able to recover from it. I assume if I do not help my kids or junior colleagues to avoid mistakes I am being irresponsible, letting them down, letting my family or company down, and that bad things are going to happen to them.

them you may be quite unsure about ("Part of me feels this *is* true, or true most of the time, but another part of me is not so sure"). However, there is some way in which you have felt, or continue to feel, that every big assumption you list is true. And you might be right. We reiterate, we are not saying all our big assumptions are false. What we are saying is that we can't explore how true or false they are until we have surfaced and tested them.

- It is clear how each of the big assumptions, if taken as true, makes one or more of the third-column commitments inevitable (e.g., if it is absolutely certain that I cannot recover from a big mistake, it then makes all the sense in the world that I would be committed to never making a big mistake). Taken as a whole, the set of big assumptions collectively makes the third-column commitments inevitable, and thus it is clear how they sustain the immune system: The third-column commitments clearly follow from the big assumptions and generate the behaviors in column 2; these behaviors clearly undermine the goal in column 1.

- The big assumptions make visible a bigger world that, until now, you have not allowed yourself to venture into. You see how your big assumptions constitute a "Danger! Do Not Enter!" sign in front of this wider world (e.g., "I could, at least theoretically, step out into a world where I am not always in control, even where I feel helpless. I could enter a world where I do not give advice when it is not asked for, where I consider that my children are more forgiving than I imagine," and so on). It is possible that all these warning signs are completely appropriate and should be heeded, but it is also possible that your big assumptions are evidence that you are limiting yourself to only a few of the rooms in the mansion of your life.

Please generate as many possible big assumptions as you can. Check them against the above criteria. This last step in developing your X-ray may inspire its own "ahas," but that is not necessary at this point. The critical threshold in creating a good map is that once you have completed the third column, you can see and feel your own version of the immunity-to-change dynamic. Having completed this step, your map should feel intriguing, illuminating, or at least interesting to you.

"Okay, okay," you might feel, after seeing your own systematic prevention of the progress you desire, "This captures my attention. Who wants to have a foot on the gas and a foot on the brake at the same time!? But now, what can I do about it?" We are about to take up that very question in the next chapter of this book. In it you will see how identifying the big assumptions, which reinforce your immune system, actually puts you in a position to disrupt it.

$$\left[\ 10\ \right]$$

OVERCOMING YOUR
IMMUNITY TO CHANGE

S EEING HOW OUR self-protective motivations systematically prevent us from achieving exactly what we most most desire is necessary. Insights can be powerful, even exciting, but they do not necessarily lead to transformation. Most people need a structure to help them channel their aspiration, test and gain distance from their big assumptions, and steadily build a new set of ways to bridge the gap between intentions and behavior. That is precisely what our immunity-to-change follow-up process is designed to do.

We begin this chapter with our own assumption—that you now have in front of you, from your work in chapter 9, a picture of your own immunity to change that intrigues you. It commands your attention and your interest. You can see yourself with a foot on the gas (genuinely and urgently wanting more success with the goal you have entered in column 1) and a foot on the brake (actively and continually producing exactly those behaviors most likely to *prevent* any progress on that goal). And you can see the very good reason *why* you are holding yourself back: You want to save your life as you know it. You can see, in your third and fourth columns, the reasons why every one of those obstructive behaviors feels necessary for your self-protection.

So, how might you proceed if you want to do something about this—if you want to overcome your own immunity to change? Before you begin you should:

- Be ready to devote a few months to this process and not expect it to happen overnight

- Choose what form of support for the journey will work best for you

- Consider the variety of tasks and activities we have developed over time that may help you, steadily and progressively, to overcome your own personal version of the immunity to change

A quick word about each of these.

First, the overcoming-immunity work will not take years. Nor will you need to devote enormous amounts of time to it over the next few months. But we do find that you need to be willing to give it your attention consistently for about thirty minutes a week, and that most people notice significant and encouraging changes in about twelve weeks. This means you should obviously not expect to make your way through this chapter in a single sitting. You may choose to read it through, just to get a sense of the road map. But if you actually want to take the trip, you will need to regularly put the book down and *do things* before you can return and carry on.

Second, it's important to decide whether you want to take the trip alone or with company. You might prefer to work through your immunity on your own (using this chapter as a guide), but you have other options. You might find a partner—best of all, someone else who wants to overturn his or her immunity to change—and debrief together as you work your way through the process. Or you may choose to work with a coach who has experience with the full "coaching arc" and can both guide you and help you stick with it. (If you want to pursue this option, let us know and we can put you in touch with one of the many people we have trained.)

Finally, whether you do this on your own, with a partner, or with a coach, you can find your own best combination of exercises from the basic set of activities people have found useful for overturning the immunity to change. We list these below in three phases, with a simple statement of the purpose of each. You have already seen many of these illustrated in prior chapters. And since each person's immune system is unique, not everyone needs to undertake every exercise.

Opening Moves: Setting the Stage

Honing your map: Review and revise your immunity map as needed, so that it feels powerful to you and you have testable big assumptions.

Initial survey: Get external input on the importance and value of your column 1 goal, and create a baseline of how well you are doing on the goal at the start of the process.

Middle Game: Digging into the Work

Continuum of progress: Envision what full success looks like in achieving your column 1 goal.

Self-observations: Tune in to the big assumptions in action and stay alert to counterexamples. Recognize when and where your big assumptions are activated, and when they are inaccurate.

Biography of the big assumptions: For each assumption, ask: When did it get started? What is its history? What is its current validity?

Testing the big assumptions: Intentionally behave counter to how a big assumption would have you act, see what happens, and then reflect on what those results tell you about the certainty of your assumption. Do this process several times, running tests of bigger scope each time.

End Game: Consolidating Your Learning

Follow-up survey: Get input (from the same people who completed your initial survey) on your column 1 goal. Compare your self-assessment of progress with what they see. Learn about the effect of your changes on others.

Identifying hooks and releases: Take stock of the current status of your big assumptions; consider how to maintain progress, guard against future slippage (the "hooks"), and recover when you do (the "releases").

Future progress: Once you are "unconsciously released" from your current big assumption, you may want to reengage the immunities process, especially around any unmet goals or areas in which you currently feel stuck or discouraged.

THE HEART OF THE PROCESS: DESIGNING, RUNNING, AND INTERPRETING TESTS OF THE BIG ASSUMPTIONS

You have seen illustrations of most of these steps in prior chapters—especially chapters 5 and 6, with the cases of David and Cathy. So we are going to devote this chapter to the heart of the process, the activities that are most iterative, take the most time, and serve as the biggest lever for overcoming the immune system—namely, designing, running, and interpreting tests of your big assumptions.

Designing Tests of Your Big Assumption

The purpose of each test you run is to see what happens when you intentionally alter your usual conduct and then reflect upon the meaning of the results for your big assumption. The purpose of a test is *not* to try immediately to improve or get better. Rather it is to get information—a very particular kind of information: "What does this say about my big assumption?" Our experience tells us that it can be hard to keep this intention front and center, so before we put you to work, we want to share with you the most common challenge in designing a test.

Remember the overly enthusiastic tendency to act (without any attention to our mindset) that we mentioned in chapter 8? It's this tendency that leads us, mistakenly, to an event-focused approach to testing the big assumption, where we assume that there is some important action that, if we were able to take it, would "solve" the big assumption and neutralize its effects.[1] A common example is having a long-delayed, difficult conversation with a boss or coworker, surviving it, and moving on.

An event-focused approach views the successful completion of the test as the *concluding* step, the hurdle overcome or the obstacle removed. Once we conduct that test (especially if it seems like a successful experience), we can feel the relief and sense of accomplishment of having completed an important task. We can savor and appreciate the work that's been done. This is all well and good, *but it is not learning*. For purposes of adaptive learning, it's important to understand that the goal in conducting the test *is not just to perform the activity specified in the test*. We need to collect data about what happens as a consequence of that action, and then *interpret those outcomes to confirm or revise our big assumption*. In other words, the test has not actually been successful until its result is connected to our work on the big assumption.

With that as a backdrop, let's put you to work. First, this exercise requires that you know exactly which big assumption you want to test. If you unearthed several big assumptions, now is the time to choose one. The two criteria for selecting are, first, that it's a powerful assumption (it has a strong hold on you and it clearly limits what you experience as "in bounds" in order to feel safe); and second, that it is testable. If you aren't immediately clear which of your big assumptions meets those criteria, see if the following questions help:

- Which big assumption jumps out at you as the one that most gets in your way?

- If you could change any single big assumption, which one would make the biggest, most positive difference for you?

- Is the big assumption so catastrophic that you could never test it? Hint: a big assumption with words like *die*, *be fired*, or *have a nervous breakdown* isn't ripe for testing quite yet. (But don't abandon that assumption; it probably has the advantage of mattering a lot. To make it testable, you may have to back up and unearth a prior assumption in the sequence that leads up to the catastrophe. For example, "I assume if I disagree with the boss I'll be fired" becomes "I assume if I say X, my boss will get angry" and/or "I assume if my boss does get angry that he will find no value in my input" and/or "I assume if my boss finds no value in my input on one occasion, he will permanently end his support of me.")

- Can you imagine some kind of information or data that would cast doubt on the big assumption? Is your assumption falsifiable?

Perhaps you are not yet sure whether your big assumption meets the "testable" criterion. To help you think this through, we are going to bring in a few real clients to serve as examples for your own comparison. We begin with Sue, the chief of staff in a large social services agency.

Sue's Test, Part 1

Sue's original big assumption was this: "If I am not accepted, then people wouldn't like me and I wouldn't have value." She turned this into a testable assumption by identifying what she thought led to her not being accepted: "If I say no, others will see me as cold and uncaring." She chose to focus her first test on the assumption that saying no would lead to damaging relationships.

Now you try it. Write down your assumption as in figure 10-1.

FIGURE 10-1

Write out a testable version of your big assumption

I assume that if . . .

Once you've chosen a big assumption to test, the next step is to design your first experiment to challenge it. Start by asking yourself: what behavior changes would give me good information about the accuracy of my big assumption? Then plan what you will actually do and/or say to make sure you have a fair test. For example, deciding *that* you will say no when asked to take on another task doesn't address *how* you will say it. You could, for instance, bark out an immediate "no," or you could say something like, "I wish I could help you, but I have an overflowing plate right now." One of these ways of saying no is clearly a better test of your assumption that the receiver will be angry at you.

Next, plan for data collection: what information should you gather when you enact that behavior? Data can be external (others' reactions to the new behavior), internal (your own reactions, cognitive and affective), or both. This is the time to consider, in advance, what outcomes would lead you to question the validity of your big assumption. This is a crucial step. If you can't think of any data that could challenge or cast doubt on your assumption, that's a sign that you don't yet have a good test. In that case, you need to go back to the drawing board.

Sue's Test, Part 2

Here's how Sue planned for testing her assumption that "if I say no, others will see me as cold and uncaring."

First, she observed that the situation that most frequently activated her big assumption was when team members confided in her about other team members.

Next, she decided to whom she would be willing to take the risk of saying no.

She then practiced what she would say. (E.g., "This is important. I feel for you; I'm disturbed to hear this. But you're looking at the wrong person. You need to take this directly to this person. How can I help you to talk directly to this person, given I know this person?" Or "I hear your concerns; this is important; I want to listen without having to feel the need to fix." Or "I can't touch this—this is not about me. Our relationship is important, our agency's relationship is important. You need to make a decision to talk directly to the person, or to go to her boss.")

Regarding data, Sue planned to pay attention to how she felt when she said no, and also see what the recipient did or said in response. If she ended up feeling insecure, or thought that the other person saw her as cold or uncaring, or if the relationship suffered, those would all be signs that her big assumption was accurate. But if she didn't feel those things, she would question the absolute truth of her assumption.

In reality, however, we know that not everyone plans their tests.

Claus's Test, Part 1

Claus provides an example of someone who did not plan his first test. This might well have been a plus for him, given that his big assumption is that he needs to be overprepared in order to be effective. When the very assumption the person wants to test risks getting activated by the planning process, test "planning" can be paradoxical. We have worked with many people whose assumptions are like this. For them, the task is to design an effective test without being controlling, overpreparing, attending to every detail in the process, and so on. In Claus's case, it would have been counterproductive to overprepare a test to see if he could be effective with less preparation!

Here is his test: over vacation, Claus decided he needed to talk with a staff member about a reassignment. He hadn't yet thought through how he would approach this person, but when he ran into him during his first morning back at the office, Claus, uncharacteristically, talked with him. "I had so much to do to catch up and I thought to myself, 'if I don't talk to him about this now, when will I?' So I talked with him right then."

What makes this a test, not just an event, is that Claus was attentive to what happened as a consequence of his acting on the spur of the moment. We will take a look at that data and how he made sense of it when we turn to the interpretation dimension of testing.

Had he not acted spontaneously, we would have encouraged Claus to focus less on preparing a test per se and more on thinking through what he deemed "safe" conditions for a test. These would be situations (certain people, topics, meetings) where he would not pay a high price if it turned out that he was ineffective when less prepared.

Having read about the purpose, common pitfalls, and features of a good test, we hope you have gained a good sense of what we are going for in this step and are ready to create your own test.

Here is the exercise. You'll find a guide sheet for completing it in figure 10-2. In this step, we ask you to create a safe, modest experiment testing your big assumption. Your test should lead you to do something different from what you ordinarily would do when routinely holding your big assumption as true. This design is *preparation* for actually running your first formal test of this assumption.

A good test conforms to the following S-M-A-R-T criteria:

- S-M: It is important that your experiment be both *safe* and *modest*. You might ask yourself, "What can I risk doing, or resist doing, *on a small scale* that might seem inadvisable if I held my big assumption as true, in order to learn what the results would actually be?"

- A: A good test will be *actionable* in the near term. This means that the test is relatively easy to carry out (ideally, it doesn't require you to go out of your way at all, but rather is an opportunity to do something different in your normal day) and can be conducted within the next week or so.

- R-T: Finally, you are clear that you are taking a *research* stance (not a self-improvement stance); you are running a *test* of your big assumption. A good test will allow you to collect data related to your big assumption (including data that would qualify your assumption or call it into doubt).

FIGURE 10-2

Guide sheet for designing a good test of the big assumption

1a. Write below what you are going to do. (Make sure you are doing something different from what your big assumption would normally have you do.)

1b. Jot down how you think your test (1a) will get you information about your big assumption.

2a. Next, what data do you want to collect? In addition to how people react to you, *your feelings* can be a very rich data source.

2b. How will that data help you to confirm or disconfirm your big assumption (BA)? (What results would lead you to believe your BA is correct? What results would lead you to question the validity of your BA?)

2c. Is there anyone you'd like to give a "heads-up" to or ask to serve as an observer who can give you feedback after the fact?

3. Finally, review your test on these criteria:

—Is it safe? (If the worst case were to happen, you could live with the results.)

—Is the data relevant to your BA? (See question 2b.)

—Is it valid? (The test actually tests your big assumption; see question 1b.)

—Are the data sources valid? (Choose sources who are neither out to get you nor trying to protect or save you.)

—Might it actually reinforce your big assumption? (Is it designed so that it surely will lead to bad consequences, just as your BA tells you? Are you setting yourself up to fail? Is there any data you could collect that could disconfirm your BA?)

—Can it be done soon? (The person or situation you need in order to enact the test is available, you are reasonably certain you know how to do what you plan, and you can run the test within the next week or so.)

As a first step, consider what behavior you could change (start or stop doing) that would yield useful information about your big assumption. Here are some options:

- Alter a behavior from column 2.

- Perform an action that runs counter to a column 3 commitment.

- Start directly from your big assumption (column 4): "What experiment would tell me whether the if-then sequence built into the assumption is valid?"

- Go to your continuum of progress (see chapters 5 and 6 for illustrations) and enact a version of a next recognizable step.

If you've completed the exercise, including question 3, terrific—you have a high-quality design for the first test of your big assumption. Now is a good time to do whatever is needed to increase the likelihood that your test goes well. At a nuts-and-bolts level, remember to contact someone from whom you want feedback. You may want to let this person in on the bigger context of your request as well as the particular kinds of data you hope he or she can give you. The clearer you are up front about what you need, the more likely this person will be able to gather valuable data. Make a plan to debrief with this person as soon as possible after the test.

Here are some things you might find helpful to do before actually running the test to get yourself in the right frame of mind.[2] Practicing what you want to do increases the likelihood you will actually feel prepared to do something that you have little, if any, experience doing.

For example:

- Prepare notes for your test.

- Practice techniques for reducing or eliminating negative "mind chatter."

You may want to imagine different ways the upcoming interaction could unfold and how you might respond and/or assert yourself according to each imagined scenario:

- Consider the implications of tone of voice, body language, choice of words.

- Anticipate how your typical ways of saying things might lead to a foregone conclusion and consider whether there is a more productive approach you could take. Role-play in your head (or with someone you trust) if at all possible.

- Be prepared with alternative strategies for handling things that are often negative triggers for you.

Finally, anticipate things that might make it hard to collect quality data. Here are a few tips to consider:

- You may experience many feelings all at once. Your feelings may change throughout your test, so try to tune in to your emotional channel frequently.

- The more a person is under the grip of his big assumption, the less skillful he is at observing other people (their behavior and their inner states). One of the most essential skills for engaging in adaptive change is the ability to see and hear what is occurring with as little judgment as possible. Seeing and hearing more clearly is where the potential for change starts.

- It is very easy to slip from noticing into interpreting another person's reactions. That invalidates a test. Try to stay attuned to what the person said or did (e.g., he said, "This makes me mad" versus "He was mad at me"). Quality data are directly observable—words and actions, including nonverbal behavior, that could be captured by an audio- or videotape.

Running Tests of Your Big Assumption

Finally, you get to take action. Go ahead and run your test! Remember to collect your data (both what you actually did and what happened as a result). If you don't end up running the exact test you planned, that's okay. Just make sure the actual test you ran still meets the criteria for an effective test (question 3 in the preceding section). If you conclude that your test was flawed, that's not a fatal problem, and it's not unusual. Just remember that you haven't yet generated data that's relevant to testing your big assumption (so whatever happened doesn't confirm or disconfirm your assumption). Your next step should be to see whether you can still do the test you originally hoped to run or you need to design a new test.

Use the form in figure 10-3 to describe your actions and the consequences. Be as neutral a self-reporter as possible. In the next section, we will turn to making sense of, or interpreting, the data.

Before moving to the next step, double check that you have assessed the quality of the actual test you ran (versus what you planned) and the quality of your data, and concluded that both are valid. Once you've done that, you're ready to interpret what happened.

FIGURE 10-3

Guide sheet for running tests of the big assumption

1. What did you actually do?

2a. What happened? What did people actually say or do when you ran your test? If you asked someone for feedback, what did she or he say? What were your thoughts and feelings at the time? (These are your data points.)

2b. Check the quality of your data to make sure it is valid. Is the data about other people's responses to you directly observable, or have you snuck in an interpretation? Would someone else in the room agree with your description? Were there any unusual circumstances in your test?

Interpreting Tests of Your Big Assumption

Designing an effective test of your big assumption is one step. Running it is a next step. Now the challenge is to look at your data for the sole purpose of understanding what it suggests about your big assumption. Remember, the purpose of running a good test is not to see whether you improved, whether your behavior change "worked" (although this is not unimportant!), but rather to use the test results to reconsider your big assumption. You will know you are on track with this exercise if you can see what aspect of your big assumption, if any, is confirmed by the data, and what aspect, if any, is disproved.

The best way to illustrate this step is to pick up where we left off with Sue and Claus so that you can see what they did, what data they collected, and how they made sense of it. After that, we will invite you to interpret your data.

Sue's Test, Part 3

This is the test Sue ran: When one of the two people she felt safe running her test with started telling her he was upset with another team member, Sue told him that she didn't want to get involved and thought it was better for him to talk directly to the other person.

Here's the data she collected. First, her inner thoughts and feelings: "I did it without feeling badly. And I didn't let it worry me that I hated the interaction because it was short and charged. It was what it was and I didn't worry about it throughout the day." The external data? This fellow later called Sue to apologize for dragging her into the issue, saying "I just wanted to tell someone what was happening."

Sue saw these results as initial disconfirmations of her big assumption. While she didn't like saying no, she didn't beat herself up for doing so, and she was glad not to be drawn into the conflict. More important, her colleague's apology led her to see that setting a limit (at least that time) was perfectly acceptable.

Claus's Test, Part 2

And what about Claus?

Here's what happened when he spontaneously talked with his employee:

He recognized the moment as "a real breakthough for me," including that he felt out of his comfort zone. As for the external data, the other person expanded on the topic, which was unusual and a surprise to Claus, given that he thought this would be a touchy issue. Claus also noticed that they were having a real conversation, with back-and-forth between them. Finally, he also was aware that he liked "that I had the guts to do this and not fear failing, even though I tested without thinking about it."

What did the data tell him about his big assumption? In his own words, "This one single experience tells me to not analyze things to death. I can more clearly articulate that I perceive wrongly that by spending more time on it or waiting, it will ripen. But it doesn't, and then I start feeling bad that I haven't done it. Lesson learned? Follow my instincts. Make sure that my head doesn't get in the way of my stomach." He sees how his big assumption creates the false sense that overpreparation is required, when the reality is that it makes him increasingly anxious. He now knows that at least in this situation, his gut feelings were sufficient preparation.

Here are a few tips to keep in mind when you start interpreting your data as in figure 10-4.

- What makes a "big assumption" more than merely an assumption is the belief, implicit or explicit, that what we assume is *always and completely* right. A big assumption automatically informs how we see reality; that is, it is "behind" the eyes, so to speak, rather than in front of the eyes.

FIGURE 10-4

Guide sheet for interpreting tests of the big assumption

1. Take a look at the data you collected. What is your interpretation of what happened?

2. What alternate interpretation can you think of for that same data? When our big assumptions have a powerful hold on us, they direct us to predictable interpretations—ones that keep the big assumption alive and well. An antidote to this tendency is to push yourself to generate at least one additional interpretation of the data.

3. What does your interpretation tell you about the big assumption you tested? What aspects of your big assumption do you believe the data confirm? Which do the data disconfirm? Did any new assumptions emerge?

4. What are your thoughts about a next test of your big assumption? Pick up on what you've learned about your big assumption. What next test could you design to learn more? If you have additional big assumptions, you might want to test those too.

- A single big assumption is rarely completely and always right or wrong. The problem more often is that we tend to overuse big assumptions and overgeneralize their applicability far beyond their scope.

- The point of a test is rarely to reject a big assumption outright, but rather to help sharpen its contours so you have a realistic, data-based version of when, where, and with whom your big assumption is relevant. Even relatively modest changes to a big assumption can overturn an immunity to change.

- It is possible to run a valuable and complete test (for this step) without having been "successful" in some action. For example, we may not have been able to hold the difficult conversation, but we gathered data that allowed us to learn something new about what holds us back, and this leads to a further refinement of our big assumption.

- No single experiment is likely to be conclusive by itself about a big assumption.

The final question in this exercise points to the iterative nature of testing big assumptions. Once we run a test and take stock of its implications for our big assumption, we design another test, one that will provide data on what we next want to learn about our assumption. David and Cathy, whom you met in chapters 5 and 6, and Sue and Claus from this chapter all conducted several tests, with each one leading the person to progressively revise the assumption. Often, the second and third tests are successive versions of the first one. What differs are the players, circumstance, or level of risk. It is the cumulative weight of several tests that, in most cases, begins to overturn the person's immunity to change—the whole purpose, let us not forget, of these exercises. Once the big assumption no longer has its force, the self-protective third-column commitment is no longer necessary, and we stop needing to generate the obstructive second-column behaviors.

Sue's Test, Part 4

Let's continue to follow Sue's next test of her big assumption, "If I say no, others will see me as cold and uncaring."

Sue heard about a blowup between two of her colleagues. She prepared herself for what she would say if one of them came to her to complain about the other. She rehearsed her lines, including saying to herself, "I know I can't fix this, it's much bigger than I am," and she primed herself to be the reflective listener she wanted to be in that situation. When one of her two colleagues, Kati, walked into her office, Sue was ready.

What did Sue do? She reminded Kati of her four-column work and her commitment to not be in the middle these sorts of conversations. "I was careful not to join her in bashing Vicki. And I was careful not to tell her what to do, but instead was a good listener."

What about the data? She paid attention to her feelings, including her comfort and anxiety levels, as well as Kati's reactions to her. She found herself feeling good during the discussion, both because she was able to act and be present in the way she wanted, and because the conversation went in an unanticipated, but very productive direction, where Sue felt that she could raise an issue with Kati. Sue felt good about making herself vulnerable and having a quality conversation that led them both to feel they got something valuable out of their talk.

Sue saw this data as contradicting her big assumption; by setting certain limits, she actually experienced a closer relationship with Kati.

As our self-observing skills get better developed, further tests of our big assumptions can occur quite fluidly. On these occasions we spontaneously act in ways contraindicated by our big assumption, but we become aware of this (at the moment or later) and use it as an occasion to ask, "What happened and what does that tell me about my big assumption?"

Sue's Test, Part 5

Sue had many "spontaneous" tests. A significant one occurred when she had an altercation with her boss, in her view the highest-stakes person to be in conflict with. The event took place in a lead team meeting, when Sue said something that led her boss, Sam, to shout angrily at her. She was bewildered about how her statement led to such an extreme and negative reaction. Imagining that he didn't hear what she said, she found herself asking what her responsibility was in the miscommunication. "I had to check in with the rest of the group—'what did I say?' They told me I was being very clear." In a follow-up conversation with her boss, Sam acknowledged that he had stopped listening.

Her conclusions: "For me personally, I hung with that conflict. I didn't freak out about it, and didn't carry it with me the whole next day. I didn't obsess with it the way I would have six months ago. I now know my relationship with Sam can withstand conflict and that I could hang with him in his clear anger that day."

Very often, future tests reflect our wish to learn about further aspects of our big assumption that revealed themselves only through earlier testing.

Sue's Test, Part 6

Again, let's follow Sue's testing to see a perfect example of testing deeper grounds. Once Sue realized that saying no was not risking relationships, she discovered a whole new learning curve: Could she say what she was really thinking without risking relationships? Could she, in other words, risk *creating* conflict?

"I did say 'I don't agree' to Beth. That was a risk. Internally, I felt that I was pushing. For me it was a risk in the relationship; I took the risk . . . and the good thing is that the relationship stayed intact. I think I can continue to say when I don't agree. But I want to be articulate in my disagreement and not just emotional! I don't think I am as articulate as I'd like to be. A bigger risk would have been to say that I thought that we were avoiding the real issue."

Now it's your turn to develop a second test. Return to the guide sheets provided earlier for the three dimensions of testing (designing, running, and interpreting).

If after a few rounds of testing, you wonder, "How do I know when I am finished?" and "How do I sustain my progress?" you are most likely ready for the following exercise, "Identifying Hooks and Releases."

CONSOLIDATE YOUR LEARNING: IDENTIFYING HOOKS AND RELEASES

Figure 10-5 shows a developmental sequence in overturning an immunity. Take a moment to think about where you are in your journey by using the descriptions of "consciously released" and "unconsciously released"—and we assume that if you are this far into this chapter, you are surely past being "consciously immune."

Which of these two descriptions speaks to you? If your self-assessment is that you are "unconsciously released," then you may find this next exercise useful for simply confirming your sense of where you are. If "consciously released" better describes your current relationship to your big assumption, then one of the following two choices will be most relevant if you want to fully overturn your immune system and succeed with your column 1 commitment.

First, consider continuing with further tests of your big assumption. This is a good choice especially if you are aware that your big assumption grabs hold of you frequently. As we said earlier, the testing process is iterative and there is no set number of tests that will overturn an immune system. If you have been working solo, you might consider finding a trusted friend or colleague to partner with you in your next test design and interpretation. Having someone to talk with can be an enormous help.

A second option is to complete another exercise, which we call "Identifying Hooks and Releases." Designed to increase the likelihood of your continued success, it asks you to take stock of the current status of your big assumption, assess your risk of getting pulled back, and plan for how to guard against slippage. It also leads you to generate the equivalent of a personalized tip sheet (see the italicized portion of "Cathy's Completed 'Identifying Hooks and Releases' Exercise").

So that you can see the potential in this exercise and get a clear answer to the question, "How do I know if I am done?" we want to remind you of the example Cathy gave us in chapter 6. As you read it

FIGURE 10-5

From unconsciously immune to unconsciously released

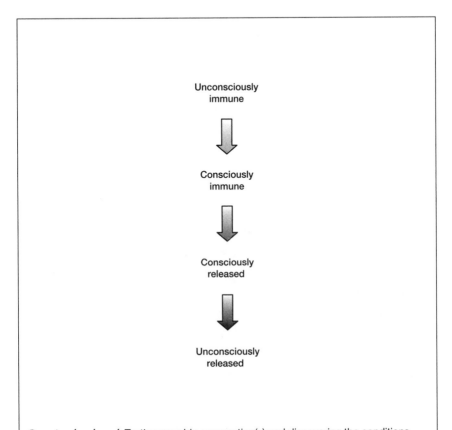

Unconsciously
immune

Consciously
immune

Consciously
released

Unconsciously
released

Consciously released: Testing your big assumption(s) and discovering the conditions under which it is and is not valid is a crucial part of this development phase. This may include discovering that the big assumption is not warranted in any situation. Often people learn new behaviors and new "self-talk" scripts as a part of this testing process. When you can act on your newly discovered knowledge to interrupt the big assumption (and the old behavior and self-talk patterns associated with it) in those situations where it is not valid, you are demonstrating the new capacity to be "consciously released" from your big assumption. This takes mindful practice. The journey is not necessarily straight or free of bumps. It is normal to fall back into old patterns associated with the big assumption. Still, knowing that you're falling back, and knowing how you can get yourself unstuck, are all signs of development. You should also see that you have made progress toward meeting your column 1 goal.

Unconsciously released: When you no longer need to stop, think, and plan in order to interrupt your big assumption, you have developed the capacity to be "unconsciously released" from it. At this point, you automatically act and think in ways that run counter to your previously held big assumption in those situations where it is not valid. New beliefs and understandings, informed and developed mindfully throughout the process, have taken the place of the big assumption. You have likely made significant progress, if not full success, toward meeting your column 1 goal.

this time, we direct your attention to the way it illustrates the benefits of identifying what *hooks* us into a big assumption, and what we can do to *release* ourselves from those hooks.

Cathy's Completed 'Identifying Hooks and Releases' Exercise

Comment on where you now see yourself on the developmental sequence.

I am somewhere between "consciously released" and "unconsciously released." I have significantly revised my biggest "big assumptions" and no longer feel run by them. Instead, I have developed new understandings about myself and my value based on my "Houston event" and continued testing over the past months. I have every reason to believe these new views about myself will keep me from falling back into the old way I thought of myself and others.

I now have a lot of ways to reduce my stress levels, including how not to get stressed to begin with. I use these tools and beliefs regularly, sometimes consciously, and others times, upon reflection, quite unconsciously.

Have you reached any conclusions or developed any hunches about conditions under which your big assumption is valid? Think about particular situations—who, what, where, and when.

I no longer see any time when my big assumption is valid.

Have you reached any conclusions or developed any hunches about conditions under which your big assumption is invalid? Think about particular situations—who, what, where, and when.

Yes. In all of my work. And even in my relationship with my husband.

Do you find your big assumption asserting itself in situations you know it shouldn't? If so, can you generalize about the conditions under which you are likely (more or less) to find yourself being sucked into the old patterns associated with the big assumption? What still sometimes hooks you?

No, my "Houston event" blasted my big assumption.
And since then, I have been learning how to help myself
not get pulled back into that kind of thinking and acting.

Have you developed key "releases" (i.e., self-talk that unhooks you) that you can readily use when facing your big assumption in real time?

I had a plan with some of my team members, which was that I would use a code word or signal to indicate that I had entered into a high-strung state. But I haven't needed my code word, because my earlier steps to interrupt the emotions have been working.

Have you developed new behaviors or ways of talking to yourself in situations that used to activate your big assumption?

Yes. Overall, I am more self-aware and more self-regulating. I am better attuned to what sends me down the path to becoming high strung, and also when I'm on the path. I now have a robust set of effective ways I use to interrupt the cycle before it even starts or to interrupt it once it starts before I become overly emotional.

> *I use my mantra "I have calm."*

> *I use de-stress balls.*

> *When I feel high-strung emotionally, I take a breath both internally and externally to reflect before acting.*

When I am in a situation where someone is saying something that gets me agitated, I tell myself, "Be respectful and calm. This is not the end of the world. You are in control of this situation. You can listen respectfully and then politely disagree."

When I feel something is wrong, I ask myself, "Is it me? Or is it something in the environment?"

When I am aware that I'm getting stressed, I ask myself, "What is in my control here and what isn't?" And then look to make choices based on what's in my control.

I ask myself: "Is this important enough to get hospitalized?"

I make more choices about what I can and can't do with my time.

When I have a timeline, I will tell the person that I don't think I can meet the deadline, or I tell them what I think I can and can't have done by that time. Or I will ask them about whether there is any flex in the timeline given what is on my plate and other commitments I have agreed to meet.

I'll say to myself, "This is what I can't make happen in order to get my priority item taken care of."

Around deadlines, I ask myself, "What will have to give, in order for me to meet this deadline?"

I conduct a process check re: my calendar. I make myself go home by a certain hour on most days and keep that promise to myself. When there are back-to-back meetings, I ask myself, "Is it important to me to attend all of these?"

When I broke my rule of going home by a certain hour, I would call Deb and say that I wasn't going to be in the next day. She was fine about that.

"Is this so important that I should jeopardize my health?"

I pay attention to the value I am adding and what I'm contributing. (And I continue to see my value as not about the product.)

I pay attention to my feelings of confidence that have emerged through this process (letting go of the fear has helped me see what value I am adding).

To what extent/how often can you use these "releases" to help you from being pulled into old patterns?

Consistently.

Think about situations in which you think your big assumption is no longer accurate. What new beliefs or understandings do you hold about "how things work" or what will happen in these situations?

One of my original big assumptions was: If I were to let myself down, then I would feel like I'm not giving as much as I should be giving. That's now changed: my definition of letting down is now different. Before it was about doing, and now it's about being. Like if I didn't speak up or share my insights. It's the act of having the insights. I would be letting myself down if I no longer had the insights or didn't believe that they are of value.

Another of my original big assumptions was: I assume that a good team member—for everyone—is giving 110 percent. I still believe it. What's changed is that 110 percent is not about checking off tasks and making sure everything is perfect. Perfection isn't about crossing every t. It's about perfection in concept, intent, and in thinking about it.

Another original assumption was: I assume a good me is 150 percent. I still think that's true, I just define it differently. Even if it's three minutes. It's a sense that I determined the necessary energy and time that was appropriate. It's the amount of time and quality of thinking that makes for excellence.

My biggest big assumption was: I assume that it's worth the risk for me to burn out than to not go the 110 percent. That's simply not true now.

Any thoughts about what has enabled you to make the changes you have?

Most importantly, I realized that my original big assumptions came out of my operating from a sense of fear. I was afraid that something I loved would be taken away from me and I felt like I had to keep proving over and over to everyone that I was good at this so they should know not to take it away. My "aha" about how my not getting accepted to medical school has kept me worried and afraid all these years was also very important. I realized I believed my not getting in was a reflection on me, that something was wrong with me. And I never voiced that belief; I just kept doing things to make sure that would never again happen to me. It's been a huge relief to unburden myself of that. Emotionally, it's exhausting to have carried that around. Now, I'm freed up from feeling that way.

This whole experience helped me to see that I actually am very good at what I do, and not only because of what I "do," but because of who I am and the unique perspectives I bring to the work. And I recognized that others see that in me too.

The "Houston event" was the catalyst for my understanding this about myself. That Teresa succeeded was a test of my not having to "do" and a confirmation of my value as someone with the particular skills, knowledge, and views I hold. Teresa succeeded because I had set it up as I did, and because I did write the objectives so clearly. My unique value was in the planning process. That newfound confidence was an enormous boost to my change.

I'm very scientific—without proof I don't believe it. It was a forced experiment—Teresa succeeding—my goals and vision were able to be realized without me doing it!

Everything followed from my letting go of my fears
and developing my confidence. I kept trying out ways
to be planful so I could reduce my stress and in the process
found different techniques and self-reminders that worked
for me.

At the very least, the answer to the question, "How do I know if I am done?" should be clear from this example. You are not "done," of course, if you have not realized significant progress on your column 1 goal. But neither are you done if you have *only* realized significant progress, and not forged a strong and continuing channel, as Cathy demonstrates, between behavioral changes and changes in your mindset—that is, changes in your big assumptions.

Now it's your turn to do this exercise using the guide sheet in figure 10-6.

Here's one last question for you if you have completed the hooks and releases exercise: How do you feel about yourself for making the gains you did on such a challenging goal?

FIGURE 10-6

Guide sheet for identifying hooks and releases

1. Comment on where you now see yourself on the developmental sequence.

2. Have you reached any conclusions or developed any hunches about conditions under which your big assumption is valid? Think about particular situations—who, what, where, and when.

3. Have you reached any conclusions or developed any hunches about conditions under which your big assumption is invalid? Think about particular situations—who, what, where, and when.

4. Do you find your big assumption asserting itself in situations you know it shouldn't? If so, can you generalize about the conditions under which you are likely (more or less) to find yourself being sucked into the old patterns associated with the big assumption? What still sometimes hooks you?

5. Have you developed key "releases" (e.g., self-talk that unhooks you) that you can readily use to help yourself when recaptured by your big assumption in real time?

6. Have you developed new behaviors or ways of talking to yourself in situations that used to activate your big assumption?

7. To what extent / how often can you use these "releases" to help you from being pulled into old patterns?

8. Consider situations in which you think your big assumption is no longer accurate. What new beliefs or understandings do you hold about "how things work" or what will happen in these situations?

9. Any thoughts about what has enabled you to make the changes you have?

FUTURE PROGRESS

Once you are "unconsciously released" from your big assumption, you may want to reengage the immunities process, especially around any unmet goals or areas in which you currently feel stuck or discouraged. All the exercises in the process are reusable. These tools can be a resource to a lifelong approach to transformative change by helping you see how you can achieve other commitments through identifying, testing, and altering additional big assumptions. Yes, the implication here is that if you look hard enough, you will find other areas in which you are unconsciously immune. Developing the capacity to identify such areas is a key to continued growth.

The very first step, of course, is to develop a new immunity map—and you can use figure 10-7 to do so as often as needed. Notice that this worksheet includes a column for generating ideas. This is where you can brainstorm goals around which you might still be unconsciously immune. Once you've done this, return to the earlier portions of your immunity work to remind yourself of the unfolding exercises and how to do them.

FIGURE 10-7

Immunity map worksheet

Generating ideas	1 Commitment (improvement) goals	2 Doing/ not Doing	3 Hidden competing commitment	4 Big assumption	First S-M-A-R-T test
			Worry box:		

These last two chapters seek to provide you a direct experience of the immunity to change in your own life (in chapter 9), and to put you squarely behind the wheel in the journey of overcoming it (in this chapter). In working with leaders it has been our experience that there is no substitute for this first-person understanding of the results the practices can bring. No matter how compelling you may find the ideas from a distance, we have found that your personal experience of the phenomenon is what will enable you to shift from merely sponsoring the work (in your organization or on your team) to being able to *champion* it—to model your own participation in it, and to have an authentic place from which to stand when the inevitable push-back surfaces.

———————

While our focus throughout chapter 9 and 10 has been on the *individual* at work on a personal improvement project, as you well know, *collectivities* (like work teams, departments, leadership groups, whole organizations) also have immunities to change. And, as you know from chapter 4, a number of such groups have benefited significantly from creating their collective X-ray. Remember, for example, the hospital clinic that was able to dramatically reduce prescriptions for drug-seeking patients, and to improve trust and confidence between the doctors and nurses in the unit—where earlier they could do neither. You or someone in your organization may want to help a group to safely and productively create a collective four-column map of its own. The next chapter will guide you in doing just that.

[11]

SURFACING YOUR
COLLECTIVE IMMUNITY
TO CHANGE

A NUMBER OF YEARS AGO, when we were first experimenting with the idea of collective immunity, we were part of a faculty running a two-week summer institute at Harvard for intact public school leadership teams. We had invited superintendents to come with their administrative teams, typically their central office colleagues and school principals. There were around fifteen teams and over a hundred people in the program. The curriculum had been put together by several collaborating faculty and, as often occurs in these situations, it was a jam-packed affair. Day after day, different faculty would involve the teams in a variety of activities in which they conscientiously and dutifully engaged.

Frequently the whole group would get an introduction to a particular exercise and then the various teams would be sent off to their own breakout spaces to try it out. We always gave them a specific time to return, so we could debrief as a collective; and day after day, session after session, every group would reappear at precisely the appointed hour.

On this particular afternoon, having some days earlier led the whole group through the immunity-to-change exercise at the individual level, we introduced them to the idea of group immunities, gave them examples and blank four-column forms, and sent them off to their breakouts with a specific time to return.

When it came time for the group to reassemble as a whole, two of the teams were not just late; they never returned! We didn't see them again until the next morning. This was our first inkling we might be onto something with this new way of using the immunity-to-change platform.

When we checked in with them, both teams told us a version of, "Sorry, the 'program' disappeared for us. We were having a work conversation the likes of which we never had before, and there was never a doubt that the most valuable thing for us to do was just to keep talking. We went right up to dinner. Hope no one was offended."

This chapter is designed to assist you if you would like to join your colleagues in creating a group diagnostic of a collective immunity to change. Why might you want to do that, and under what conditions?

- You are part of a group that has a desire to get better in some aspect of its functioning or ongoing performance. Perhaps the group has an important goal it knows it is not accomplishing, or for which progress feels much too slow. Perhaps it is aware of a particular collective dysfunction, such as: "We make great plans but we don't follow through"; "We don't take each other to task"; or "We are each too focused on protecting our own turf."

- Your group has an appetite, at best, or the willingness and tolerance, at least, to engage in a little collective introspection for purposes of better self-understanding.

- Whatever tensions, factions, or distrust may exist, the present level of group discord is not so great that all intragroup conversation becomes an opportunity for overt or covert hostilities; that is, the group does not have to be highly collegial but it cannot be an active battleground.

As we saw in chapter 4, there are many possible designs for undertaking a group diagnostic. Your preference will be a function of the nature of your collective and people's availability and/or interest in participating. Here are a few things to consider:

- If your group does not have clearly identifiable subgroups and is not larger than twelve or so (for instance, if you're all members of a single department or a peer-oriented project team), you can undertake the diagnostic together.

- If your group does not have clearly identifiable subgroups but is *larger* than twelve or so (say you're the partners of a large firm, or all the senior faculty of a large department), you can divide into arbitrary subgroups of around eight people (each a microcosm of the whole), construct several possible diagnostics, and then compare them in the whole to create one collective map that captures the best of all the earlier drafts.

- If your group consists of clearly identifiable subgroups (for example, the different tenure levels of a firm, or different departments of an organization), each subgroup can meet separately to construct its own diagnostic, and then when the whole group reconvenes the purpose is not to create one map that best captures the whole (as above), but to better understand the various pieces of the whole to which all belong.

- If your entire group is not present (if, perhaps, not everyone is available or interested, or the full group is simply too large), a representative work team can meet to propose a collective diagnostic either for the smaller group's own self-understanding or to be shared subsequently—in a tentative and inquiring stance—with the whole.

- If not a single other member of your subgroup is available, you can still undertake a collective diagnostic for your own personal illumination, keeping in mind that all your entries are best guesses of what the group as a whole would enter if it were being completely forthcoming, and that the picture you create is, at best, a provocative possibility, not a certain uncovering of a heretofore unrecognized truth.

Obviously, different designs will enable or limit what can happen after you create your collective diagnostic. So, to the extent possible, it is important to begin with the end in mind, and consider what you are hoping for before you start. For example, if you are looking for greater understanding *of* your group, it may be sufficient to work out a propositional diagnostic with a representative subset of the whole group. In contrast, if you are looking for greater understanding *within* your group, it is far preferable to have the whole group participate so that the understanding includes all the stakeholders in its creation and syndication.

Whatever design you choose, we recommend that all participants first map their own individual immunity to change before creating a collective one. We have been asked by groups if it is okay to skip the individual four-column activity and just jump right into a collective diagnostic ("because we are really more interested in group improvement than individual self-reflection").

Making one's way through the exploration of *group* immunities presumes the set of skills and conceptual familiarities provided by putting oneself through the rigors of the *individual* assessment. Once you understand the idea of taking responsibility for your own self-protective, competing commitments, you tend to take this for granted as you work your way through an analysis of your group immunity. But if people try the latter without this first-person understanding, their analyses tend to be shallow, at best, and, more frequently, a new means of carrying on intragroup warfare, at worst.

If, for whatever your reason, you decide to ignore our advice, we strongly recommend that you find some way to introduce the group to the concept of individual immunity to change before asking them to do a collective self-assessment. You might want to show them examples of good individual and collective X-rays—which you can find in this book—so they know what they are aiming for. When you're ready to move to the collective exercise, you can take the step-by-step approach to group diagnostics we describe next.

STEP 1: IDENTIFYING YOUR COLLECTIVE IMPROVEMENT GOAL

After you have determined which of the many possible designs makes the most sense for your purposes, your group needs to identify its specific collective improvement goal. In some cases, the group already knows the goal, and everyone is clear that they are entering into the activity because "we need to do a better job by our junior associates" or "we need to overcome the siloed nature of our leadership team" or whatever your group's collective change challenge may be.

More often, though, a group will generate too general or too operational an improvement aspiration—"we need to close the achievement gap"; "we need to improve communication on our leadership team"—and the group can really benefit from getting more specific (for example, "we need to improve how we teach"; "we need to handle conflict more effectively"). Here it can be most helpful to give everyone a version of the empty map similar to figure 10-7, the individual template with a brainstorming column. You can distribute copies of the blank collective map (figure 11-1) and ask people to

FIGURE 11-1

Worksheet for building your collective immunity map

Improvement focus— brainstorming possibilities	1 Our improvement goal (collective commitment)	2 Our collective fearless inventory (doing/not doing instead)	3 Collective competing commitments	4 Collective big assumptions
			Worry box:	

take a few minutes, on their own, to enter into the left-most shaded column their candidates for the group's focused improvement goal.

Next, your group needs some time to consider everyone's column 1 entries and agree upon a single collective goal. Many groups have found just this step alone, even before they get into the challenge of uncovering contradictory commitments, to be illuminating and valuable. This is often the case when everyone in the group can quickly tell you the thing "we need to get better at" ("we need to be a more inspirational leadership team for our younger associates"; "we need to be more entrepreneurial"), but if you asked five people separately what this really means, you would get five different answers. For instance, one person believes the team will be more inspirational by being bolder, and another believes the issue has little to do with the leaders' magnetism and more to do with their willingness to give their time and attention to their younger colleagues. Or one person believes *entrepreneurial* means hunting new clients or kinds of clients, and another believes one can be just as "entrepreneurial" with established clients.

Once your group has settled on a likely improvement goal, have members assess its alignment with the key column 1 criteria for collective immunities:

- Do we agree we are not doing well enough at this?

- Do we agree *we* are significantly implicated in this—that the problem here cannot be largely laid at the feet of parties or forces *external* to the boundaries of this group?

- Is it *important* to us to get better at this? Are there big payoffs (or big costs averted) if we do?

As with the individual immunity map, the value of this exercise depends on the quality of the column 1 entry. The more urgent and important the goal, and the more shared this perspective, the better. After your group has finalized its goal using the criteria for a good entry, you should enter it in the first column of a large newsprint version of a four-column map displayed on the wall, so everyone will be able to see the diagnostic as it takes shape over time.

STEP 2: TAKING A FEARLESS INVENTORY (OF BEHAVIORS CONTRARY TO THE IMPROVEMENT GOAL)

Next we recommend giving people several minutes on their own to consider what they personally think should be your *group's* answer to the question, "What are the things we collectively do, or fail to do, that work *against* this goal?"

When everyone is ready, your group can then take up the collective conversation as to what should go from people's own drafts onto the single, group-sanctioned map.

In a disarmingly nonponderous way, then, the social task of filling each column has the effect of shifting the group's conversational context *each time* into a quite different, increasingly introspective territory. In this way, unlike the work of creating one's individual map, people are not waiting until the third column to experience the novel value of the process. Each column provokes conversation that has value for the group's collective understanding and cohesion.

As you consider possible entries for the public map, apply the criteria for good column 2 entries you already know from doing your individual map:

- List concrete behaviors—what the group actually does or fails to do.

- The more entries and the more honest you are all willing to be, the greater the power of your developing map—so take a deep dive, and tell on yourselves. Remember, the purpose is not to shame or embarrass the group. You will all see shortly that the richer you make this column, the bigger the eventual payoff.

- Make sure that everything you enter provides a picture of the group working *against* its own goal in column 1. No doubt the group is also doing things *on behalf of* your column 1 goal. Good for you, but remember that is not the nature of the column 2 assignment. You aren't looking for balance here. The most value will eventually be found in the things you do, or fail to do, that have the effect, perhaps quite unintentionally, of undermining your group's improvement goal.

- Don't get into *why* you are doing these things or start forming ideas or plans for how to stop doing them and get better. The urge to problem solve—to explain your ineffectiveness and/or to devise strategies to cure yourselves of wicked ways—is often very strong at this point in the process, and must be resisted. It's understandable, since for many of us it is uncomfortable to confront a list of our foibles, and we want to do something immediately to make it go away. Understandable, but resist these impulses. For now, you are just trying to go for descriptive depth and honesty. Just the behaviors themselves in all their embarrassing glory.

One final criterion is particular to developing a collective diagnosis:

- These are behaviors you *all* are engaging in or failing to engage in, rather than "those of us who don't get it," "that faction," or "those adversaries." The *whole group* acknowledges its *collective* ineffectiveness.

If this last criterion is not understood and observed, your collective diagnosis risks devolving into accusatory infighting. On the other hand, when it *is* understood and observed, it can create a refreshingly safe, nonrecriminatory space for the group to tell on itself. Recall the second-column list of the professional services firm in chapter 4, which had the improvement goal of creating greater trust and mutual support within its partner ranks:

- We don't listen very well to each other; we'd rather tell each other.

- We talk behind each other's backs.

- We feel that if we haven't been consulted it wasn't a decision.

- We let our individual agendas trump the collective agenda.

- We don't assume the best intent in ambiguous situations; on the contrary, we often tend to assume bad intent.

- We avoid difficult conversations with each other.

- We don't extend ourselves to really understanding each other's agendas.

- We don't share information.

- We create and perpetuate an incentive structure that rewards individual over collective achievements.

- We are very judgmental and critical of each other.

- We form cliques and continue to collaborate within our small circles.

- We are all out there scurrying for clients, staying busy, hedging against downturns and lean times.

- We compete for junior associates to join our particular projects.

Or consider this list from the school district leadership team that aspires, in its first column, to create a plan, based on research and data, that better addresses the needs of English Language Learners:

- We make plans but don't follow through on our commitments.

- We have district materials but people use them or not as they choose.

- There is no ongoing training for teachers.

- We don't consistently reinforce teacher skills and strategies/techniques.

- We don't have the expectation that we put into practice what we train staff to do.

- We don't continuously support programs with district resources.

- We don't systematically monitor best practices.

- We don't demonstrate our commitment to uninterrupted times for critical instruction.

- We [the district] are not clear in communicating to our schools what is negotiable or not.

- We don't analyze program success.

- We don't involve teachers and principals in change reform by connecting current practice with data about results as evidence for a need to change.

- We want districtwide programs, but only if we like them for our own school!

As we believe you will find when your own group has a chance to determine its second-column entries, this form of discussion paradoxically does not create discouragement but more typically relief that you are finally naming and taking responsibility for something you all know to be true. You are doing it in a way that makes no one person the villain or victim, and you are surviving this hard look in the mirror. If anything, a group usually feels more cohesive after this fearless inventory than before.

Take whatever time your group now needs to discuss and create your own second-column entries and place them in the public map visible to all.

STEP 3: UNCOVERING YOUR COLLECTIVE COLUMN 3 COMPETING COMMITMENTS

Your next move, if successful, will bring into view your collective immunity to change. The key here is to create powerful, often provocative, third-column commitments that make visible a bigger range of social motivations than your group has previously been able to acknowledge.

Consider the examples we have already seen, especially those in chapter 4. The senior faculty genuinely wants to create a more hospitable professional home for its junior members, but before it can, it has to discover it is *also* in the grip of a commitment to preserving the privileges of seniority. The fire starters genuinely want to reduce their own fatalities, but before they can, they may need to acknowledge that their commitment to avoid feeling overwhelmed or out of control is actually preventing their learning the very things that will make their deaths less likely. What about the school districts that genuinely want to do a better job by their English Language Learners? We saw one of them recognize that they also had a commitment to protecting their little charges from the burden of high expectations they might not be able to meet; to preserving, in their own words, a "*povrecito* culture."

The other school leadership team that created the long, brave list of second-column behaviors? They were most interested in the discovery that they had a commitment to having someone to blame other than themselves. ("If we get everyone doing what they should, and *still* do not succeed, we will have no choice but to conclude that the real problem is *us,* that there will be no one else to blame, and we will be shown to be ineffective.") They needed to discover, in other words, that in order to avoid the *overt* conclusion that they were ineffective leaders, they *covertly* led ineffectively.

When people see a collective immunity map constructed by others they often say, "It's amazing a group would be that honest with itself! I don't think my group would be able to go that far together." But we remind you that when groups begin the process of creating their collective maps, they usually have no idea they are going to be able to open up so much to each other, and "honesty" is not actually the issue. In most cases, the group, even most of its individuals, is *unaware* of its self-protective motivations (its third-column commitments). They magically appear like a photographic image on contact paper, urged on by the collective energy that's released in the overturning-immunities process.

The relief of the second-column conversation is that people are finally talking collectively about the counterproductive things they all know they do. But the liberation of the third column comes from seeing something they hadn't known—that all these behaviors have a perfectly good reason behind them, that they are highly productive on behalf of other shared motivations.

Your group will get to its own third-column discoveries by leveraging its fearless inventory, all those second-column confessions of ineffectiveness relative to your goal. Keep the group quiet and have each member, working on his or her own preliminary map, fill in the "worry box" at the top of column 3: "What do I think our group would be most worried about if we tried to do the opposite of every second-column entry?"

When everyone has had a chance to think about this for themselves, your group can turn to its third shared conversation:

- Consider each worry or fear offered by a group member.

- Convert it into a possible third-column commitment (e.g., "We worry that the ownership group will think we are not 100 percent committed to the work" becomes "We are committed to never running the risk the ownership group feels we are slacking off." Or "We worry, if we trust the group to make decisions, that our own self-interest will not be protected" becomes "We are each committed to having a say in every decision in order to protect our own self-interest.")

- Enter each possible third-column commitment on the public map.

As you make your entries in your shared map, we invite you, once again, to apply a group-oriented version of the same criteria we used when filling out this column on the individual map:

- Each of your third-column commitments is clearly a commitment to *collective self-protection.* Each is tightly tied to a particular collective worry or fear. The partners of the professional services firm in chapter 4 identified in their second column that they regarded any decision for which they were not consulted as "not a real decision." When they discussed the worry that arose when considering an opposite action, the consensus was, "To regard these as real decisions, even when we are not consulted, we would have to really count on each other to be holding our own agendas and interests in mind. We would have to believe we each had each other's back. We worry about making ourselves that vulnerable to, or reliant upon, each other." The collective worry or fear is clear. The competing commitment it led to—"We are committed to not having to rely on others, to never having to depend on others"—is clearly a commitment to collective self-protection.

- Each commitment makes some of the obstructive behaviors in column 2 perfectly sensible. You can all see how, given the commitment you are now about to enter in column 3, the behaviors you previously entered in column 2 are just exactly what any group might do. (The professional service partners could see how, if they share a commitment to never having to depend on each other, it makes perfect sense that they cannot allow anyone other than themselves to weigh in on each important decision.)

- Your group can now see exactly why trying to succeed merely by eliminating its second-column behaviors is not going to work, because those behaviors are serving a very important purpose.

- Finally, the group sees how it is actually trying to move in two opposite directions at the same time, and understands why everyone feels stuck in this conundrum.

As its map began to take shape, the professional services group, for example, could see how the partners' genuine commitment to greater degrees of internal collaboration was stymied by their equally genuine, but less visible (until now), commitment to not depending or relying on anyone other than themselves. And with each of its third-column entries, the group could link back to its original improvement goal and, in essence, see yet another layer of its immunity to change. You should now be able to do the same with your map. It should be clear to your group how each hidden commitment in column 3 motivates an obstructive second-column behavior; how each hidden commitment provides a braking action against the gas pedal of the first-column improvement goal.

There is one more dimension that we want to make sure your group is experiencing. It is possible to draw a cognitively whole picture, but still not feel like the mapping has revealed something powerful for most members of your group. You might feel, "We have done as instructed, but the map doesn't really grab us. It doesn't seem to blow open any doors to new insights. It doesn't have that 'Gosh, it's amazing they were so honest!' quality."

If this describes your group's experience, what can you do about it? Remember that an immune system comes into being to take up a critical mission in a dangerous world. It seeks to protect you from what you think might kill you. If your immunity map lacks punch at the moment, it is because the life-and-death drama your group has been brilliantly—and invisibly—handling has not yet been made sufficiently visible. It is because the danger your immune system believes is lurking out there, ready to end your life as you know it, has not yet been framed in your third-column commitments.

This is likely so for one of two reasons. Either you didn't get down to the bone in identifying the fears connected with doing the opposite of your column 2 behaviors, or you did name your real fears, but then failed to capture this discovery in your third-column commitments. Let's quickly illustrate each of these failings, and discuss how you can repair them.

Recall the school leadership team that eventually made the powerful discovery that they were committed to overprotecting their children. They came to see that they were constrained by this mindset: "We must not hold out high expectations for our students because it will be one more burden in an already overburdened life, contributing to more experience of failure." It was valuable for them to bring this line of collective thinking to light, but recall that they did not get there on their first go at things.

In drafting their first map, they did not get down to the biggest fears surrounding the prospect of ramping up the rigor of their curriculum and instruction. They said they would worry about the extra work they would have on their plates and the initial feelings of uncertainty or incompetence as they took on new materials and new methods. Their map, strictly speaking, met all the formal criteria but still had no charge. They needed to go deeper with their fears. You will remember they were taken there by one courageous member of the group who surfaced the idea of the *povrecito* culture: "We are afraid to put more weight on their little backs." If your map does not yet feel powerful, if it doesn't raise provocative possibilities about your group's collective mindset, your first option is to direct the group's attention back to the worry box in column 3: "Have we gone deep enough in surfacing our fears about what would happen if we were to do the opposite of any or all of the column 2 entries?"

There's a second option, illustrated by our work with a group of research university librarians. They were committed to being less on the periphery, to being less on the receiving end of faculty and administrative decisions, to being more of a full partner in the governance of the university. What kinds of things did they do that worked against this desire? They did not actually press for a seat at the various tables that ran the university. They did not speak up when given the opportunity to influence decisions. They did not proactively develop their own positions on impending issues of importance to them. What fears kept them from doing so? After a few early takes on this that didn't get anything spinning below the neck, they came up with: "We worry that if we are given more of a voice we will be exposed as frauds or dismissed as naive; that we really only know what we know about—the library." This was certainly getting down to the bone, but their map still had no oomph for them after three columns (as it should) because their third-column commitment lost all the danger that lived in their fears: "We are committed to sticking with our strengths." The map had a whole different feel for them when they stayed closer to their fears in drafting their competing commitments:

- We are committed to taking no action that may expose us as frauds or naive.

- We are committed to not being embarrassed in front of our "clients" and bosses.

- We are committed to not discovering we lack what it takes to be real partners in the governance of the school.

The librarians' map felt much more powerful to them now, not just because they were naming something they had never before looked at together, but because they had a much stronger picture of the "braking action" that countered their improvement goal. They saw the dangers from which they were protecting themselves, and they saw how utterly sensible and self-sealing their immune system was.

So this is the second way to ensure your map is powerful: If the fears *do* reflect worrisome risks, threats, and dangers to the group's psychological and material safety, then you have succeeded with this step; now you should look to see whether the way you translate your anxieties into competing commitments retains (even elaborates upon) the full force of those fears.

If you've addressed all these potential pitfalls, your group map should now register powerfully with both head and heart: You can all *see* a coherent system that successfully manufactures nonchange; and you all *feel* intrigued, provoked, and engaged with the picture you have created. If this is so, you should also have a strong interest in answering this question: *How do we get out of this?* This brings us to your group's next move and next conversation.

STEP 4: UNCOVERING YOUR COLLECTIVE BIG ASSUMPTION

If you have a gripping picture of a collective immunity to change, the final two steps of group work will help you build a bridge from diagnosis to prescription for overturning your immunity to change. As you know, the overturning-immunity process provides an *adaptive* means of addressing an adaptive challenge. It turns an improvement goal into a "good problem"—the kind that "solves you." Your group, like all others, will be tempted to improve by immediately reducing the second-column behaviors—by embarking on a *technical* means of addressing an *adaptive* challenge.

As with overturning individual immunities, you need a point of entry that can enable your group to impact and alter the system, rather than being recaptured by the system. When one partner from the professional services firm said he was so relieved to be in an offsite that didn't end with people standing and pledging to change, he was speaking from years of experiencing his group trying to solve an adaptive challenge (becoming more collaborative) by a technical means. Sincerity and even urgency are not enough. The collective mindset that is "protecting" your group from progress on its goal needs to change. When you begin to address that immunity, you will unleash a cascade of unplanned, unpledged behavior that sweeps up the improvement goal and usually moves far beyond it. (Remember the cases in part 2 of this book.)

The next step and the next group conversation serve to create the optimal entry point for overturning your group's collective immune system. Take a few minutes of quiet and let everyone work on the fourth column of your preliminary map. Look at the column 3 entries on the wall and ask yourselves, "What are the assumptions we must be taking as true if we hold these competing commitments?" (Or, more accurately, "if we are *held by* these competing commitments?")

The collective map in figure 11-2 offers an example from the university librarians we just mentioned.

When everyone has had a chance to think for a bit on their own, you can reconvene for a fourth group conversation and listen to each other's fourth-column assumptions. Enter on your shared map the ones that meet the following criteria:

- It is clear how each big assumption, if taken unquestioningly as true, makes one or more of the third-column commitments inevitable (for example, if it is absolutely certain that our relationship with our university colleagues will be irretrievably ruined if we say something stupid once, it makes all the sense in the world that we would be committed to never being embarrassed in front of them). Taken as a whole, the big assumptions collectively make the third-column commitments inevitable, and thus it is clear how they sustain the immune system. (The third-column commitments follow clearly from the big assumptions; the third-column commitments sensibly generate the behaviors in column 2; and these behaviors clearly undermine the goal in column 1.)

- The big assumptions make visible a bigger world that, until now, the group has not allowed itself to venture into. You can all see how your big assumptions constitute a "Danger Zone" sign as you contemplate exploring this bigger world. The librarians could, at least theoretically, step out into a world

FIGURE 11-2

The university librarians' collective immunity map

1 Our collective commitment	2 Doing/not doing instead	3 Our collective competing commitments	4 Our collective big assumptions
To be less on the periphery, to be less on the receiving end of faculty and administrative decisions, to be more of a full partner in the governance of the university	We do not actually press for a seat at the various tables that run the university. We do not speak up when given the opportunity to influence decisions. We do not proactively develop our own positions on issues of importance to us even when we know they are coming down the pike.	We are committed to taking no action that may expose us as frauds or naive. We are committed to not being embarrassed in front of our "clients" and bosses. We are committed to not discovering we lack what it takes to be real partners in the governance of the school.	We assume faculty and administrators would have very high expectations of us, expect us to meet them immediately, would think much less well of us if we didn't, and that we probably can't meet them. We assume if we say something stupid once, all is lost—this is how we will be regarded forevermore. We assume we must be experts at everything right off the bat, that we are permitted no "learning curve" on anything. We assume that "what it takes" is a fixed or inherited trait; you've either got it or you don't. It cannot be developed.

where they feel like amateurs at thinking systemically and holistically about the university. The professional service partners could, at least theoretically, depend on each other more. They all *could* do these things, but their big assumptions tell them not to. It is possible that all these warning signs are completely appropriate and should be heeded, but it is also possible that their big assumptions are in some way distorted, and that they are limiting their collective life to a very restricted space in the wider world they could be inhabiting.

It is important in this fourth conversation for everyone to understand that the purpose at the moment is *not* to problem-solve or debate the validity of a given big assumption. Some of the assumptions you hear may seem unquestionably true ("What do you mean we *assume* some bad thing will happen? Believe me, some bad thing *will definitely* happen!"). Some of them you may want to argue are definitely false ("But we know, if we take a rational look at this, that there is plenty of evidence that this is not true"). And some of them you or the group as a whole may be quite unsure about ("Part of me feels this *is* true, or true most of the time, but another part of me is not so sure").

However, the point is not, for the moment, to settle any of these questions. Rather, the point is to see that, accurate or not, the collective knowing system—the group mindset—is operating as if all your assumptions are always true (and that is what makes them big assumptions). The question before the group, once the fourth column has been completed, is not, "Are these things really true?" but rather:

- Do we feel that these aspects of our mindset are seriously impairing our effectiveness?

- Do we feel like it could make a big difference if we were able to release ourselves from these group beliefs?

- Do we feel that we owe it to ourselves to see if we *can* alter any of these?

If the answers to these questions are negative, then however interesting your group may have found the experience of creating a collective diagnosis, the exploration is probably going to end here. There will be no collective will to move from diagnosis to treatment because the illness doesn't feel that serious. There will be no urgency to overturn an immunity to change because the *lack* of change is judged not to be that costly. In effect, this is the moment where your group has a second chance to do a gut check and decide how important the column 1 improvement goal you distilled really is.

In most cases, however, the answers to these questions are vigorously in the affirmative. The original improvement goal feels as important as it did before you began, and now you can see the contours of the mindset that are actively preventing progress on the precise goal you all hope to achieve. This should motivate you to take the final step in preparing your group to overturn its collective immunity.

STEP 5: PREPARING TO TEST YOUR BIG ASSUMPTIONS

The best way to conclude the collective diagnostic process is for group members to leave full of enthusiasm for running one or more specific experiments or tests that can yield information about the big assumptions. You generate this enthusiasm by having people brainstorm thought experiments and action tests that could conceivably yield information or experiences that shed doubt on, or disprove, one of the big assumptions. Have them brainstorm first individually, with their own preliminary maps, and then collectively.

As with the individual tests we described in chapter 10, your first collective tests or experiments should have S-M-A-R-T designs:

- They should be *Safe* (if things go badly, your group will survive to run another experiment another day).

- They should be *Modest* (your group is just taking a first step beyond the Danger Zone sign; it is not relocating to some destination miles beyond that sign).

- They should be *Actionable* (the group, or its appointed delegates, should be able to run the test or experiment in a timely fashion so that momentum is not lost).

- The test or experiment should constitute a kind of *Research* program to get *data* (rather than an improvement program to get *better*).

- The plan should be evaluated for its likely benefits as a *Test* of a big assumption (rather than how promising a strategy it is for improving behavior).

You will remember that the professional service firm partners planned a thought experiment and an action test. To unpack the whole category of entrepreneurialism for starters (recognizing it had multiple meanings within the firm), their intention was to examine each of the different elements they came up with, and then to assess which were and were not threatened or constrained by collaboration, and in what fashion. They explored whether any of the elements might actually be *aided by* the collaborative ethic.

As an action test, they decided to identify ten entrepreneurial projects (new clients they wanted to serve, or new projects they wanted to pursue with existing clients) that they would undertake collaboratively rather than as sole practitioners, to test whether they could form new coalitions and succeed at generating new business while breaking down familiar cliques and looking out for the individual agendas of each member.

There are several things to be said about these planned activities, and they all apply to the tests you and your group will design as well. First, they are undertaken to get information about the big assumptions, not for the group to immediately "get better." This group disposition—to take action so as to explore its mindset rather than immediately to improve—is as important as the particular design of the test or experiment itself. We have mentioned the age-old debate as to whether you should bring about changes by first changing mindset (the preference, e.g., of insight-oriented therapists), or by "grabbing people up by the scruff of their behaviors" and letting the mindset follow after (the preference of the behaviorists). Our approach, you will recall, is a third way. We believe that the mindset *is* the mother of behavior, but we believe that mindsets can change as a result of specific behaviors undertaken with specific goals—namely, behaviors that give you information (both cognitive and affective) about the mindset—in short, the behaviors of a self-reflective learner rather than those of a social engineer.

Therefore, after the experiments and tests have been run, it is important to bring the results back to the group to connect them to the question, "What do these results mean for our big assumptions?" rather than "Are we making progress on our goal?" Rarely will the result of a single experiment allow you to heave a sigh of relief and conclude you now know that your big assumption is utterly false. But if your group's results do challenge a big assumption in some way (and often they will), this should at least create positive momentum to explore a little further. ("Well, sure, that worked out fine under all those very favorable conditions, but would it also work out if we did X, or did it with Y?")

In actual practice, these planned tests are just a way of getting started. As "action research" they offer a culturally friendly way for action-oriented groups to begin integrating the discipline of a learning organization into their routines. Ultimately, your most transformative group experiments tend to grow out of the recurring recognition that "here we are again, operating out of that big assumption." As people get sharper at recognizing their big assumptions in action, their insights often prompt spontaneous tests and experiments. "What if we deliberately act somewhat contrary to that big assumption and see what happens? Is there a way to do this safely? What, exactly, is the information we would be looking for, if we thought of this also as a kind of test? Is the plan we've come up with likely to get us this information?"

Our experience is that the most powerful foundation for significant progress on seemingly intractable organizational challenges combines two strands of work: Individuals working on their personal immunity to change as it relates to a group improvement aspiration, combined with the group as a whole developing a picture of its *collective* immunity to change around this *same* aspiration. Groups often spend a lot of unproductive time talking—with no sustainable results—about their most difficult challenges. If that same time were used to build supports for overturning the individual immunities, and to create opportunities for the group to explore its big assumptions as part of its shared language and collective routines, then the immunities framework can become a robust structure for linking personal learning to organizational success.

As the cases in part 2 of the book suggest, the likely outcome, if your group decides to take on this work and succeeds, will far transcend just delivering on your first-column improvement goal. Working *adaptively* on adaptive challenges means helping to bring about—even in adulthood—the ongoing growth of the mind. It means building increasingly complex capabilities, individually and collectively, which are portable to all regions of one's living. If this looks like something of interest to your group, we cheer for the success of your journey, and hope you will let us hear about your discoveries along the way.

GROWING YOUR OWN

How to Lead So People Develop

E VERY JANUARY the World Economic Forum creates the hottest ticket on earth. For four days, by invitation only, from all parts of the globe, some two thousand heads of companies, heads of state, heads of universities, TV talking heads, and eggheads gather in the small Alpine village of Davos, Switzerland, to consider what is happening in the world.

A few years ago we were invited to attend the proceedings. It's a lot of fun, especially if you like nonstop stimulation and a crash course in global dynamics with learning companions you usually only read about in newspapers or see on television. Underneath all the talk and the tinsel, though, there is really only one topic: change. "The world is changing, your business is changing, and if you have any sense, you'd better be changing, too." Morning, noon, and night—in small groups and full assembly, over meals and on the shuttle buses—there is constant talk of change.

But with so many heads in attendance, it is perhaps no surprise that the conversations pay too little attention to the world below the neck—to the feelings, anxieties, and motivations that spur passionate commitments *not* to change. You can spend four days at Davos and not find a single session addressing *why* change is so difficult or what we can do about it.

In this book we have tried to distill twenty-five years of research and practice into a practical account of a single phenomenon we believe is at the heart of individual and collective change prevention—and what you can do to overcome it. In our view, leaders and organizations that master the immunity to change will be dominant in their sectors in the new century. They will set the standard in terms of accomplishing their own goals. They will be the most admired by their competitors. They will have the greatest loyalty and commitment of their internal constituents.

HOW LEADERS CAN LEAD THE WAY

How can your organization become a home for the continuing transformation of talent? How can you help more people make the leaps you have seen here, leaps that can unlock their fuller potential?

To foster real change and development, both the leader and the organizational culture *must take a developmental stance*, that is, they must send the message that they expect adults can grow:

"We can all keep growing."

"We will *need* to, in order to accomplish our goals [as an organization, department, or team]."

"We will *want* to, in order to experience the greatest vitality and satisfaction in our work."

What are the features of a genuinely developmental stance? We have identified seven crucial attributes:

1. It recognizes that there is "life after adolescence"; that adulthood, too, must be a time for ongoing growth and development.

2. It honors the distinction between technical and adaptive learning agendas.

3. It recognizes and cultivates the individual's intrinsic motivation to grow.

4. It assumes that a change in mindset takes time and is not evenly paced.

5. It recognizes that mindsets shape thinking *and* feeling, so changing mindsets needs to involve the head *and the heart*.

6. It recognizes that neither change in mindset nor change in behavior alone leads to transformation, but that each must be employed *to bring about the other*.

7. It provides safety for people to take the kinds of risks inherent in changing their minds.

As we consider each of these a little more deeply, we invite you to take inventory—for yourself and for your team or organization. But we suggest you do this not in the spirit of a checklist, where you may feel prompted simply to answer yes or no. Instead, think about each of these features as a continuum, and as you locate yourself or your group within each, consider what would constitute a single next step along that continuum. What would it look like in your case? How easy or challenging would that next step be? Which steps are most important for you to take first?

1. IT RECOGNIZES THAT THERE IS "LIFE AFTER ADOLESCENCE;" THAT ADULTHOOD, TOO, MUST BE A TIME FOR ONGOING GROWTH AND DEVELOPMENT

As long as we believe that mental development is the province of the young, we will conceive of formal learning as a *preparation* for adulthood, or the launchpad of a career's trajectory. Successful leaders in the new century will act on the recognition that organized learning is, yes, an essential preparation for adult life, but is just as essential for promoting the growth of mental capacity *throughout* adult life.

It is our experience that the culture of professional development in most organizations—in private and public sectors—actually differs significantly from this kind of expectation, although interestingly, many leaders do not realize it. While the language of "growth" and "development" is widespread, the actual practices we see tend to be grounded in a transmission model (rather than a transformational model) of learning, with a goal of transferring knowledge from one person (typically an expert) to the learner. The expectation is that the learner will "add" more to his mind rather than reconstructing it to achieve greater mental complexity: more files and applications for the operating system; no significant enhancements to the operating system itself.

As leaders act to include more transformational models in their settings, they will ultimately render quaint our current manifestations of organizational learning—punctuated training programs, executive education, corporate universities, episodic "professional development" events—all of which unwittingly apply the forms and functions of youthful schooling arrangements to an adult realm that is not about "preparation for the journey" but "life along the road."

We do not imagine these existing forms of professional development will vanish, nor should they. They are an adequate means of *informational* training to help workers input new skills and meet technical challenges. What will vanish is our sole reliance on these to meet a variety of learning needs.

If you look at the delivery systems for learning in your own organization, what implicit picture of "the mind at work" do they reveal—a system whose repertoire can be enhanced, or a system that can itself be transformed as well?

2. IT HONORS THE DISTINCTION BETWEEN TECHNICAL AND ADAPTIVE LEARNING AGENDAS

Our current designs are not adequate means for promoting the *transformational* learning that is necessary to meet adaptive challenges. At the beginning of this book we mentioned Ron Heifetz's assessment that leaders' biggest and most frequent mistake is to try to meet adaptive challenges via technical means. We believe the day will come when those responsible for organizational learning will look back and say a similar thing about their first-wave response to the need for learning at work: "We used technical learning designs and expected them to deliver adaptive results."

One of our own clients responsible for his company's corporate university has already said to us, "The line managers send us their people, hoping they will come back able to do things they cannot now do. But in most cases, in order for us to really satisfy these hopes, we would have to be set up to support transformational learning, and we are not. I don't know any corporate university that is."

Consider the kinds of learning that leaders today—in business or social sectors—hope for from those who work for them. A unit CEO of a financial services company in Switzerland tells us, "The world is changing. I need our account managers to literally reconceive their jobs. For twenty years they have been managing their clients' portfolios. They are good with financial instruments, with numbers, with analysis and forecasting. Now they need to be good with people and their feelings. They need to be able to talk to their clients about their *lives,* about whom they love and what they care most about in the world, and how they want to use their assets accordingly. It's a whole different job."

We heard almost an identical thing from a school superintendent in Cincinnati: "The world is changing. I need our principals to reconceive their jobs. For twenty years they have been excellent plant managers. They know how to coordinate a variety of operations that make for a safe and efficient building. Now they need to be leaders of instructional improvement. They need to get closer to the 'point of practice,' into classrooms, watching what their teachers are doing, and they need to figure out what their teachers need to better promote their students' learning. It's a whole different job."

Now consider the contrast between the way even the best leaders tend to meet these learning needs today, and the way they could meet them tomorrow. Let's say the account managers are attending a series of programs at the financial service company's state-of-the-art corporate university. The school principals are attending an intensive summer institute at a world-class university that also provides some follow-up via webinars and coaching visits from university faculty to the job site.

Even in these best possible cases—strong, deliberate responses by the leaders at these settings; heavy investments in resources to support employee learning; engaged and committed participation by the employees themselves—everyone in these scenarios is still battling against long odds. They are all expecting, without realizing it, that a learning delivery system originally designed for children will somehow meet the needs of adults.

The school principals and the account managers alike find themselves in *classes*, first of all—artificial, temporary groupings of people who have no collective purpose or accountability to each other and who, after a predetermined and relatively brief period of time, will likely never see each other again. The people to whom they *are* accountable sent them to these programs dearly hoping for that elusive thing that hangs over all contemporary professional development programs—"transfer," the ability of people to take what they learn in these work-distant groups and apply it to their real work settings when they return.

Whether due to their recognition that groups so constituted are unsuitable for deep dives into participants' constraining mental models, or a general discomfort with a more personal curricular focus under any circumstances, the designers and deliverers of these classroom-based programs are unlikely to provide opportunities for the bigger forms of learning the participants will need to significantly change their behavior.

Successful leaders of organizational learning in the future will embrace outcome-driven, rather than course-driven, approaches to adult development, as summarized in figure C-1. They will recognize that learning programs trying to solve "the problem of transfer" are probably lost the moment they begin. They will prefer programs that "start at transfer"—designs that are rooted within real, intact operational work groups. In these groups the members have a purpose and mission beyond their collective learning, to which that learning is tightly linked. Because they work at real challenges together every day, they naturally have a continuing and self-interested need to see

FIGURE CONC-1

Moving learning from the classroom to the work team: High-level design features for organizational learning

20th-century features	21st-century features
Course-driven	*Outcome-driven*
1. Learning In artificial groups (classes)	*plus* Learning in real work groups
2. "Time out" apart from work flow	*plus* Infusing learning within work flow
3. Time-limited	*plus* Time-elastic
4. Indirect learner accountability	*plus* Direct learner accountability
5. Informational/technical	*plus* Transformational/adaptive
6. Seeking transfer of learning	*plus* Starting at transfer
7. Serving team-leaders	*plus* Coteaching with team leaders
8. Tight boundary between learning personnel and line personnel	*plus* Loose boundaries/adjunct faculty
9. Loose connections to overall corporate strategy	*plus* Tight connections to strategy
10. In prep for an initiative	*plus* In support during an initiative

change and improvement in each of their colleagues, and are automatically inclined to appreciate it when it occurs.

So where might our school principals and account managers find themselves when they are engaged in organizational learning in the future? Imagine a superintendent's or a CEO's leadership team that meets regularly, as it does today, to drive the organization toward the accomplishment of its goals. Much of the time it carries on in straight-ahead work mode, just as it always has, but with a significantly greater level of effectiveness than before. And why is that?

It is because the team has *also* developed a robust and continually accessible second channel. At regularly scheduled intervals, and spontaneously when the need arises, it can shift from an operational to a learning mode. Team members are aware of their own and others' immunities to change, and of the group's collective tendencies to protect itself from the very progress it seeks to make. In this second mode the group is a place to conduct personal-learning experiments and to debrief experiments conducted elsewhere. The group is an incubator of new capacities to remake the "airplane" at the same time it is flying it —precisely the task of adaptive work.

The group is not always a comfortable place to be. The risks people run require courage. The learning at times is scary. But if you asked any of its members, even those who initially were most skeptical or resistant, you would be hard-pressed to find someone who wants to return to business as usual. Learning that leads to our own continuing development is very precious. It causes us to feel more alive. We remake ourselves as we remake our organizations.

At one end of this continuum a workplace sees organized learning as something that goes on primarily away from the job; at the other end, organized learning is infused into the meat and muscle of the way work gets done on the job each week. Where would you place your setting on this continuum?

3. IT RECOGNIZES AND CULTIVATES THE INDIVIDUAL'S INTRINSIC MOTIVATION TO GROW

It is worth thinking about what your organization or its culture regards as a *continuous* (versus a periodic) priority. The Golden Gate Bridge in San Francisco, we are told, is continuously being repainted. The day after its full repainting is completed, its next repainting begins. The city places a premium on continuously preserving its welcoming golden gleam. What does your leadership or organization show it wants to keep its eye on *continuously*?

It is ironic to us that even those organizations that have been influenced by the quality movement and think about "continuous improvement" of operations and systems usually do *not* think about continuously developing human capability. Since most systemic improvements are adaptive challenges, they require more than structural or operational redesign: they require transformations in talent to *sustain* the redesign. This is exactly the reason so many brilliant strategy consultations lead to little despite the client organization's appreciation for the good advice and its leaders' sincere intention to carry it out.

In contrast, most organizations look at the development of talent as a priority that can be met in a punctuated or periodic fashion. It is not one of the organization's Golden Gates. We "send people off." We create breaks from the work from time to time. We send them to the corporate university, to executive education programs, to leadership development institutes, like the bankers and the school principals. We give people sabbaticals.

In our work across public and private sectors the only real difference we see here is in *how long* you can get people to take these breaks. School administrators will come to a program in the summer for two weeks. CEOs may be reluctant to come for more than a few days. But this is not a big difference. The basic model is exactly the same—go off for a while, once in a while, get the batteries recharged with some good content, and bring back a new burst of energy to your organization. This is a model that sounds an awfully lot like another familiar work design, called *vacation*! Does it make sense to you, here at the dawn of the twenty-first century, with all we know today about developmental potential in adulthood, that our basic model for talent transformation should look, more than anything else, like our model for periodic rest and recovery?

What would your leadership or your organization look like if it were at the other end of this developmental continuum? It would pass this multipart test:

- We could come into your setting, randomly select several employees, including you perhaps, and everyone could answer the following question: What is the one most important thing you personally are working to get better at?

- Everyone, at every level, whether new to the place or the company founder, would be working on *a good problem* for personal learning. A good problem is one you are working on not so much to solve it, but for it to "solve you." People's answers, in other words, would name something that will require them to grow in order to accomplish it (versus some new technical skill they are seeking to acquire).

- They could tell us a way in which they continually have an opportunity to work on this growth.

- They could tell us the name of at least one other person in the organization who knows the goal and cares whether they accomplish it.

- Finally, each could tell us why it matters to them personally that they accomplish the change, how becoming different in just the way they describe would be a boon not only for the organization but for them individually.

There is no more perfect marriage of interests—between the needs of an organization and the needs of its individual members—than the ongoing growth of people at work. No "benefit" an organization provides its employees is a better investment than one that meets our deepest human hunger, to experience the continuing unfolding of our capacities to *see* more deeply (inwardly and outwardly) and to *act* more effectively and with greater range. The immunity-to-change diagnostic is a device to turn a hard-to-reach improvement goal into a "good problem," the sort that, if examined, will solve us before we will solve it.

Do the employees in your setting each have a good problem "that is working on them"?

4. IT ASSUMES THAT A CHANGE IN MINDSET TAKES TIME AND IS NOT EVENLY PACED

We're going to give it to you straight: the transformation of talent takes a while. There is no McDonald's drive-through window for adult development. Offers to deliver this to you overnight should be treated like fund-transfer solicitations from widows of Nigerian finance ministers. You might think your self-assessment question here is, "How patient are you willing to be?" It's not.

If you are anything like every leader we have worked with in both the private and public sectors, a better question is, "Why are you so impatient?" In our experience the usual answer is "because I haven't got the time!" Sorry, we promised to give it to you straight: if this is your answer, it just isn't true. For any given employee, the cumulative amount of time you have already shown yourself willing to devote to traditional training—what is actually a series of punctuated training investments and management work-arounds, each one comfortingly brief—is likely *considerably greater* than the single investment of the few months needed to help someone overcome an immunity to change. You have the time, more than enough time. It just doesn't look like it.

Why does it take time? Because we are in the world of human cultivation, not human engineering. We are not speaking of flipping a light switch. We are speaking of the evolution of mental complexity, of the gradual process of mental differentiation and reintegration, of *looking at* a way of making meaning we used to only *look through,* of shifting *subject* to *object.* You have no problem with longer time horizons when you are talking about any other major initiative in your organization; why do you expect overnight success in this one?

"But it's so *obvious* that he needs to trust his own gut more," you say, "and be less fixated on what everyone else thinks. If I can't sit him down and explain this to him in an hour, surely there must be someone in my organization who can!" Well, it may be obvious from your plateau. However, if he is shaping a world from the plateau of the socialized mind, believe us, to him it isn't so obvious.

But our message here—and this is very important—is not that you will need patience to take up a developmental perspective; *it's that taking up a developmental perspective will give you patience.* You get impatient because you think it *can* go faster. When you take up the perspective our developmental research illuminates, you usually find you can be more patient. You know the future of a tulip bulb is to blossom into a tulip; you know the future of a caterpillar is to sprout wings and fly. But you are not impatient with the tulip bulb or the caterpillar.

Nor are you without means to actively be of help. Adopting the developmental perspective does not mean resigning yourself to simply sitting still and waiting. There remain crucial, but different, actions for us to take. We cannot pull on the bulb or train the caterpillar to fly.

But we *can* make sure the first has good soil and the latter moist, leafy food. "Good problems"—the kind of internal conflicts the X-ray illuminates—and the opportunity to actively explore the big assumptions that preserve these conflicts: these are what nourish the transformation of mindsets.

When it comes to people development in your setting, how well matched are the outcomes you hope for and your expectations for when they will be realized?

5. IT RECOGNIZES THAT MINDSETS SHAPE THINKING *AND* FEELING, SO CHANGING MINDSETS NEEDS TO INVOLVE THE HEAD *AND THE HEART*

We know we don't have to ask whether you consider your own and other people's feelings an important part of what is going on at work. We don't think leaders are clueless as to the existence and importance of the emotional world. We just find that most leaders feel at a loss for how to engage this powerful dimension in ongoing, constructive, productive, and appropriate ways. The inclination, as a result, is either to ignore it and hope it takes care of itself, or relegate it to a cordoned-off space ("HR or executive coaching will take care of that") or time ("We'll have an offsite and bring in someone who is good at this").

Understandably so. What other models have been provided for you? You know you're not a psychotherapist and you do not aspire to be one. You may even be unsure how much those who *are* trained psychotherapists belong in your workplace. All fair enough. Taking a developmental perspective on transforming talent does not mean you should turn your workplace into the Esalen Institute or that you need to become the leader-as-Dr. Phil.

But it does mean recognizing that the difference between *efficiency* and *effectiveness* is as important in this realm as it is in any other, and it is a bad bargain to gain the first at the expense of the second. A developmental perspective means understanding that, messy and time-consuming as it might seem, learning designs that do not get to the constraints of participants' mindsets are relatively power-less to transform the way that work is done. It means, as we have said about the leaders you have met in these pages, not forgetting that people bring their humanity to work with them every single day, and that until we find a way to engage the emotional life of the workplace we will not succeed in meeting our most important goals. It means recognizing that hard-and-fast divisions between the public and the private, between "the work realm" and "the personal," are naive and unproductive.

Consider the experiences of Peter Donovan and Harry Spence, whom you met at the beginning of this book. What they each found of value in the immunity-to-change approach was the common language, the shared framework it afforded for both bringing the world of private feelings into the workspace and binding it tightly to the accomplishment of targeted, focused personal improvements that were highly valuable to the organization and to the individual.

In your own setting, are critical feelings brought to the table or kept in the closet? When they are on the table, do they support personal and collective learning, or hinder it?

6. IT RECOGNIZES THAT NEITHER CHANGE IN MINDSET NOR CHANGE IN BEHAVIOR ALONE LEADS TO TRANSFORMATION, BUT THAT EACH MUST BE EMPLOYED *TO BRING ABOUT THE OTHER*

There is, as we have said, an age-old battle among philosophers of personal change. Are we better off trying to "reflect our way" toward transformation, expecting eventual changes in behavior as the out-come of our hard-working contemplation? Or would we be better off taking up new behaviors as best we can and trusting that our minds will catch up with the realities of our new experience? In the world of psychology, for example, the insight-oriented approaches reflect the first school, and the behavioral modification approaches reflect the second.

Our answer is: neither. Our answer is that the whole thesis-antithesis structure of the question needs itself to be transcended in order to reach a new synthesis that amounts to something very different than just a combination of the two.

Our experience is that we cannot simply contemplate our way out of the mindset our immunity X-ray reveals, but neither can we simply elect to alter the behaviors of our second column. Rather we must take up an activity technically known as *praxis*—practice specifically designed to explore the possibility of altering our personal and organizational theories (the theories that reside in our big assumptions).

As you saw in part 2, the people we worked with transformed their talent through behavior change *designed to bring about mindset change* and through mindset change *designed to bring about the lasting behavior changes* that enabled them to reach their goals.

Now here is your inventory opportunity for this dimension: This may come as a surprise, but it is our experience that most people— even people who would describe themselves as comfortable with the reflective as well as the "doing" mode—have never engaged in focused, structured, persistent, and active reflection. What they have experienced is more like "time to think" or being led through a set of interview questions directing their attention to a particular time, experience, or event. Would this be true of you?

7. IT PROVIDES SAFETY FOR PEOPLE TO TAKE THE KINDS OF RISKS INHERENT IN CHANGING THEIR MINDS

We have yet to import to the new frontier of adult development much of what we've learned from a century of work on mental transformations in childhood. Among the most robust of these findings is what it takes for the mind to grow: challenge and support. Good problems, the sort that reveal the limits of our current way of making meaning; and support to bear the anxiety that goes with realizing we may not know ourselves or the world as well as we thought—these are as crucial for our growth today as they were when we were young.

The immunity-to-change process is a factory for converting every unfulfilled ambition into a good problem for transformational learning. But if you import only the "challenge" without tending to the anxieties it arouses, we promise you are going to be disappointed with the results.

Even if you are supporting people taking up this work in the complete privacy of a one-to-one coaching relationship, it is still important to recognize that what they are undertaking—if it works at all—will lead to some coming apart before it leads to an enhanced way of coming back together. When you are watching Al deliberately venture outside his zone of competence and comfort, and you are having some misgivings about his current performance, remember your skeptical belief that "Al will always be Al," and there is no way he can change. Well, take a look; what you are seeing, awkward though it may be at the moment, are the first signs of the very change you thought impossible. We know it may not yet resemble something worthy of a prize, but it is definitely worthy of—and very possibly in need of—your supportive recognition and affirmation.

However inexpert Al's first new moves may look to you, they are the result of his courage and willingness to tamper with the anxiety-management system that has successfully enabled him to come as far as he has. You may have some worries about his recent departures from the Al you have always known, but believe us—he is much more worried than you are. He is entering spaces his big assumptions have been telling him, probably for years, he should never venture into. Your understanding could be crucial to his continuing the journey.

But if you are also thinking to support the overcoming-immunities work in the context of a team—the kind of thing where people let each other into their own maps—you will almost certainly need to take deliberate actions to make the team a little safer and more trustworthy than it currently is. This is not hard to do; you just need to know to do it.

Remember Peter Donovan's executive staff? When they first started in the work one of the braver skeptics spoke for several others when he said, "I've been in corporate life for many years. I have a lot of misgivings about this. When you let other people know about your own weaknesses, you're giving them ammunition. It might all feel fine today because we are all getting along. But how do we know that sooner or later somebody doesn't load this stuff into a gun and shoot us in the back with it?"

Peter thanked him sincerely for his courage in speaking up. He acknowledged that what he was proposing was a risk. He was truthful in saying that nothing he could do or say could reduce the risk to zero. He also reminded them that every other great thing their company had achieved included some risk. And most important, he helped them to create a norm that said anyone who uses another person's one-big-thing as a club, or disrespects it in any way, is violating a sacred tenet of the group. A year later Peter told us that one of the most enthusiastic proponents of the work was the brave guy who had raised this concern at the start.

Remember Harry Spence's senior staff? It is as easy to identify a deliberate move that was necessary to make that group, as well, a safer space for this work. The issue here was not about what members would do with each other's privileged information. The concern was with evaluation, and what would or would not go in people's files. These veteran public servants knew that commissioners come and go, and however reasonable and respectful the current chief's written comments about their personal and professional development might be, how did they know future employers might not take it differently? It was one thing to be talking about such real things in the current group. It was quite another to assume that such frankness would not put them at a disadvantage in some future context.

Harry acknowledged immediately, as soon as the issue arose, that a clear norm here was absolutely necessary. The group elevated its level of safety by agreeing to, and holding to, a norm that said however much the work might find its way into members' conversations with each other, including conversations of an evaluative nature, nothing of the work would ever find its way into anyone's permanent file.

Challenge and support—the two must go hand in hand. Do you have a sense of the ways your own setting might need to be safer to insure that anyone and everyone who takes up this work is not making a mistake in doing so?

Seven different dimensions to being a developmental leader—if it feels like that is too much of a challenge, we have some support to leave you with as well: In our experience, the best way to stay connected with all seven of these is to make sure you are working to overturn your own immunity. Knowing (and feeling) what the journey is like from the inside can only enhance your capacity to lead in a setting where others can successfully and safely unlock their own potential as well.

We wrote this book with one conviction and one purpose.

Our conviction is that there is no expiration date on your ability to grow. No matter how old you are, the story of your own development—and the stories of those around you—can continue to unfold.

Our purpose is to put in your hands a new conceptual and practical means to unleash capabilities in yourself and your colleagues.

As you think of engaging the immunity to change you may wish to consider Peter Donovan's words: "Whatever you tell leaders," he said, when we spoke with him last about this book, "tell them this: the courage to make these kinds of changes is energizing and contagious. I saw people inside and outside my senior team go from 'This is too personal!' to 'I want to do this too!'"

We wish you big leaps and safe landings.

NOTES

CHAPTER ONE

1. S. Milgram, *Obedience to Authority* (New York: Harper and Row, 1974).

2. I. Janis, *Groupthink* (Boston: Houghton Mifflin, 1982). P. t'Hart, *Groupthink in Government* (Baltimore: Johns Hopkins University Press, 1990).

3. K. Eigel, "Leader Effectiveness: A Constructive-Developmental View and Investigation" (PhD diss., University of Georgia, 1998).

4. Bartone compared level of mental complexity and leadership performance rankings among graduating West Point cadets and found a significant positive correlation. (P. Bartone et al., "Psychological Development and Leader Performance in West Point Cadets," paper presented at AERA, Seattle, April 2001). Benay assessed the mental complexity of eight leaders in a midsized food distribution company and found the same upward-sloping relationship with a multifactor leadership measure assessing "transformational leadership abilities." (P. Benay, "Social Cognitive Development and Transformational Leadership: A Case Study" (PhD diss., University of Massachusetts, 1997)). Bushe and Gibb studied sixty-four consultants and found that their level of mental complexity was strongly and significantly associated with peer ratings for consulting competence via a seventy-seven-item instrument tested for reliability and validity. (G.R. Bushe and B.W. Gibb, "Predicting Organization Development Consulting Competence from the Myers-Briggs Type Indicator and Stage of Ego Development," *Journal of Applied Behavioral Science* 26, [1990]: 337–357).

5. N. Branden, *The Six Pillars of Self-Esteem* (New York: Bantam, 1995), 22–23.

6. C. Argyris and D. Schön, *Organizational Learning* (Reading, MA: Addison-Wesley, 1978), 21.

7. Ibid.

8. J. Loevinger and R. Wessler, *Measuring Ego Development* (San Francisco: Jossey-Bass, 1970).

9. R. Heifetz, *Leadership Without Easy Answers* (Cambridge, MA: Harvard University Press, 1998).

CHAPTER THREE

1. R. Kegan and L. Lahey, "The Real Reason People Won't Change," *Harvard Business Review,* November 2001.

2. R. Kegan and L. Lahey, *How the Way We Talk Can Change the Way We Work* (San Francisco: Jossey-Bass, 2001).

CHAPTER FOUR

1. We have drawn this vignette from our collectively authored book on school reform: T. Wagner, R. Kegan, L. Lahey et al., *Change Leadership: A Practical Guide to Transforming Our Schools* (San Francisco: Jossey-Bass/ Wiley, 2006).

2. This vignette is drawn from research presented by Peter Ham, MD, Dan McCarter, MD, Nina O'Connor, MD, Andrew Lockman, MD, University of Virginia, Department of Family Medicine, presentation at the Society of Teachers of Family Medicine (STFM), Chicago, Spring 2007.

3. Indeed, the facilitator said he chose the immunity-to-change process intentionally as a "carrot" approach, rather than the more typical "stick" of trying to change people's behavior through draconian departmental policies or disincentives. He viewed the latter approach as ineffective, and likened it to smoking cessation counseling, saying, "Heavy-handed approaches may only solidify resistance to change."

4. This vignette is drawn from C. M. Bowe, L. Lahey, R. Kegan, and E. Armstrong, "Questioning the 'Big Assumptions': Recognizing Organizational Contradictions That Impede Institutional Change," *Medical Education* 37 (2003): 723–733.

5. R. Heifetz, *Leadership Without Easy Answers* (Cambridge, MA: Harvard University Press, 1998).

6. C. M. Bowe, et al., op. cit., 727–729.

7. Ibid., 730–731.

8. Ibid., 731.

9. Ibid., 731.

10. Ibid., 732.

11. Ibid., 732–733.

12. Ibid., 732.

13. Ibid., 733.

CHAPTER FIVE

1. Heller gives us a flavor for the supposedly straightforward nature of delegating: "The process begins with the analysis—selecting the tasks that the manager could, and should, delegate. When the tasks are selected, the parameters of each should be clearly defined. This will help the delegator to appoint an appropriate delegate and to provide as accurate a brief as possible. Whatever the role, proper briefing is essential—you cannot hold people responsible for vague or undefined tasks. Monitoring of some kind is also essential, but should be used for control and coaching rather than interference. The final stage is appraisal. How well has the delegate performed? What change, on both sides, needs to be made to improve performance?" (R. Heller, *How to Delegate* [New York: Dorling Kindersley, 1998], 7.) Gerard Blair has even more explicitly encouraging words for the newly promoted: "The good news is that the first steps to becoming a really great manager are simply common sense . . . Put simply, things normally go wrong not because you are stupid but only because you have never thought about it before . . . In the leisure of your own armchair, you will think about issues without pressure and learn from what others have thought before you. Then, when a management problem occurs at work, you will have already thought about something similar and you will be able to apply your common sense. (G. Blair, *Starting to Manage: The Essential Skills* [Piscataway, NJ: Institute of Electrical and Electronics Engineers, 1996], 1–2).

CHAPTER SEVEN

1. We were invited to partner with our colleague, Dr. Robert Goodman, who had long been helping Nascent Pharmaceuticals with team development.

2. The interview contained eleven open-ended questions (e.g., asking about the team's strengths and weaknesses, especially related to communication; their personal contributions to these; and the team leader's strengths and weaknesses) and five Likert scale items (trust levels, ability to surface and handle conflict, effectiveness of decision making, and appreciation of individuals' contributions).

3. With the exception of asking that Chet partner with one particular team member, all pairs were spontaneously created.

4. People surveyed only their fellow team members, since their goal was specific to improving their team's performance.

5. I. B. Myers, *Introduction to Type: A Guide to Understanding Your Results on the Myers-Briggs Type Indicator* (Mountain View, CA: CPP, 1998).

6. In addition, people's individual preferences can be combined to create a team profile. This shows a collective picture of the team's preferences and can be

used to identify ways the team may be lopsided and for which it needs to compensate. This was a secondary objective.

7. R. Ross, "The Ladder of Inference," in P. Senge, A. Kleiner, et al., *The Fifth Discipline Fieldbook* (New York: Doubleday, 1994), 243.

8. Especially A. S. Bryk and B. L. Schneider, *Trust in Schools: A Core Resource for Improvement* (New York: Russell Sage Foundation, 2002).

9. This is not to suggest that people kept all their appointments, or that they were able to prepare fully for every session. Some rescheduling and flexible meeting agendas are inevitable, and do not interfere with a motivated learner's progress. This is also not to suggest that people found it easy to make time. This person was probably not alone when she said, "Many times it was difficult to focus on this work. It was a difficult time in the year with upper management, projects, etc., and hard to step away. It was fast paced and sometimes hard to keep up with what they wanted us to do within ourselves. The pace of my job is hard."

CHAPTER TEN

1. We are indebted to our Harvard colleague Matt Miller for the distinction between an event-focused and a process-learning-focused approach to testing our big assumptions.

2. Our appreciation to Barbara Rapaport for these preparation suggestions.

INDEX

ABOUT THE AUTHORS

ROBERT KEGAN is the Meehan Professor of Adult Learning and Professional Development at the Harvard University Graduate School of Education. His thirty years of research and writing on adult development have contributed to the recognition that ongoing psychological development after adolescence is at once possible and necessary to meet the demands of modern life. He is the recipient of numerous honorary degrees and awards. His seminal books, *The Evolving Self* and *In Over Our Heads,* have been published in several languages.

LISA LASKOW LAHEY is Research Director of the Change Leadership Group at the Harvard University Graduate School of Education and coauthor of *Change Leadership: A Practical Guide to Transforming Our Schools.* A developmental psychologist and educator, she led the research team that created the developmental diagnostic, now used around the world, for assessing adult meaning systems. Her writing and practice focus on the joint goal of helping teams to better support individuals' development and of helping individuals to enable teams to perform more optimally.

KEGAN and LAHEY have collaborated in research and practice for more than twenty-five years. Together they founded Minds At Work, a client-serving group supporting the personal and professional development of senior leaders and their teams in public and private sectors. The authors of *How the Way We Talk Can Change the Way We Work* and the widely distributed *Harvard Business Review* article, "The Real Reason People Don't Change," Kegan and Lahey are credited with the breakthrough discovery of a hidden dynamic that impedes personal and organizational transformation. This work (on what they call "the immunity to change") has now found its way into the practice of leaders and senior teams in business, governmental, and educational organizations in the United States, Europe, and Asia. Joining past recipients Warren Bennis, Peter Senge, and Edgar Schein, they received the Gislason Award for exceptional contributions to organizational leadership from the Boston University School of Management. They can be reached at www.mindsatwork.com.